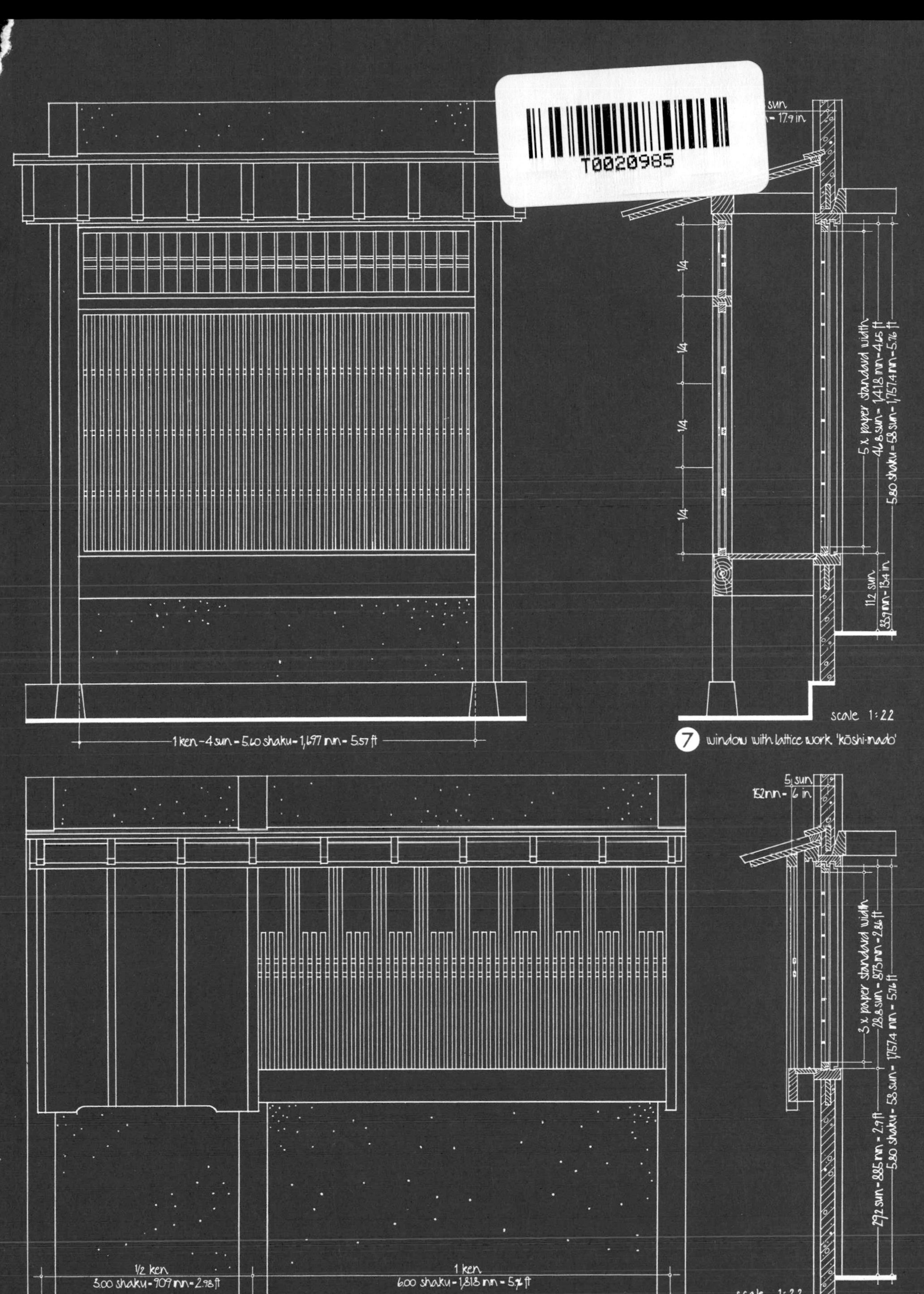

7 window with lattice work 'kōshi-mado'

MEASURE AND CONSTRUCTION OF THE

JAPANESE HOUSE

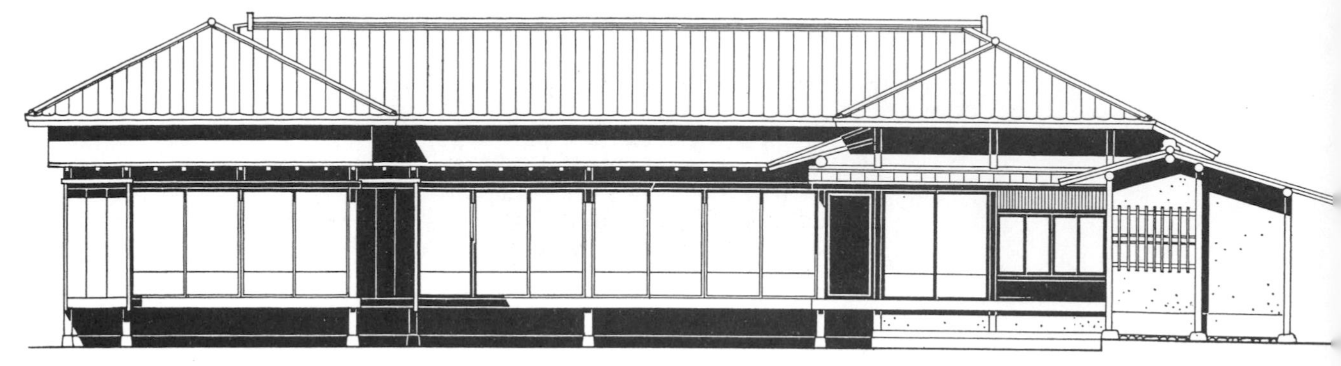

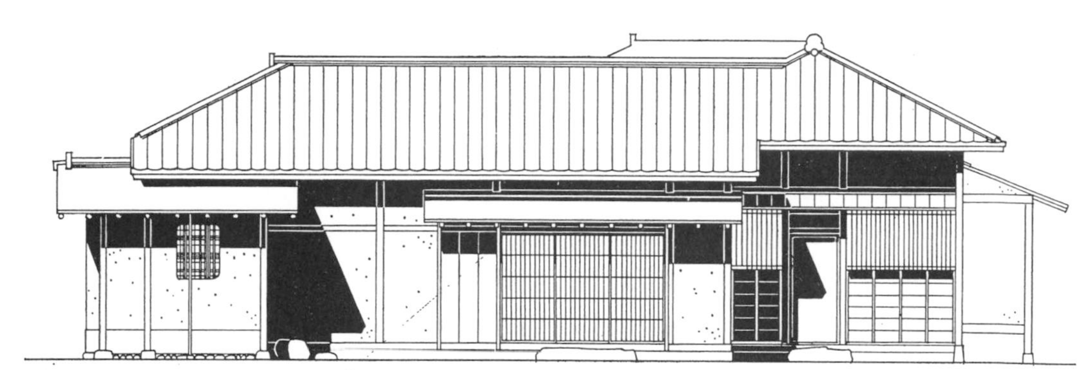

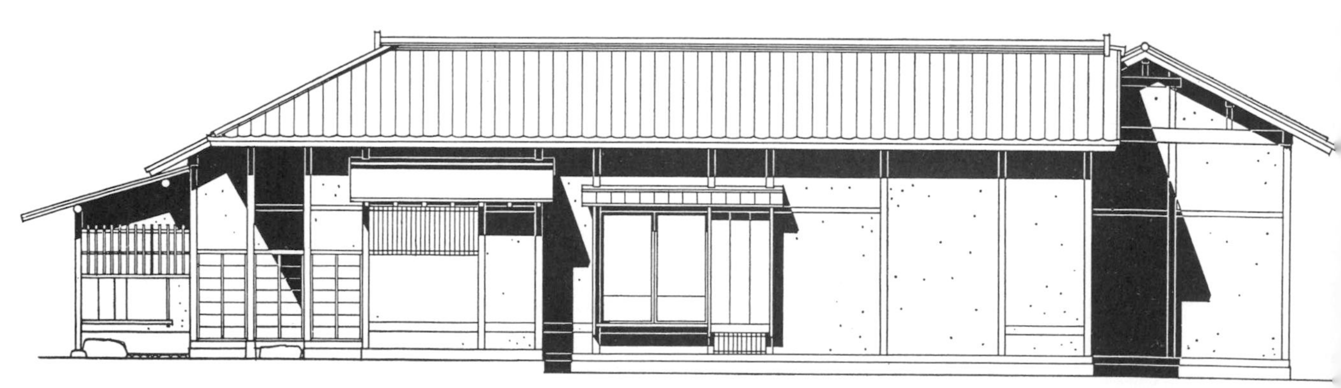

MEASURE AND CONSTRUCTION OF THE

JAPANESE HOUSE

HEINO ENGEL

WITH A NEW FOREWORD BY

MIRA LOCHER

TUTTLE Publishing

Tokyo | Rutland, Vermont | Singapore

to ERNST NEUFERT *sensei*
my teacher in architecture

Published by Tuttle Publishing, an imprint of Periplus Editions (HK) Ltd.

www.tuttlepublishing.com

LCC Catalog Card No. 84-051859

ISBN 978-4-8053-1646-7

First edition, 1985
This edition, 2020

Distributed by

North America, Latin America & Europe
Tuttle Publishing
364 Innovation Drive
North Clarendon,
VT 05759-9436 U.S.A.
Tel: 1 (802) 773-8930
Fax: 1 (802) 773-6993
info@tuttlepublishing.com
www.tuttlepublishing.com

Japan
Tuttle Publishing
Yaekari Building, 3rd Floor,
5-4-12 Osaki, Shinagawa-ku,
Tokyo 141 0032
Tel: (81) 3 5437-017
Fax: (81) 3 5437-0755
sales@tuttle.co.jp
www.tuttle.co.jp

Asia Pacific
Berkeley Books Pte. Ltd.
3 Kallang Sector #04-01
Singapore 349278
Tel: (65) 6741-2178
Fax: (65) 6741-2179
inquiries@periplus.com.sg
www.tuttlepublishing.com

25 24 23 22 6 5 4 3

Printed in Malaysia 2112TO

table of contents

list of illustrations

figure

publisher's note

The text and drawings of this presentation, except for minor alterations in their sequence, have been taken unchanged from the larger volume *The Japanese House: A Tradition for Contemporary Architecture,* which was first published in 1964 and has gone through eleven printings. The decision of the publishers to single out the two chapters "Measure" and "Construction" from the fifteen of the original volume and to publish them as a separate book is, on one hand, a response to the growing trend in architecture to apply features of distinctive architectural styles of the past in contemporary design, and on the other, simply to provide a book more accessible to those interested in these two fundamental considerations. It is our hope that with this edition Dr. Engel's excellent work will gain an even wider audience.

foreword to this edition

By Mira Locher

First published in 1985, *Measure and Construction of the Japanese House* remains in print and sought-after for 35 years, read and consulted by architects, students, and others interested in Japanese architecture. The book is the result of both the author's careful and passionate study of Japanese culture and architecture as a recent university graduate and also his later reconsideration of some of the early ideas compelling his in-depth research. Although the initial publication date of *Measure and Construction of the Japanese House* is 1985, the book has a history that started more than 30 years prior, and its publication occurred at a moment when Japan and Japanese architecture were starting to undergo immense changes. In those proceeding 35 years, it is interesting to consider how this book has remained a top reference for the study of traditional Japanese houses.

Since the history of *Measure and Construction of the Japanese House* is much longer than the 35 years it has been in book form, this printing provides an opportunity to delve a bit into the history of the author and the work. First published as a standalone book in 1985, *Measure and Construction of the Japanese House* originally was part of Heinrich "Heino" Engel's larger work, *The Japanese House: A Tradition for Contemporary Architecture*, published by Charles E. Tuttle Co. in 1964. *The Japanese House* in turn drew from Engel's 1959 PhD dissertation, *The Japanese Home and Modern Living*. Engel developed his ideas during his extensive travel and research in Japan, influenced and encouraged by both his mentor, Ernst Neufert, and Neufert's mentor, Walter Gropius.

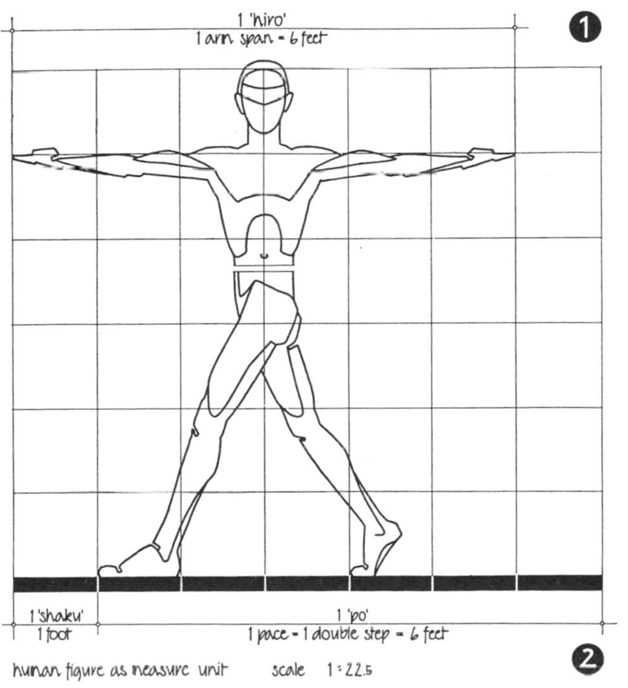

Born in Germany, author Heino Engel studied architecture at the Technische Universität (TU) Darmstadt in the years following World War II. He was highly influenced by one of his professors, Dr. Ernst Neufert, who was active as an architect designing industrial buildings in post-war Germany. Neufert studied under Walter Gropius at the Bauhaus and, after traveling in Spain for a year, joined Gropius' studio and then later worked as an architect for several companies. In the years prior to WW II, Neufert designed housing, as well as office and factory buildings, and became interested in the potential of standardization in design and construction. This interest led him to write *Architects Data*, a standardization handbook for architects first published in 1936, which remains a classic reference book for European architects, space planners, and contractors. Neufert was appointed to teach at TU Darmstadt in 1946, where he influenced a great number of students of architecture, including Heino Engel. Neufert's greatest impact on Engel may have been his encouragement to travel and see the world after completing his studies, but Neufert's important work on standardization no doubt also was an inspiration for Engel's future career.

In 1952 Heino Engel left Germany to travel in the Middle East and Asia. He spent three years in Japan, from 1953–56, and for at least part of that time lived with a family in Otsu, not far from the historical capital of Kyoto. It was there that he first learned about Japanese culture and began seriously studying the architecture. While many Japanese towns and cities suffered severe damage in the war and rebuilt using contemporary materials and forms, Kyoto's historic districts remained relatively intact. Engel no doubt spent a good deal of time examining the existing buildings in Kyoto as well as in the countryside. When Walter Gropius visited Japan in 1954, Engel had the opportunity to meet with him. Gropius encouraged Engel to delve deeply into his investigation of Japanese architecture and culture, and thus Engel "proceeded to explore the aesthetic, environmental, cultural, and design details of wood dwellings,"[1] paying close attention to "the degree of emotional delight humans are capable of deriving from environment." In an essay discussing Japanese environmental aesthetics, Barbara Sandrisser describes Engel's ideas as "idealistic, perhaps, yet how humane and civilized. The young Engel was passionate about Japanese environment, recognizing the significance of culture to architecture."[2]

While in Japan, Engel published what appears to be his first essay on Japanese architecture, the article "One Thought on Japanese Residential Architecture," for the Japanese architectural journal *Shinkenchiku* in 1956. In the essay, Engel expressed concern that architects were no longer learning from the past, and that modern architecture dealt only with the present conditions—a "standard" based on mass production. He pondered "whether or not the art of building . . . could become also a mere technical

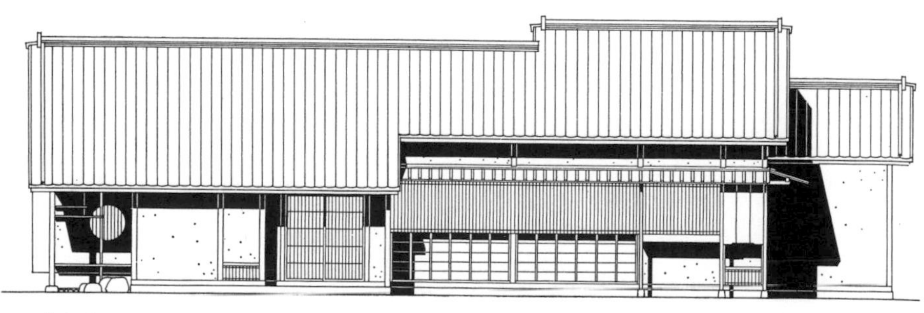

north elevation

product itself and cease to be a work of art."[3] Engel discussed the "Japanese-unique"[4] architectural qualities of the historic buildings in Japan—in particular the residences, and how often they are misinterpreted by outsiders with minimal knowledge of Japanese culture and the historical development of the architecture in relationship to political, societal, and environmental factors. He lamented the architecture being "imitated as a superficial decoration or fashion" and suggested that Japanese architecture could indeed be a model for creative expression within standardization—but only with a clear understanding of "the backgrounds, conditions and influences that proved decisive in the formation of the essential characteristics of the traditional residential architecture."[5]

Engel's interest in Japanese culture and architecture and his investigation of the development and design of historic Japanese houses led him to purse a PhD at TU Darmstadt, with Professor Neufert serving as an advisor. Engel focused his research on the building materials and construction methods of Japanese homes from the 17th and 18th centuries and completed his 124-page dissertation, titled *Japan Wohnhaus für die Gegenwart* (translated as *The Japanese Home and Modern Living*) in 1959.

After returning from Japan and while working on his dissertation, Engel was hired by the University of Minnesota to teach in the School of Architecture, where he initially served as a lecturer in 1956 and later as an assistant professor. He left Minnesota in 1964, returning to Germany and starting an architectural practice in Offenbach, where he had spent at least part of his youth. That year, 1964, also was the year he completed his first book, *The Japanese House: A Tradition for Contemporary Living*, published by Charles E. Tuttle Co., with acknowledgment to Ernst Neufert, who "inspired interest in Japanese architecture and encouraged research."[6] Engel derived the first chapter of *The Japanese House* directly from his doctoral dissertation, and he expanded the work with the goal for *The Japanese House*, as he discussed in his preface, to examine historic Japanese residential architecture as an example of "the establishment of organic relationships between man, society, technique, and shelter," which he strongly believed should be integrated with "contemporary ethics" to produce an appropriate contemporary architecture—what he termed "architecture in the industrial society."[7]

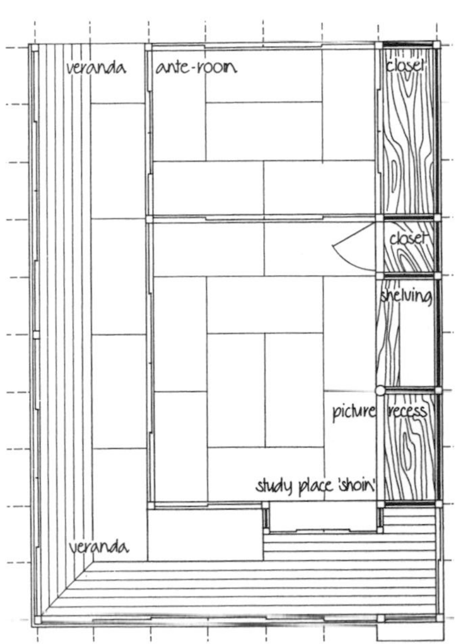

The Japanese House included an enthusiastic foreword by Walter Gropius, emphasizing the significance of the Japanese house in which "the design conception had started from the very bones of the building and not merely at its skin as a cosmetic play. Spiritual and practical requirements of living had been coordinated into an artistic approach that represents one of the most valuable contributions to a universal philosophy of architecture."[8]

In his introduction, Engel lamented the loss of "the humanizing force that art gives" to "the forms created by science and technique" and believed the "commoners'" residential architecture from 17th and 18th century Japan could serve as a good example. He stated unequivocally that "there is no other architecture equally suited to demonstrate the principles of cultured living and building and to stimulate contemporary design as is the dwelling of the common people in Japan."[9] Regarding *The Japanese House*, Engel explains,

> This treatise thus aims at making an architecture of the past seizable [sic] for the contemporary. It is an attempt to interpret the outstanding achievements of a prior architecture, not as forms with obscure causes and motivations, but as forms that actively state a particular order of values. By discussing architectural causes rather than merely comparing architectural forms, the analysis of Japanese residential architecture will deal with the very core of the problems in contemporary architecture.[10]

Walter Gropius concurs in his foreword, emphatically stating.

> This book offers the key to the understanding of this profound approach to design. It will interest every teacher and student of architecture and architectural history, every creative architect and designer in East and West alike. To the Western architect it will show up the missing ingredient in our own civilization, the coherent effort at attaining unity in diversity. It

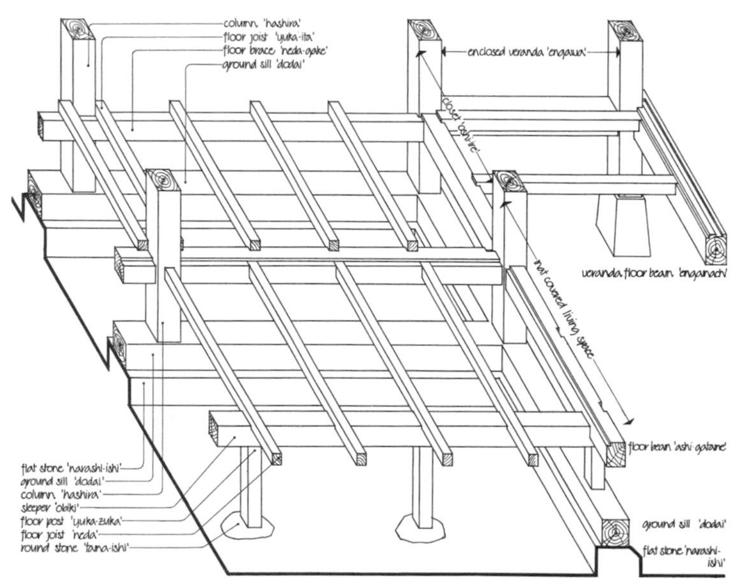

> will make him conscious of the necessity to develop a philosophy of common purpose, able to absorb and give focus to the manifold experiments in technique and aesthetics as they bewilder him today. To the Japanese architects it will give support to their new outburst of creativity, the fruits of which must already now be considered to be contributions to modern architecture of the highest rank."[11]

At almost 500 pages in length, *The Japanese House* is hardly a concise introduction to Japanese culture and architecture. Nor is it meant to be a compendium of all historical forms of Japanese architecture, instead focusing specifically on the architecture of Japanese Edo-period commoners' houses. At the time that Engel wrote *The Japanese House*, he was not interested in form for form's sake, but rather understanding and communicating "the motives that produced the form,"[12] and he aimed for thoroughness.

> Only a comprehensive study of all the factors involved in the evolution of the Japanese house can lay the basis for comprehension, interpretation, and final utilization. As wrong as the overestimation of mere analytical recording is, it would be equally wrong to do away altogether with any methodical investigation and depend alone on intuitive assumption.[13]

Engel also noted that the book was not meant for casual perusal, rather it "is directed toward those readers who take a serious interest in Japanese and contemporary architecture and do not shy away from strenuous reading and tedious studying."[14] No doubt the size of the volume and the complex presentation of a number of the ideas may have been off-putting to some readers. Even the publisher seemed not completely convinced and included an unusual note stating "no amount of editorial primping can make a

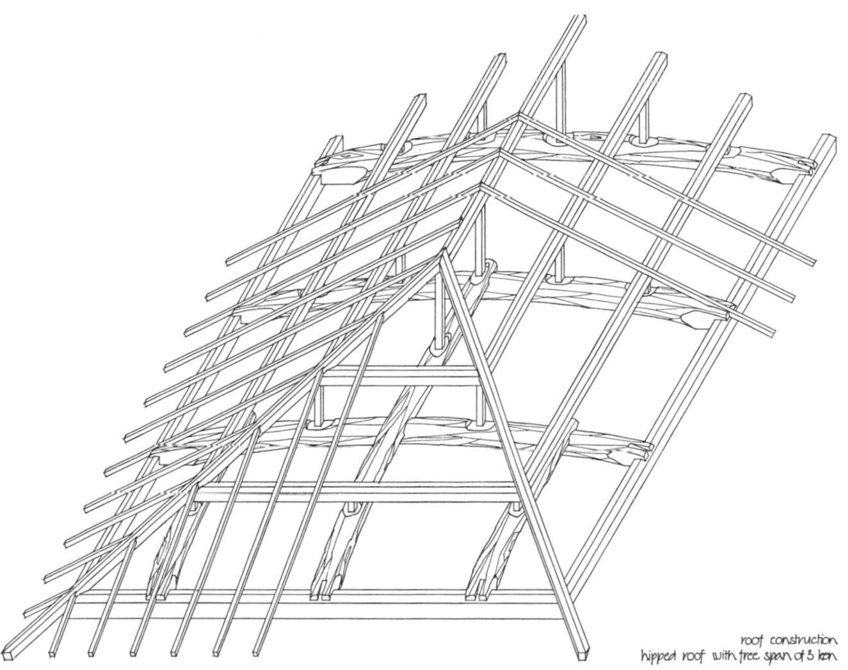

book more or less than what it is."[15] Nonetheless, for many years *The Japanese House* was considered "the 'Bible' of Japanese vernacular architecture because of the intermingling of photographs and detailed drawings with contextual, historical, cultural, and aesthetic notions."[16]

During his time at the University of Minnesota, while also working on *The Japanese House*, Heino Engel developed a secondary area of research that stemmed in part from his architectural education at TU Darmstadt, which included a strong background in structural approaches to architecture. He produced a series of lectures and research that evolved into a particular study of architectural structures, which he published as his second book, *Tragsysteme—Structure Systems*, in 1967. As with his mentor Ernst Neufert's famous book on architectural standards, Engel's book became—and remains—a classic book for learning about architectural structural systems. *Tragsysteme* initially was published in German and English (Stuttgart, Deutsche Verlags-Anstalt) and later translated into other languages. In 1997, Engel revised and enlarged the book, stating that

> Only when the essence and causality of structures in building is realized, only when the full scope of structures is measured, and only when the features of their behavior and of their structure forms are understood, only then can the planner of building—architect or engineer—creatively bring the potential of structures to bear in the development of architectural ideas of today.[17]

In 1970 Engel returned to the University of Minnesota School of Architecture to serve as a short-term visiting professor. At that time, the University of Minnesota noted that Engel "is the principal architect of Engel Architects and Planners in Offenbach, specializing in commercial, entertainment, housing, recreational and institutional buildings." While at the University, he gave three public lectures which reflected the three major themes of his research and teaching: "Toward an Integral Theory of Architecture,"[18] "Physical Control System: Bearing Structures," and "Systems Architecture: The Japanese House."[19]

Based on the title of his third lecture, it seems that Engel's interest in architectural structural systems may have had an influence on his thinking regarding the architecture of the Japanese house. In 1985, most of the initial sections of *The Japanese House: A Tradition for Contemporary Architecture*, nearly one-fourth of the book, was published separately under the title *Measure and Construction of the Japanese House*. After so passionately arguing for broad comprehension of Japanese culture prior to utilizing the architecture as a model, it is interesting to note Engel's change of heart. *Measure and Construction of the Japanese House* deals with just those areas—the systems of mea-

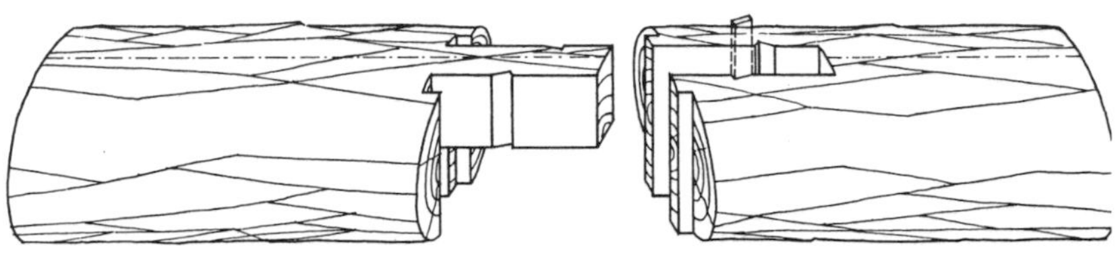

surement and modules along with the architectural elements and fittings used in the construction of historic Japanese dwellings, with an eye toward what contemporary architects can learn from them. Engel elucidates,

> The broad acceptance of an alien architectural achievement three hundred years old might be considered an astonishing phenomenon. It is not really so, however, if one realizes the particular features that distinguish the traditional Japanese house: the modular order of system and form; the flexibility of space partitions and room functions; the compository potential of the floor mat; the expressive diversity within comprehensive standardization; the integrative quality of Japanese architectural forms. Indeed, it is for these features that the Japanese house seems to be better suited to serve as a pattern for contemporary housing than any other form of residential architecture.[20]

While the reader of *The Japanese House: A Tradition for Contemporary Architecture*, might be surprised at what seems like a major shift in thinking, Engel clarifies in his introduction to *Measure and Construction of the Japanese House* why he believes his prior viewpoint "has become debatable."[21] He explains the difficulty of an approach requiring a comprehensive understanding of the culture and circumstances shaping the development of an architecture and that "with such an approach only a fraction of past cultural achievements could be made accessible and thus become part of our world today."[22] He continues,

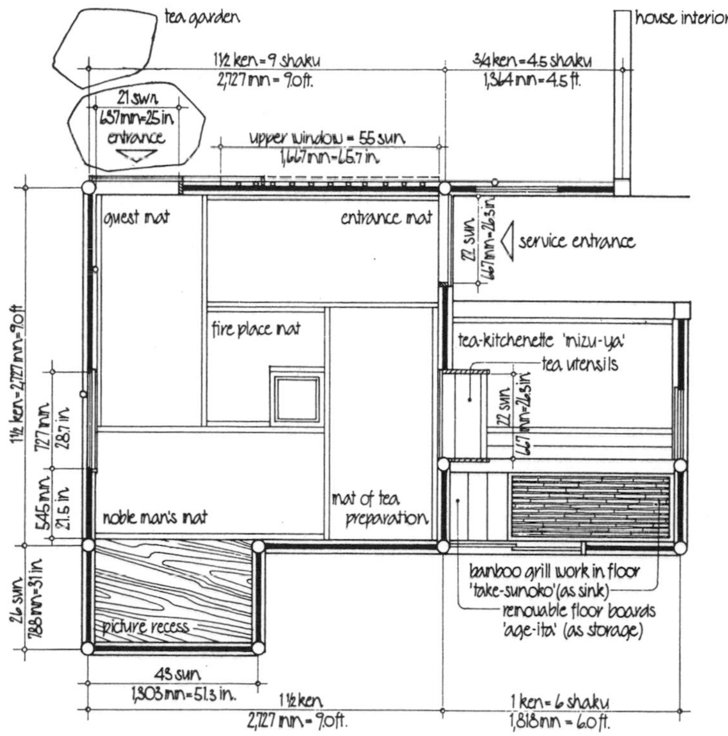

floor plan of standard tea-room with 4½ mat = 2¼ tsubo = 7.44 sq.m. = 80 sq.ft. and tea-kitchenette

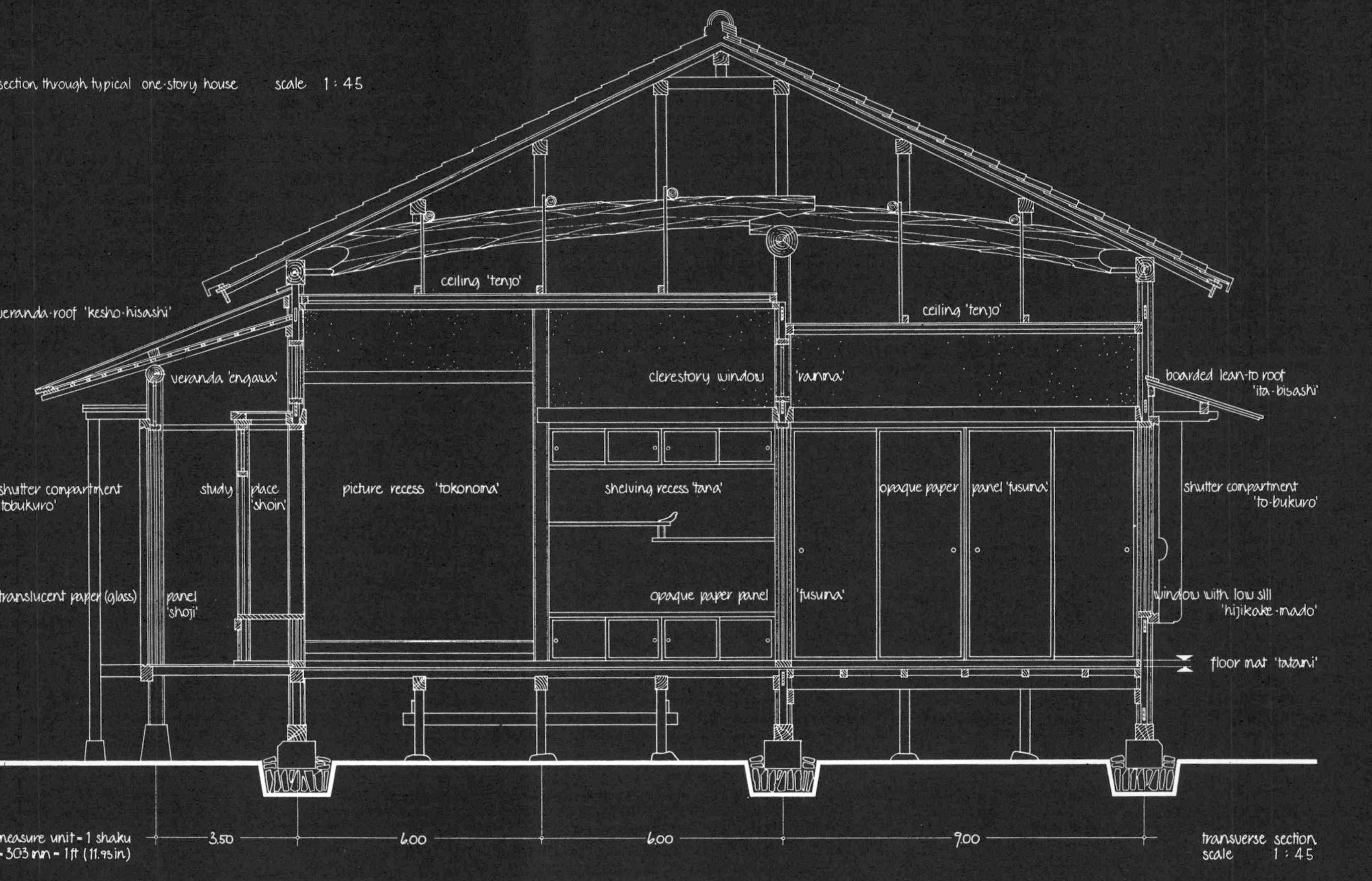
section through typical one-story house scale 1 : 45
ceiling 'tenjo'
ceiling 'tenjo'
veranda-roof 'kesho-hisashi'
veranda 'engawa'
clerestory window 'ranma'
boarded lean-to roof 'ita-bisashi'
shutter compartment 'tobukuro'
study place 'shoin'
picture recess 'tokonoma'
shelving recess 'tana'
opaque paper panel 'fusuma'
shutter compartment 'to-bukuro'
translucent paper (glass) panel 'shoji'
opaque paper panel 'fusuma'
window with low sill 'hijikake-mado'
floor mat 'tatami'
measure unit = 1 shaku = 303 mm = 1 ft (11.93 in)
3.50
6.00
6.00
9.00
transverse section scale 1 : 45

> Therefore there may be good reason for a second axis of approach to historical evaluation, namely to experience and appraise objects and forms spontaneously and apart from the knowledge of their origin, i.e., through the eyes and a mind that are not preconditioned, but which rely on unbiased reaction alone. The legitimacy of this approach is confirmed through the course of history itself: the transfer of cultural goods from one territory, one time, or one generation to another was frequently a transport of form, tool, or technique separate from the forces and functions that led to their origination. In fact, there may be an element of truth in the view that the reenacting and the reinterpretation of those "imports" in the new environments functioned better the less they were still associated with their original *raison d'etre*.[23]

Engel completes his argument by stating that the "independent existence" of *Measure and Construction of the Japanese House* "confirms the validity of the thesis in a very practical manner and is evidence that the claim and title of the book of twenty years ago is indeed very much alive: The Japanese house *is* tradition for contemporary architecture."[24] Whether or not Engel remained appalled at the "superficial fashion" in which architects borrowed forms and elements from historic Japanese architecture (as he described in his initial article in *Shinkenchiku*), he did not articulate it in the introduction to *Measure and Construction of the Japanese House*. However, by 1985 the architecture world was deeply entrenched in postmodernism, with its visible reaction to the tacit certitude of scientific knowledge and its regular appropriation of historic forms.

It is interesting to note that 1985 is important in the history of Japanese architecture—it marks the start of Japan's infamous "bubble economy" with its "practically unlimited investments in construction and urbanization."[25] Sparked by the effort to increase the export of goods from the United States through the devaluation of the U.S. dollar, the value of the Japanese yen abruptly increased. Within a very short period of time thereafter, relaxed banking laws and increased exports led to Japan's economic boom and a shift from a post-war catch-up mentality to a mood of unprecedented prosperity.

In what architect and Japan scholar Botond Bognar calls "the hyperactive bubble years between 1985 and 1995,"[26] Japanese architects experimented with diverse formal and philosophical responses to the generally indistinctive post-World War II urban development and the chaotic economic conditions caused by ballooning land values. "Architecture in the fast lane,"[27] is how Bognar describes the situation. With the escalated cost of land in the late 1980s, buildings were seen, in a sense, as disposable. Even architect-designed buildings would be replaced much more quickly than ever before (or after)—sometimes in less than ten years after completion. A 1986 Washington Post article aptly described the cityscape of Japan's capital as "the contrast between staggering clusters of nondescript or actively ugly modern buildings and a street life so hypnotically vivid that architectural esthetics hardly seem to count."[28] In this uncharted territory, architects experimented with formal responses, some verging on the bizarre and others more refined. Considering the quantity and design variety of the buildings constructed in Japan in the late 1980s, it is easy to imagine that interest in Japanese architecture from outside Japan increased as the "bubble" expanded.

For those looking to learn about what came before the sometimes brash and always self-confident "bubble architecture," *Measure and Construction of the Japanese House* provided an answer, perhaps even an antidote. Once the bubble burst and its effects wore off, Japanese architecture experienced a more pragmatic phase, constrained by the post-bubble economic recession, before turning again toward exploration and experimentation as the economy recovered. Throughout these shifts of the last 35 years, no other work has replaced Engel's meticulous text on historic Japanese domestic architecture. *Measure and Construction of the Japanese House* remains an indispensable resource for anyone interested in Japanese building culture.

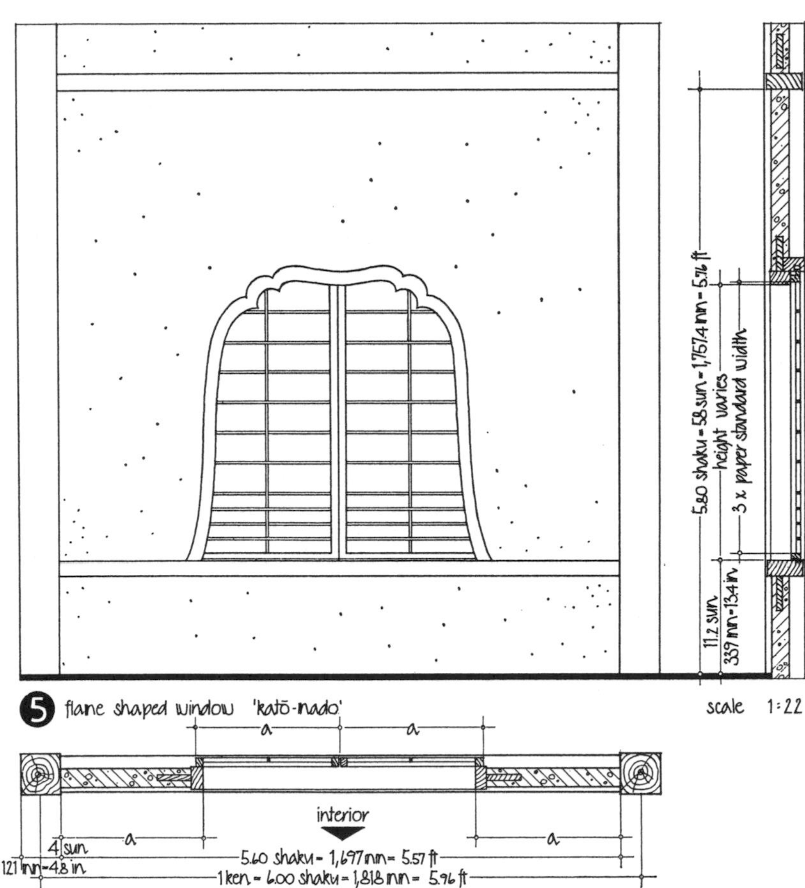

5 flane shaped window 'katō-nado'

Endnotes

1 Sandrisser, Barbara, "Cultivating Commonplaces: Sophisticated Vernacularism in Japan," in *The Journal of Aesthetics and Art Criticism*, Vol. 56, No. 2, Environmental Aesthetics (Spring, 1998), 210.

2 Sandrisser, 203.

3 Engel, Heinrich, "One Thought on Japanese Residential Architecture," in *Shinkenchiku*, vol. 31, No. 8 (August 1956), 60.

4 Engel, *Shinkenchiku*, 61.

5 Ibid.

6 Engel, Heinrich, *The Japanese House: A Tradition for Contemporary Living* (Tokyo and Rutland, VT: Charles E. Tuttle Company, 1964), 19.

7 Engel, *The Japanese House*, 21.

8 Gropius, Walter, "Foreword" in Henrich Engel, *The Japanese House: A Tradition for Contemporary Living*, (Tokyo and Rutland, VT: Charles E. Tuttle Company, 1964), 17.

9 Engel, *The Japanese House*, 23.

10 Engel, *The Japanese House*, 24.

11 Gropius, *The Japanese House*, 18.

12 Engel, *The Japanese House*, 25.

13 Ibid.

14 Engel, *The Japanese House*, 26.

15 "Publisher's Note" in Henrich Engel, *The Japanese House: A Tradition for Contemporary Living* (Tokyo and Rutland, VT: Charles E. Tuttle Company, 1964), 16.

16 Sandrisser, 210.

17 Engel, Heino. Tragsysteme Structure Systems (Ostfildern, Germany: Hatje Canst Verlag, 1997), 13.

18 "Toward an Integral Theory of Architecture" was published as a book by the University of Manitoba, Canada, in 1973.

19 University of Minnesota, "University of Minnesota Events" press release, January 9, 1970, https://conservancy.umn.edu/handle/11299/51864. Accessed November 11, 2019.

20 Engel, Heino, *Measure and Construction of the Japanese House* (Tokyo and Rutland, VT: Charles E. Tuttle Company, 1985), 13.

21 Ibid.

22 Ibid.

23 Engel, *Measure and Construction*, 14.

24 Ibid.

25 Bognar, Botond, as quoted in Melissa Mitchell, "Japanese architectural trends reflect unique realities, scholar says," University of Illinois News Bureau, March 9, 2009, https://news.illinois.edu/view/6367/206006. Accessed November 13, 2019.

26 Ibid.

27 Ibid.

28 Forgey, Benjamin, "Tokyo's Great Spiral" in *The Washington Post*, October 4, 1986; https://www.washingtonpost.com/archive/lifestyle/1986/10/04/tokyos-great-spiral/5ec06c00-9968-49a8-97cb-51c5d24f1401/. Accessed November 13, 2019.

introduction

This book is concerned with a residential architecture that not long ago encompassed the building of a whole nation, of the rich and the poor alike: the house of the Japanese. The purpose of this edition is to describe what the Japanese house is and how it is built, not to explain why the Japanese house is as it is.

The broad acceptance of an alien architectural achievement three hundred years old might be considered an astonishing phenomenon. It is not really so, however, if one realizes the particular features that distinguish the traditional Japanese house:

the modular order of system and form;
the flexibility of space partitions and room functions;
the compository potential of the floor mat;
the expressive diversity within comprehensive standardization;
the integrative quality of Japanese architectural forms.

Indeed, it is for these features that the Japanese house seems to be better suited to serve as a pattern for contemporary housing than any other form of residential architecture.

The author has thus limited this publication to the presentation of considerations of the form, system, and detail involved in how space in the Japanese house is laid out, how the components of the Japanese house are dimensioned, and how the Japanese house is then pieced together. Naturally, with such a content the presentation is concerned with the external, physical features of the Japanese house, not with the deeper causes and roots that gave birth to them.

Doubts, therefore, may come forth regarding whether an approach to presenting architecture for direct intake into house design has any legitimacy. Can imitation or adoption contribute substantially to the quality of contemporary architectural work? Might not morality in architecture seriously be injured in that the causative linkage of function, form, and meaning is interrupted, and the truth and readability of our contemporary environment are afflicted?

The conviction held until recently by the author was that the only way to experience architecture of the past or present and to make it work in one's professional or personal development is to study the full realm of environmental circumstances that have brought about this architecture. Only then, so the position was, can the past remain a living agent of our time and can tradition really function.

Plausible as this argument may appear, to the author himself this extreme viewpoint has become debatable. For it would mean that the "correct" application or appreciation of any cultural achievement would require an advance study of the total material and spiritual environment in which the object originated. Certainly, with such an approach only a fraction of past cultural achievements could be made accessible and thus become part of our world today. Moreover, it seems very unlikely that any study of the social or technical backgrounds will ever allow us to view and experience, even less to reenact, an architecture of the past in the same way as did the people then and there.

Therefore, there may be good reason for a second axis of approach to historical evaluation, namely to experience and appraise objects and forms spontaneously and apart from the knowledge of their origin, i.e., through eyes and a mind that are not preconditioned, but which rely on unbiased reaction alone. The legitimacy of this approach is confirmed through the course of history itself: the transfer of cultural goods from one territory, one time, or one generation to another was frequently a transport of form, tool, or technique separate from the forces and functions that led to their origination. In fact, there may be an element of truth in the view that the reenacting and the reinterpretation of those "imports" in the new environments functioned better the less they were still associated with their original *raison d'etre*.

Consequently, this book is deliberately an invitation to probe the possibilities of utilizing this architectural achievement of the Japanese as form, component, or system directly in modern living and building. It is true that the book seems to contradict the basic premise of the larger volume from which it has been taken. However, it by no means stands in contradiction to the former's underlying thesis of the model quality of the Japanese house. On the contrary, through its independent existence it confirms the validity of this thesis in a very practical manner and is evidence that the claim and title of the book of twenty years ago is indeed very much alive: The Japanese house *is* tradition for contemporary architecture.

definitions

measure

MEASURE IN BUILDING is the order that controls the scale, proportion, and form of the building. It relates the parts to the whole and in turn makes the whole dependent on its parts.

MEASURE IN BUILDING means standard. The standard of man's body was the earliest measure. Incorporation of various standard units of the body into one system by relating them in simple ratios effected the first measure system.

MEASURE IN BUILDING precedes construction. Before man could build, he had to conceive of measuring. Measuring is one of man's first intellectual achievements. It distinguished man's house from the animal's den.

MEASURE IN BUILDING is the essential means by which man brings building into precise relationship with himself. Measure is the element which humanizes man's environment.

MEASURE IN BUILDING thus is manifestation of culture. For standard of culture is determined by the variety and depth of emotional intercommunication of man and man-made environment, i.e., by the degree of human measure in his environment.

MEASURE IN BUILDING also contains measures of aesthetics, fabric, and technique and thus constitutes in itself a compromise between these frequently opposite forces. The character of this compromise reflects the purpose of a building.

MEASURE IN BUILDING manifests the skill, taste, and thought of builders. Ancient cultures possessed an elaborate order of measure that determined building. This order was based primarily on visual aesthetic principles.

MEASURE IN BUILDING, then, is the instrument by which man masters the basic fabric of building. Thus, it is his "measure" to organize the elements of building into an entirety and to create the human environment called architecture.

The question of measure in building is as old as building itself. In fact, the history of architecture is but the history of man's quest for the secret of measure, in proportion, number, scale, and form. Not only architects, but artists, mathematicians, and philosophers as well, have participated throughout the ages in the search for a "measure" that would both physically and spiritually establish the complete harmony between man and the world.

This striving for the appropriate measure is evidenced by the many geometric as well as arithmetic methods that architects of various periods developed in order to determine the proportions of their buildings. Usually simple grids (square, rectangular, triangular, or circular) or more complex geometric patterns were employed as a reference system for the dimensioning of the building. Numbers themselves were thought of as possessing mystical and aesthetic significance. The golden number, the golden section, the divine proportion, all representing the irrational number which is the positive root of the equation $x^2 = x + 1$ and whose value is approximately 1.618, essentially controlled such modular design.

Whereas these traditional efforts were prompted by man's search for visual beauty and not by an immediate necessity for living, the problem of measure in the contemporary industrial society is concerned with the very substance of building. Even though increased mechanization in most industries has initiated mass production of most of the important goods and has thus raised the standard of living, the building industries have yet to emerge from the medieval method of handicraft production. Therefore, assimilation of building to the machine industry is one of the main tasks of contemporary architecture and the first step toward this goal is the establishment of standard measures that are all based upon one single common measure, the module. The module should fulfill the practical demands of both building and living and should control design and production of building whatever be its purpose or size. Coordination of all activities connected with building and of all building components in accordance with the module, i.e., modular coordination, is a necessity in the machine age.

Especially in the face of the largely unchecked and impersonal authority of the machine industry over the production of building elements and the dehumanized environment created by their assemblage, the control of measures in the building industry is one means of re-establishing the emotional accord of man to his creations, without which there is no true culture.

construction

CONSTRUCTION IN BUILDING is both the act of building and the structural system, translating into reality what theretofore has been idea, conception, or design. Construction in building, therefore, is a means rather than an end.

CONSTRUCTION IN BUILDING, thus, is the materialization of design. As such it comprehends the total range of factors that condition design—the practical, technical, functional, environmental, and spiritual aspects of architecture.

CONSTRUCTION IN BUILDING demonstrates architectural growth in its transformation and evolution. Architecture began with purposeful construction of human shelter and developed in direct interdependence with technical improvement.

CONSTRUCTION IN BUILDING reflects the level of civilization and thereby gives clues as to the conditioning society and the philosophic background. Thus, construction marks cultural epochs as distinctly as does literature, painting, or music.

CONSTRUCTION IN BUILDING is closely interrelated with form, expression, and sensation of building. Stimulating certain forms and preventing others, it is an element that gives character and substance to architectural space and thus renders architecture distinctive.

CONSTRUCTION IN BUILDING also influences the psyche of man. Influencing architectural form and space, it invites a particular mode of living. Thus, it not only orientates the taste and customs of the inhabitant but also influences the ethics and morals of family and society.

CONSTRUCTION IN BUILDING is dependent on various factors. Utilitarian purpose of building, distinct idea of design, climatic-geological conditions, also traditional methods and thoughts, all decisively influence construction in building.

CONSTRUCTION IN BUILDING, then, is an essential element in both building process and building structure. Though it is not architecture itself, yet, it is the decisively formative medium in the earliest shelter as well as in contemporary building.

Not only has the system and form of construction undergone essential changes throughout the ages, but the proportional contribution of construction in the ensemble of architectural factors has been a subject of widely different interpretations. Some epochs unconditionally subjugated construction to spatial ideas, while others indiscriminately adopted the form dictated by construction. Such extreme and opposing conceptions also characterize contemporary architectural work. After the period of eclecticism in the 19th century, characterized by an alienation of architectural form from construction, contemporary architecture obviously tends toward constructivism. Under the watchword "structural integrity" construction is ostentatiously displayed and architectural idea often is no longer primary conception but mere constructional result.

In the light of such extreme tendencies, an analysis of the role of construction in the Japanese dwelling should be attributed more importance than that of mere record, because Japanese residential architecture throughout its evolution has preserved a unique balance between form, space, and construction. Indeed, construction in the Japanese house is an essential component of space, as well as the major source of form. Architectural accentuation is attained mainly through constructional means, and architectural décor is derived from constructional device.

Although for an assessment of the structural qualities of the Japanese house it should suffice to analyze only the overall system of construction, a study of constructional detail is also required in order to gain that broad understanding which alone can become the basis for a substantial evaluation. Studying the details of one house without forsaking their general validity for the total domestic architecture of Japan is possible only because all constructional features are employed uniformly throughout the nation. In fact, with the description of a single house, the entire residential architecture of Japan is covered, both in system and detail, a unique phenomenon in the history of architecture.

But it is both unnecessary and impossible to describe every constructional detail and its variations. Basically, they are the same all over Japan. However, local differences, especially climatic adaptations, even carpenters' personal preferences, have emerged. Moreover, Western methods have effected modifications through use of metal. The original construction, however, that is to say, the classic performance (the subject matter of this book), was constructionally free of any metal support or joinery.

Such general application was possible only because of the particular order of the feudalistic society. Constructional procedure, dimension, and detail were written down on paper scrolls and kept by the master carpenter. As the profession was hereditary, the scripts were handed down from father to son. In the Tokugawa period (1600–1867) they were woodblock printed and thus provided an exchange of new methods as well as universal dispersion. The measurements as they appear in these rules are not absolute, but are moduled by column distance and column section. Since both are standardized, measurements of constructional detail for residences have become fairly fixed.

In describing constructional detail, this book employs the same depictive methods as those that appear in the traditional carpenter manuals, for there is hardly another method so simply executed and so easily comprehended as is the illustrative technique of the Japanese carpenter.

This analysis, then, with a short description of historic precedence and architectural evolution, is intended to provide a scale for better judgment of contemporary affairs. It should also shed light on the role of construction in the creation of architecture, which is so much disputed and so much abused in contemporary building.

1 measuring system and module

measure of man

The earliest and most primitive architectural space was the minimum volume required to contain the family. Its dimensions, therefore, were but human measurements in their multiple, modified by interior functional activities and by the limits that material and technique imposed. These basic factors of space in residential architecture have not essentially changed and are also prerequisite to adequate architectural space in contemporary design. This is not meant to challenge the importance of other less primitive-practical factors in the creation of architectural space such as its ideal or psychological aspect. No doubt, these are decisive for the quality of architectural space, but in residential architecture they can only be attributed secondary importance in comparison to the fulfillment of man's mere physical requirements for space, i.e., requirements for sitting, working, and sleeping.

The cause and idea behind space in residential architecture, therefore, is primarily functional-practical and only secondarily emotional-ideal. Of course, space may occasionally function to satisfy man's aesthetic-spiritual wants rather than his physical wants, but the dominant function of space in residential architecture is the fulfillment of man's practical requirements. Therefore, thorough knowledge of the measure of man's physique is essential for both analysis of the existing and creation of the new.

This is of even more importance in the case of Japan, where social conditions have imposed on the common classes the utmost of limitation and curtailment of space in building that has no equivalent in Western architecture. In fact, the relationship of human and architectural measurement is so immensely close that one may well speak of their being identical. It effects a strong interrelationship of man and house and is the major reason why the Japanese house appears dwarfishly small in comparison with Western residences, the difference being far greater than the difference between Japanese and Western figure would indicate.

Measurements of the average-sized human have little significance for architectural dimensioning. For building, no matter of what type, is not for the individual alone but for the majority of people. Consequently, architectural dimensioning has to prove adequate for all, i.e., it must be determined by the size of the average tall person so that convenience is provided for all others. Only the height measurements of furniture are exempted, because, here, the measurements of the average small person reversely prove adequate for all others. Therefore, the two extremes, the tall and the small human figure, have to be considered in architectural dimensioning. However, since furniture is very rare in the Japanese house, only measurements of the average tall Japanese are of value.

The dominant Japanese physical type is Mongoloid. In relation to the total figure height, the head is large and the limbs are short; also the face clearly manifests the Mongolian type.The main physical differences from the Caucasian type, having architectural importance, are the following:

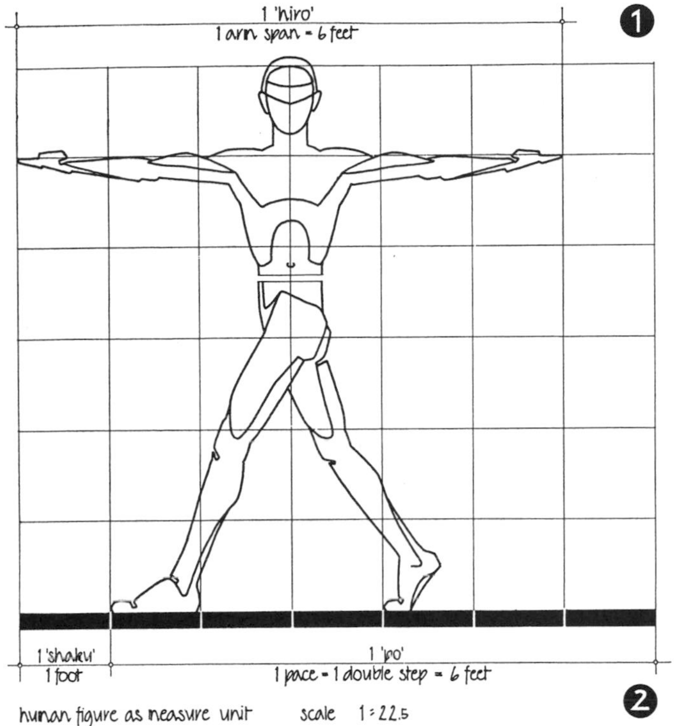

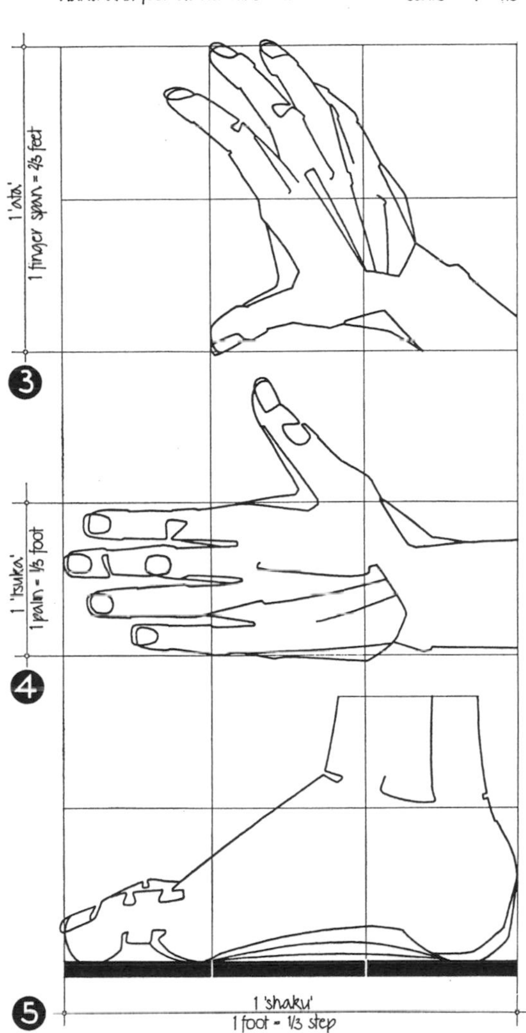

early human standard measures in relationship to foot unit
1 foot = about 275 mm = 10.8 in.

FIGURE 1: The human figure as standard for measure units.

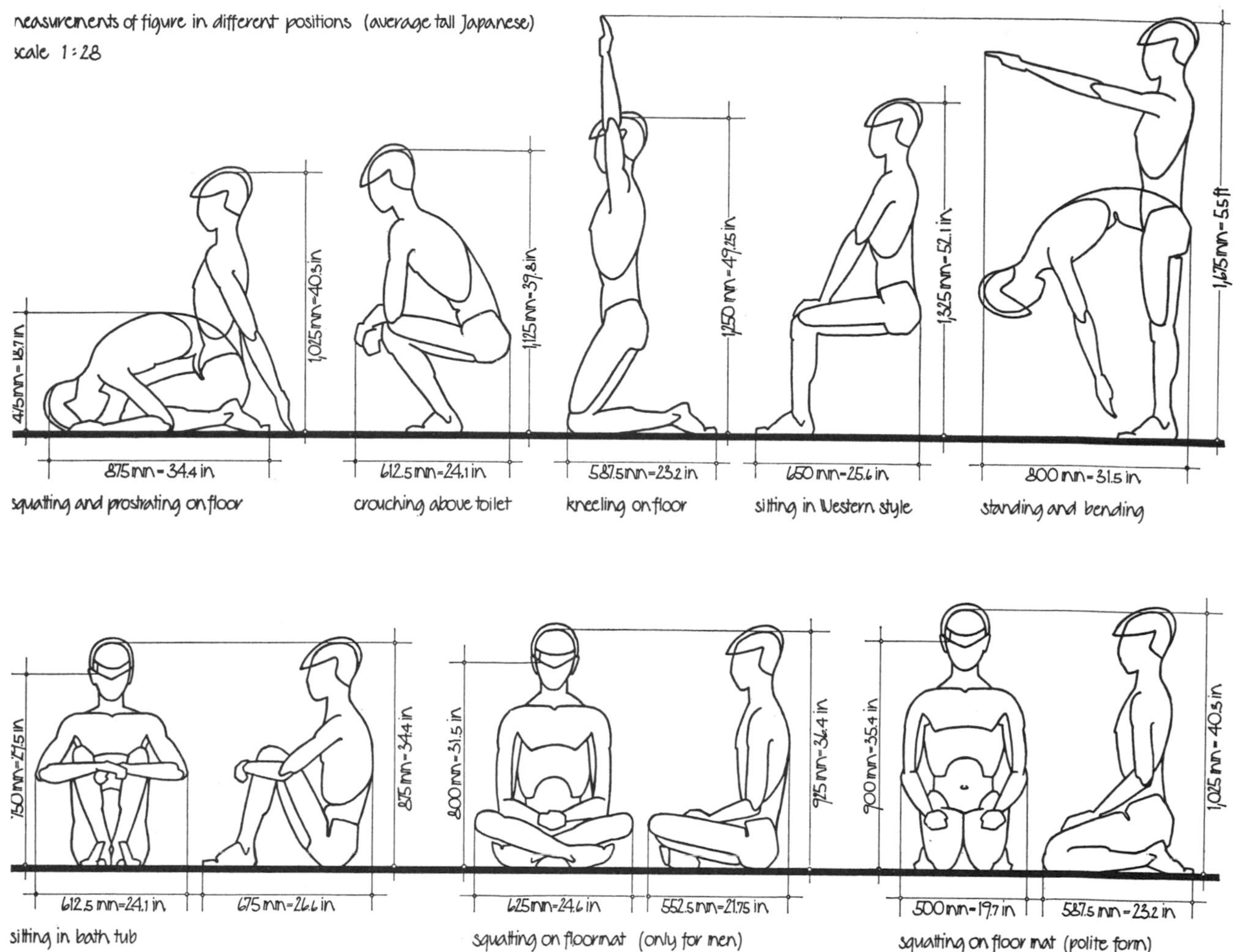

FIGURE 2: Space requirements of the Japanese figure in various postures.

1. The average height is about 6 *sun* smaller (187.5 mm. = 7.4 in.).*
2. The whole body height is between 6½ and 7 times that of the head height, while in Western countries the average is 7½ to 8 times.
3. The body crotch is much lower than the middle of the body whereas the Caucasian type has the crotch about at half height.
4. This results in particularly short legs and other limbs, which are already shorter because of smaller body height.
5. Thus the torso has about the same height as the Caucasian counterpart, i.e., sitting on the same base, the eye level of both is about the same.

* The height difference between male and female is about 4.5 *sun* (137.5 mm.= 5.4 in.).

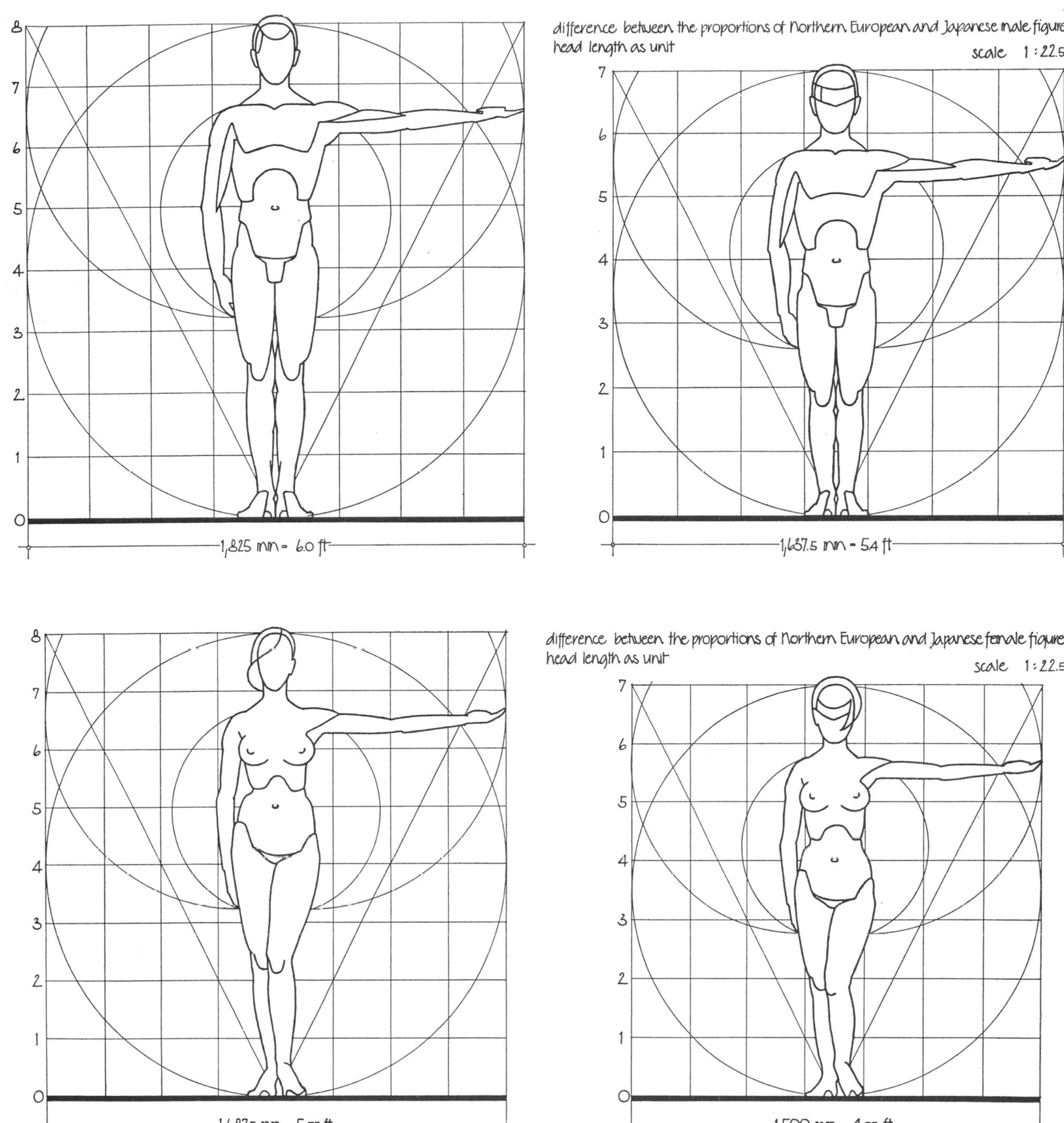

FIGURE 3: Comparison of standard human figures of Northern Europeans and Japanese.

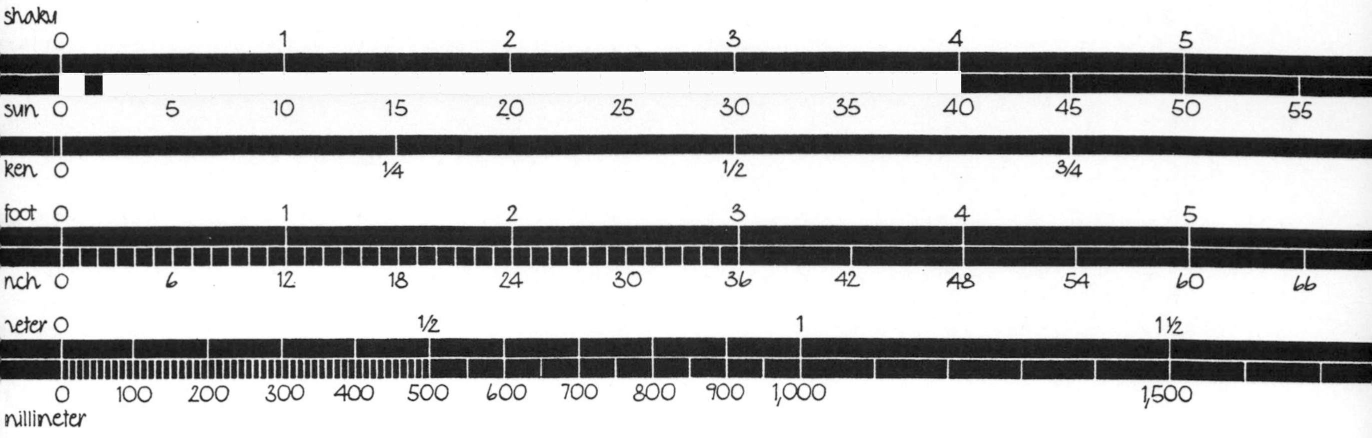

comparison of traditional japanese length units with foot/inch-system and metric system

1 shaku = 10 sun = 303 mm = 11.93 in. 1 foot = 12 in. = 1.01 shaku = 10.1 sun = 30

building measures

Though in Japan the metric system has been in use since 1891, the ordinary residence is still controlled by the traditional measure system.Its basic unit is the Japanese foot called *shaku,* almost identical with the English foot. The structure of measures was taken over from China and in its original subdivision was consistently decimal.

1 *ri* = 150 *jō* = 1500 *shaku*
1 *jō* = 10 *shaku* = 100 *sun*
1 *shaku** = 10 *sun* = 100 *bu*
1 *sun* = 10 *bu* = 100 *rin*
1 *bu* =10 *rin*

In the latter half of Japan's Middle Ages another length unit, the *ken,* appeared. *Ken* originally designated the interval between two columns of any wooden structure and varied in size. However, it became standardized in residential architecture very early and was used as a measure unit in the cities. After various transformations the *ken* finally emerged as the unique design module, although in two essentially different applications: the *kyō-ma* method and the *inaka-ma* method. Both have affected the measures in residential architecture up to the present time, but only the *ken* of the *inaka-ma* method of 6 *shaku* (1,818 mm. = 6.0 ft.), which relates to center-to-center distance between columns, eventually replaced the *jō* unit of 10 *shaku* used in handicraft and for common use and was incorporated as the official unit of the Japanese system of measures. The primary reasons for this development were the *ken* measure's intimacy with daily life, its close relationship to human measurements, and its practicality in use.

The Japanese system of length measures is comparatively simple:

1 *ri* = 36 *chō* = 2160 *ken* = 3,927,165.12 mm. = 12,884.40 ft. = 2.44 mi.
1 *chō* = 60 *ken* = 36 *jō* = 109,087.92 mm. = 357.90 ft.
1 *jō* = 10 *shaku* = 3,030.22 mm. = 9.94 ft.
1 *ken (inaka-ma)* = 6 *shaku* = 1,818.13 mm. = 5.97 ft.
1 *shaku* = 10 *sun* = 303.02 mm. = 11.93 in.
1 *sun* = 10 *bu* = 30.30 mm. = 1.19 in.
1 *bu* = 10 *rin* = 3.03 mm. = 0.12 in.

* The *shaku* measurement in use at that time was probably the *kōrai-shaku,* which is 1.17 times the size of present *shaku* measurement (approximately 355 mm. or 14 in.).

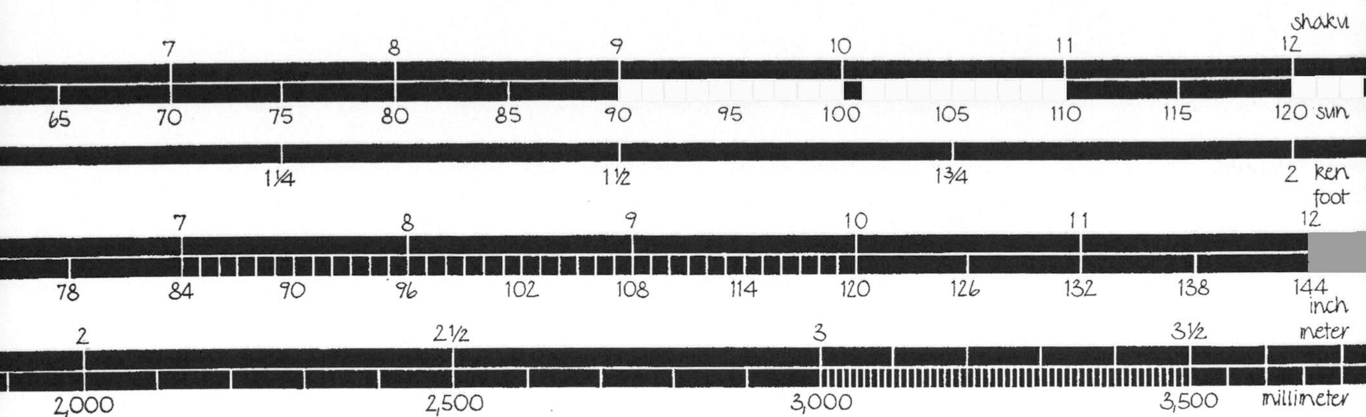

FIGURE 4: Comparative scales for *shaku*, foot-inch, and metric systems.

The units *ri, chō,* and *jō* are applied only in field measurements and city planning. Yet, as the construction of cities systematically subjected blocks, streets, and houses to a common order, these large units also affected the single residential site and therefore, though indirectly, the houses too.

While the above length units constitute exact measurements, the Japanese square measures for residences are conspicuous by their vagueness. Two units are used to denote room area, but neither can be expressed in exact measurement.

The one unit, *jō* (not to be mistaken for the length unit *jō*, which has a different Chinese ideograph), is actually the area covered by one mat. The latter, however, being dependent on the standard *ken* unit with its two design methods, varies not only with different room sizes but also with local practice. In spite of this, *jō* denotes room areas corresponding to the number of mats, e.g., 3, 4, 4½, 6, 8, and 10 *jō*. The only correct identification of *jō*, then, is that it is the area covered by one mat, which may be anywhere between 6.5 x 3.25 and 5.8 x 2.9 *shaku* (approximately 2.00–1.54 sq. m. = 21.1–16.8 sq. ft.).

The other unit for architectural square measurement is *tsubo.* Being the area of one square *ken*, it also has inherited all those differences that characterize the two methods of the *ken* module. Moreover, since the *ken* of 6 *shaku* is a center-to-center column distance, the *tsubo* only gives the amount of the area as marked by the constructional *ken*-grid. It does not de note the actual floor area because walls are placed on center of this grid and their thickness subtracts from the floor area. Still *tsubo* is used indiscriminately for both interior and exterior areas of residential sites, taking into account neither the different sizes and methods of the application of the *ken* nor the discrepancy between constructional distance and open width. The actual size of 1 *tsubo,* thus, may vary from 6.50 x 6.50 to 6.00 x 6.00 *shaku* (3.9–3.3 sq. m. = 42.3–36.0 sq. ft.).

These, then, are the measure units which have exerted an influence upon, and also have emerged from, Japanese living and building. Among them certainly *shaku* and *ken* are the most important and therefore are given closer examination in the succeeding pages.

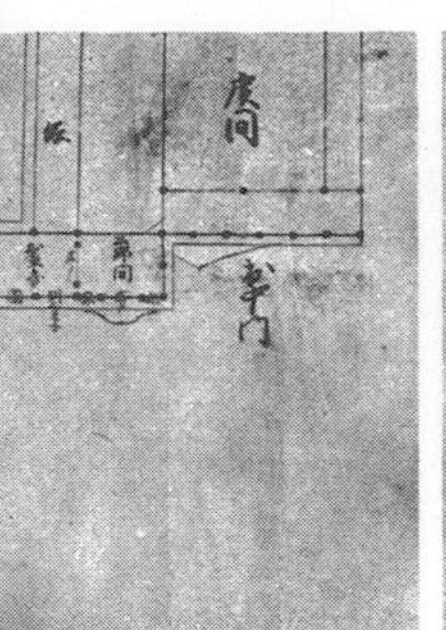

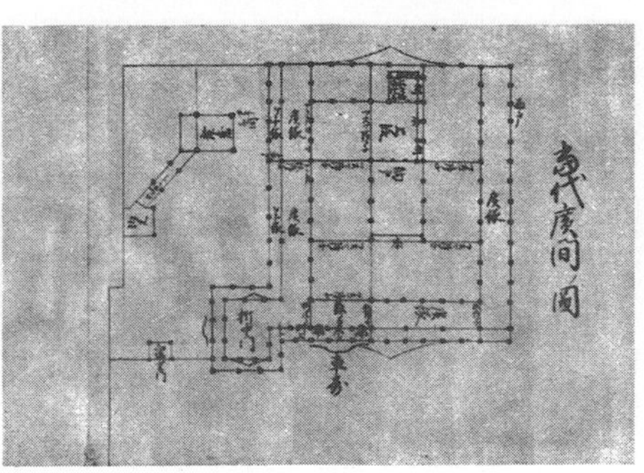

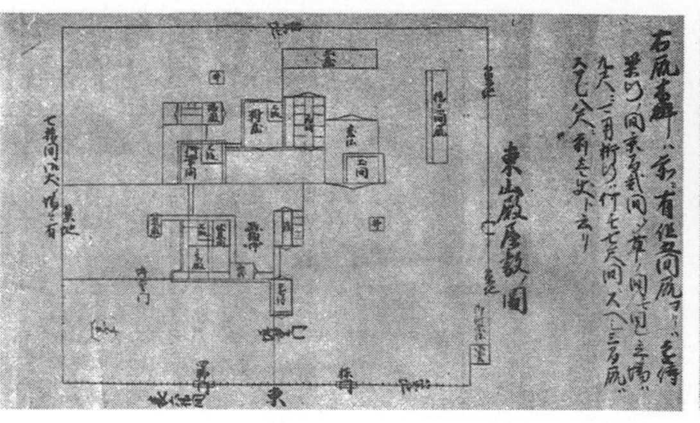

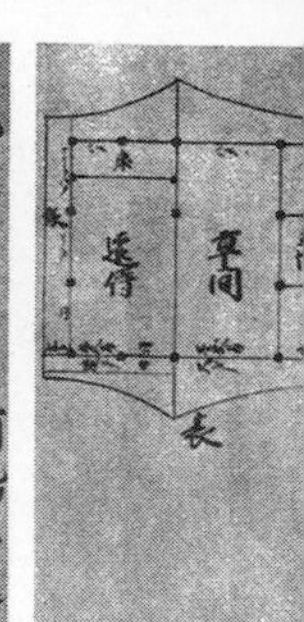

ken measure and module

The term "module" stems from the Latin "modulus" (little measure) and has been used in building ever since the time of Vitruvius (1st century B.C.). It denotes a basic length unit in building from which all other dimensions of measurements are derived. In the classical Greco-Roman temple the module was the diameter of the column and in the Chinese temple it was the width of the rafter. In Classic architecture the module was not an absolute measurement but varied according to the size of each building. It was meant to control aesthetic-visual proportions and was conspicuous by its independence from any other material or human-utilitarian measurement.

Industrialization of contemporary building has again prompted the search for a single measurement that would at the same time be a convenient unit for architectural design and a practical unit for industrial production. Because of its analogy with the Classical "order," this measurement is called "module"; the comprehensive coordination of all building activities and building components according to this unit is called modular coordination. It differs from the past module in that it is not an aesthetical but a practical-functional measure and in that it is no longer relative to the size of each building but is an absolute measurement.

This modern meaning of module, however, has an outstanding precedence in Japan, where for the last two to three hundred years the ordinary houses of the entire nation have been built on the basis of a modular order which is unique in the history of world architecture. Indeed, the Japanese *ken* module is an extraordinary phenomenon in architecture without equivalent elsewhere; and, though its complicated past is anything but clear, its uniqueness among all architectural measures, modules, and standards, past and present, cannot be contested.

The history of the Japanese residence is the history of the *ken.* When the *ken* was consciously applied for the first time, Japanese architecture struck one of its most distinct features, order. What contemporary architecture hitherto has striven for so unsuccessfully emerged in Japan logically: a unit universally applied in living as in building, a standard distance for construction and economy, a module for aesthetic order, a six-fractioned measurement in decimal system, a length related to human proportions, even a link between city and domestic planning. Even though other forces may have contributed to its evolution, the *ken* is mainly the carpenter's achievement. No other feature in the Japanese house is likely to better demonstrate his mastership of the total range of his profession.

The Chinese ideograph *ken* means "distance" or "interval," and major column distance was the original meaning of the *ken* as used in house construction. Remains of the earliest dwellings confirm that this distance was fairly well fixed even before a regular system of measures existed. But it was only after organization of the feudalistic society,

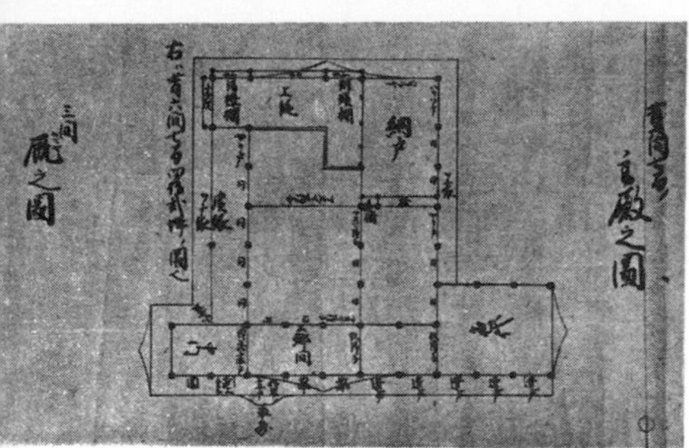

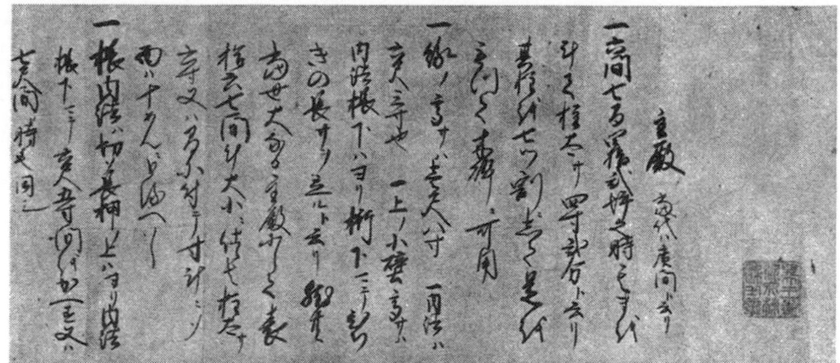

FIGURE 5 (right to left): The *Shōmei* scroll, 1608, by Masanobu Heinouchi. The part depicted shows plans of standard structures and layout of the Higashiyama Palace.

patterned after the Chinese, that the rise of cities and the growth of artisan professions effected more systematic residential building in the city. There is no doubt that this early standardization was based on economic-constructional considerations rather than on man's exact spatial requirements. Definitely, no visual-aesthetical considerations were involved. Logically, the typical column distance was the decisive measurement and it is, therefore, probable that the *ken* measurement came into being as an independent dimension of residential construction and not as the multiple of an existing smaller length unit.

Accordingly, this *ken* must have been applied predominantly in the cities, a theory that is supported by the fact that early records always refer to the "*kyō-maken*," which literally means "column distance in metropolis measurement." Apparently this denotation of the *ken* was made to distinguish it from *ken* as employed outside the towns, where residential building was not yet a matter of a particular and organized craft and also where residential design was not limited by a rigid street and block pattern. Thus, the column distance *ken* that previously had varied between 7½ and 6 ft. was established at 6½ ft.; the changeable constructional distance *ken* became exact measurement.

Doubtless, in the design of buildings, the increasing influence of the carpenter himself played a decisive part in the evolution of the *ken.* In pace with the social transformations that took place at the end of the Middle Ages in Japan, the carpenter also began to design temples and aristocratic mansions, a privilege that previously had been limited to the priest and nobleman. Conceivably, stimulated by ancient proportional rules of Buddhist architecture as inherited from China, the carpenter also developed a canon of aesthetics for the various buildings of the influential warrior class for whom he had to work. The essential and, as it proved, decisive change in this order was that all measurements were brought into direct ratio to one unit, the *ken* of the cities, the *ken* in *kyō-ma* measurement of 6.5 *shaku* (1,970 mm. = 6.5 ft.); the constructional measurement *ken* became aesthetic module.

In the meantime a different *ken* unit emerged outside the cities and towns, the *ken* in *inaka-ma* measurement (column distance in countryside measurement).

1 *ken* in *kyō-ma* measurement (original) = 6.5 *shaku* (1,970 mm. = 6.5 ft.)

1 *ken* in *inaka-ma* measurement = 6.0 *shaku* (1,818 mm. = 6.0 ft.)

Many theories have been set forth about the origin of the *ken* of 6 *shaku* and how the difference in measurement between *kyō-ma* and *inaka-ma* came about. All of them lack evidence, but there is much probability in the theory that in areas outside the influence of the organized towns, an independent system of design evolved which was different from the urban pattern. For building in rural areas was not tied to city planning nor subjected to aesthetic-conventional rules of guilds, and therefore could develop strictly along economical-practical lines. Certainly an even unit of 6 *shaku* is a more practical standard length for design and constructional layout with divisions into halves and quarters than the odd *ken* of *kyō-ma* measurement of 6.5 *shaku*.

Because of such advantages, the employment of *ken* in *inaka-ma* measurement also gradually spread into the cities. A governmental regulation of March and August 1657 concerning reconstruction and building in Edo (Tokyo) mentions both *ken* measurements; yet, later on, the *ken* of 6 *shaku* became dominant in the entire northern part of Japan. Because of its practical advantages rather than its functional appropriateness as length, the 6-foot *ken* was incorporated into the existing measure system; the architectural measurement *ken* became official unit of length.

The architectural advantage gained was extraordinary. The consistent sequence of decimal subdivisions was interrupted at a decisive point, thereby permitting an important multi-divisibility into 2, 3, and 4 (room width is usually 2 *ken* or 12 *shaku*) without sacrificing the merits of the decimal system. Moreover, the intimate relationship between living and building effected complete adoption of this architectural measurement in everyday living, replacing the former *jō* of 10 *shaku*.

Nevertheless, the use of the *ken* in *kyō-ma* measurement continued regardless of its odd subdivision. The former imperial capital, Kyoto, as well as the major part of Japan, still uses *ken* in *kyō-ma* measurement. It is used even in Hokkaidō, the most northern island, which was settled in more recent times. The reason for this preference is the greater absolute length of the *ken* in *kyō-ma;* for the *ken* standard of 6 feet has the disadvantage that its half, the 3 feet fraction, is slightly too small for minimum spaces such as corridor, veranda, toilet, and bath. In the *inaka-ma* system, therefore, the ½-*ken* module is frequently not applied for the small rooms, in favor of either 3.5 *shaku,* or even 4 *shaku.*

The differences in the two *ken* measurements had further consequences. After both constructional standard distances had established themselves as exact measurements, usage of the rigid floor mat gradually became common among the lower classes. Since the mat was prefabricated and often was taken along with change of domicile, it became necessary to standardize floor area instead of structural interval. Thus in the *kyō-ma* method of design, the system of measuring column distance *ken* from center to center was upset and spacing of columns was determined by the standard mat size, measurements of which originally had been subjected to the regular center-to-center distance of the columns.

Whereas *ken* in *inaka-ma* maintained its congruity with constructional distances, from this time on, the measurement of *ken* in *kyō-ma* was no longer constant, but was variable depending on the interior room width which was determined by the mat units. As will be explained later, due to this transformation, the two measures of *ken* came to denote particular systems of plan technique; the length unit *ken* became a method of design.

With this the *ken* terminated a rather complicated development: transmutation and differentiation from varying column distance to two different but exact measurements—to aesthetic module in the one case and to official length unit in the other; dissolution of the original meaning of the *ken* as actual column distance; and, finally, emergence of two essentially different design methods, one of which even nullified the role of the *ken* as absolute measurement.These transformations, then, are the source of the many misinterpretations of the architectural meaning of *ken.* At different times *ken* meant different things, just as it does at present in different areas of Japan.

traditional standards

Since the unforeseen onset of the machine revolutionized the basis of architectural creation, the standardization of building elements on a modular basis has become a matter of increasing importance in contemporary architecture. Agreement exists that standardization, i.e., the finding and determining of large and small units of excellence in contemporary architecture, is inevitable not only because of the need for economic use and control of the mass-productional machine, but also because it constitutes a creative medium in architectural expression. However, opposing viewpoints and vague conceptions exist about the possible consequences of standardization upon architectural creation, as well as upon life in general, because the West, throughout its history, has not produced an architecture with a comprehensive physical standardization that would allow a study of the effects of standardization.

On the other hand, since the early Middle Ages the East (India, China, and Japan) possessed an elaborate standardization that controlled residential architecture. Only in Japan has this standardization survived to the present. It penetrates the universal range of architectural work to a degree paralleled as yet by no other modular system of residential building in the contemporary West. In fact, everything that is a component of, or contributive to, the erection of a Japanese house is standardized: fabric, measure, design, and construction; even the garden. The integral unit is standardized as is the total organism. That is to say, they all have been developed to a level of excellence that from the viewpoint of the traditional Japanese life does not ask for further improvement. This comprehensive standardization, then, not only holds the value of instructive comparison with contemporary architecture, but also should remove many misconceptions and thereby promote a better understanding of the potential of standardization and prefabrication in building. For in its history of more than three hundred years, Japanese modular coordination has produced certain results that have immediate relationship to modern standardization:

1. Since architectural creation is no longer concerned with individual room, material, construction, detail, façade, not even with the dominating silhouette of the roof, design is concentrated on that which is solely decisive for architecture in general: organization of space by means of composing rooms of fixed sizes, choosing among a limited number of materials and techniques, and interrelating outdoors and indoors. Free from the entanglement of constantly developing anew individual units of space, form, or construction, and given cohesiveness by the discipline of the *ken* grid, architectural creation becomes an immensely free play with spaces in space.
2. Since the house is decided in all its components, everyone is familiar with both design and construction of a building, even in detail. Therefore, residential architecture is not a particular craft or art to the Japanese, but is just a part of daily life of which everyone has sufficient knowledge to be his own architect. Consequently, the professional architect, as he emerged with the introduction of the West's new materials and constructions, is as recent as he is little respected, and he is not at all necessary for the design of traditional residences.
3. Since residences of any size and room arrangement are built with identical units, the component parts are prefabricated at the carpenter's workshop. As a result, the actual building process consists of merely assembling the various units, and requires a minimum of time and labor. Removable building parts such as windows, doors, mats, and ceiling components can readily be bought on the market so that deteriorated parts can easily be replaced. With equal simplicity the house can be extended as old parts can be used for new construction.

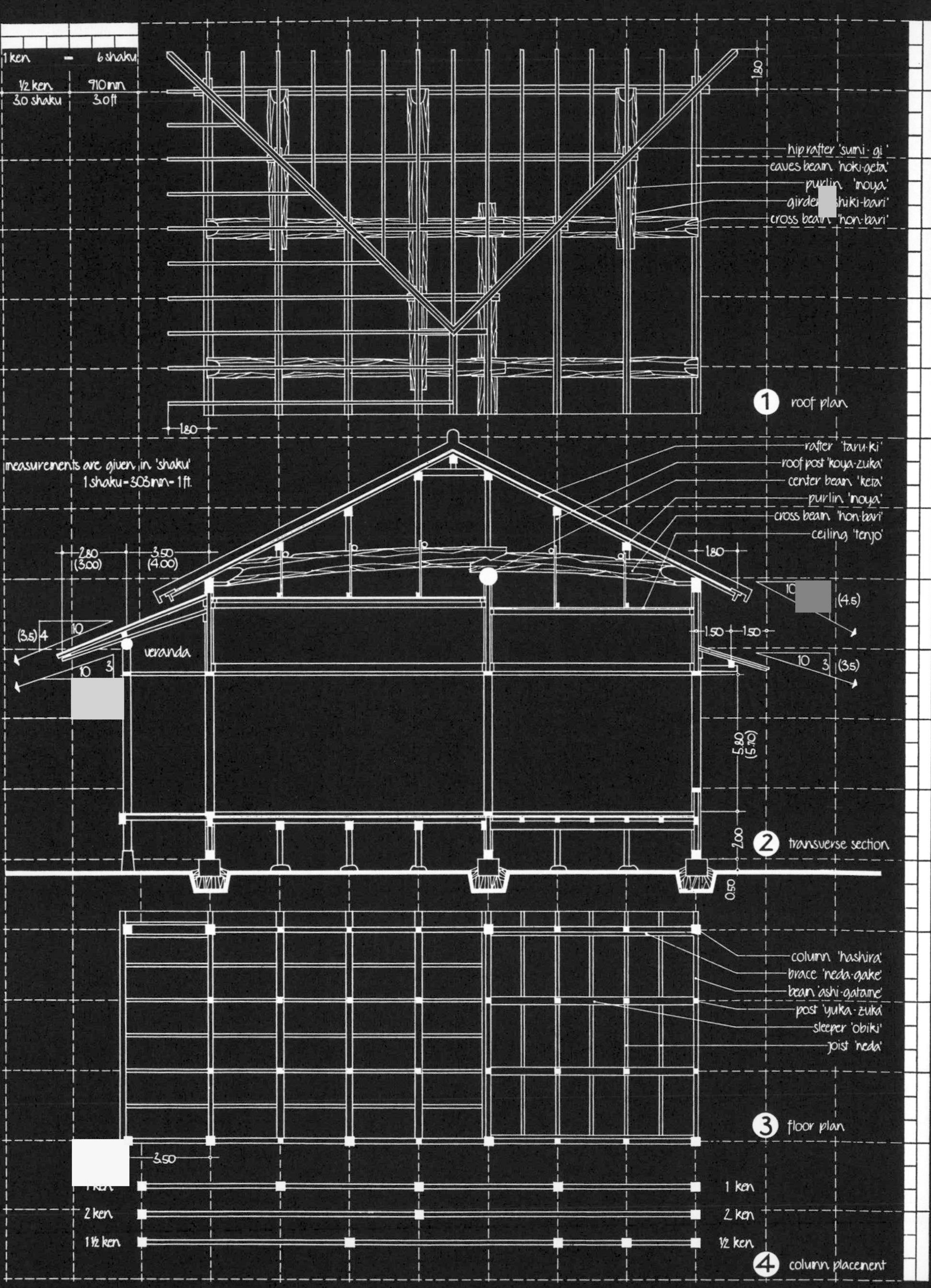

FIGURE 6: The modular order of the Japanese house.

4. Since in his work the carpenter is confined to only a few standard forms and methods, he attains exacting technical precision and skill and accomplishes highly qualified work with a minimum of time and material. He does not need working drawings, nor is he concerned with constructional problems. Instead, he concentrates his creative instinct solely on the refinement of that which standardization has not yet reached. This accounts for the extreme refinement of the Japanese residence, which, by the same reason, is more evident in detail than in entirety.
5. Since on the other hand, the carpenter is subjected to an order, the alteration of which both social environment and his own professional belief forbid, he does not attempt to improve the standards his forefathers creatively developed. Throughout centuries, therefore, method and construction have remained stagnant at a primitive stage and have essentially strangled progress in building and living. Thus the present residence constitutes a strange contrast of primitivity in essence and perfection in performance. In this instance, the Japanese house clearly demonstrates a defective tendency caused by standardization.

Though standardization in the Japanese residence actually covers all phases of architectural work, only the standard measurements of the house anatomy will be studied. Among them the absolute measurements are of less interest than those which are incorporated into a particular order or system such as the dimensions that are in ratio to either the *ken* or the column section of 4 *sun.* If the *ken* is the basis of such an order, actually two groups of standards have to be considered, i.e. the standards based on:

ken in *kyō-ma* measurement = 6.5 *shaku* (on the average), and

ken in *inaka-ma* measurement = 6.0 *shaku.*

Only the *inaka-ma* system is exemplified in the drawings, since the *kyō-ma* measurements are more complicated and also are somewhat modified by different design methods.

It is evident that all horizontal structural distances are in direct ratio to the standard length *ken.* This modular order of *ken* is then consistently subdivided into fractions of ½ or ¼, i.e., into smaller intervals of 3 or 1½ *shaku.* Thus the order of *ken* also controls the details. Yet, this order is not slavishly adhered to in all instances. As the standard unit of ½ *ken* (3 *shaku* = 909 mm. = approx. 3 ft.) is rather small for the width of corridors, toilets, and verandas, the width of these minimum spaces is frequently enlarged to 3.5 or 4.0 *shaku,* the adjustment being easily accomplished by the handicraft technique.

The standard heights in the Japanese house show greater variety, yet the mere fact that they are standardized is of interest rather than the actual length, which may differ very slightly from one carpenter to the other. In the drawings, measurements most frequently used are listed, while those used less frequently are set in brackets. Deviations are given in percentages. The measurements of roof projections show the greatest local deviations, probably due to particular climatic circumstances. However, they are strictly observed within the particular locale. Most of them are not in ratio to any basic unit, but are absolute measurements.

Actually, the organization of the ceiling exemplifies the only module in the composition of standards that changes relative to room size. But here too, the former flexible ceiling height has become constant measurement in many areas, and so has the market size of the ceiling board. Present carpenter manuals contain only absolute measures.

The module for the ceiling, both in its height above floor and its subdivision, is the floor mat *tatami.* However, the mat itself does not function as module, but only the number of mats contained in each room; i.e., room size determines ceiling height and organization. As the ceiling is suspended by perpendicular ties to the main beams above, these height variations within a single house can be accomplished without additional time, work, or material.

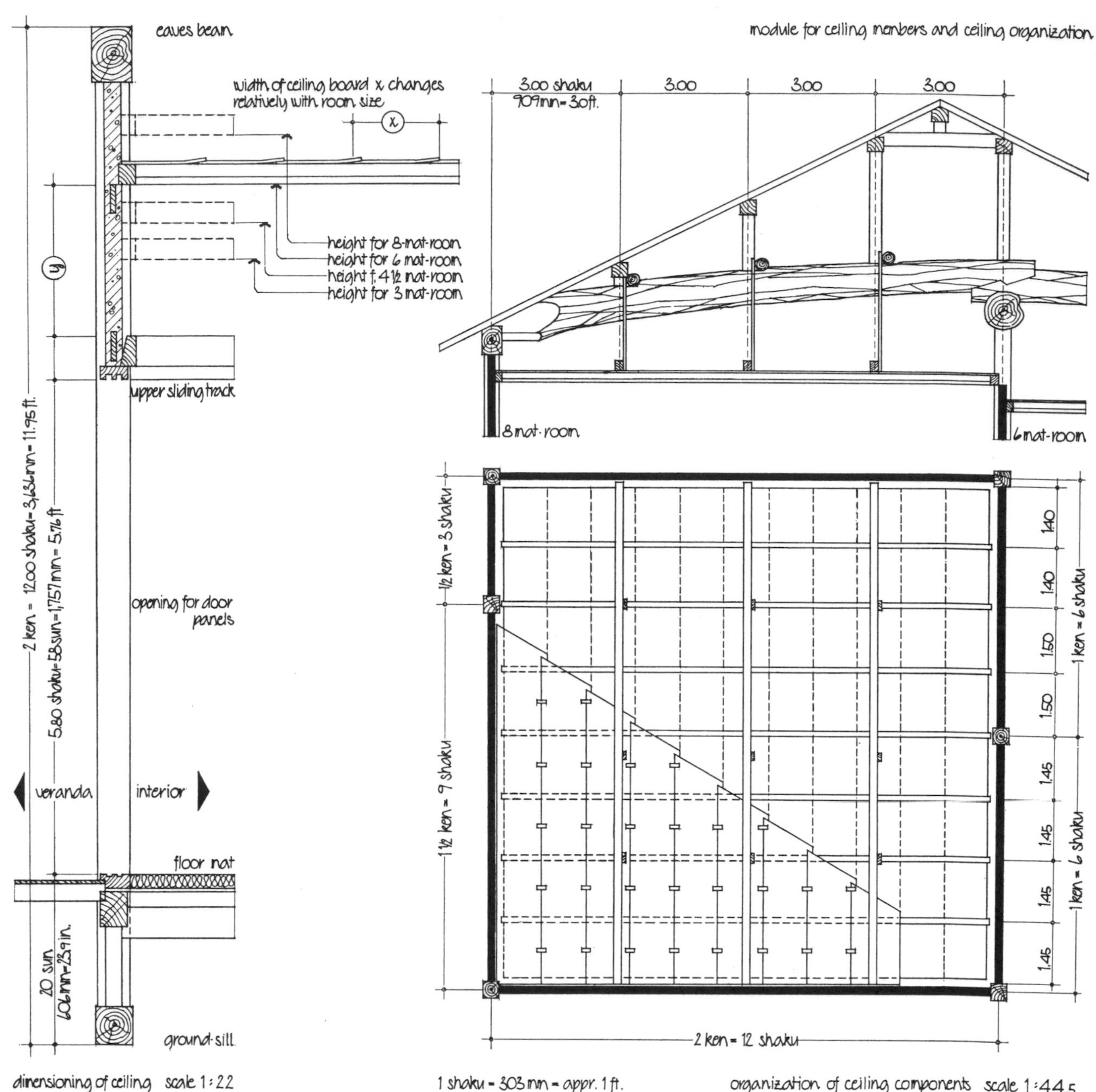

FIGURE 7: The modular order of the ceiling.

Ceiling height from top of frieze rail (*nageshi*) to underside of ceiling ledge (*tenjō-mawaribuchi*), i.e., height of upper wall (*kokabe*):

height measured in *shaku* = number of mats x 0.3 (0.25)

Dimension of ceiling boards, *tenjō-ita,* i.e., board width:

width for 4½- and 6-mat rooms = 1.0 *shaku* (303 mm. = 11.9 in.)

width for 8-mat room = 1.2 *shaku* (364 mm. = 14.3 in.)

width for 10-mat room = 1.5 *shaku* (455 mm. = 17.9 in.)

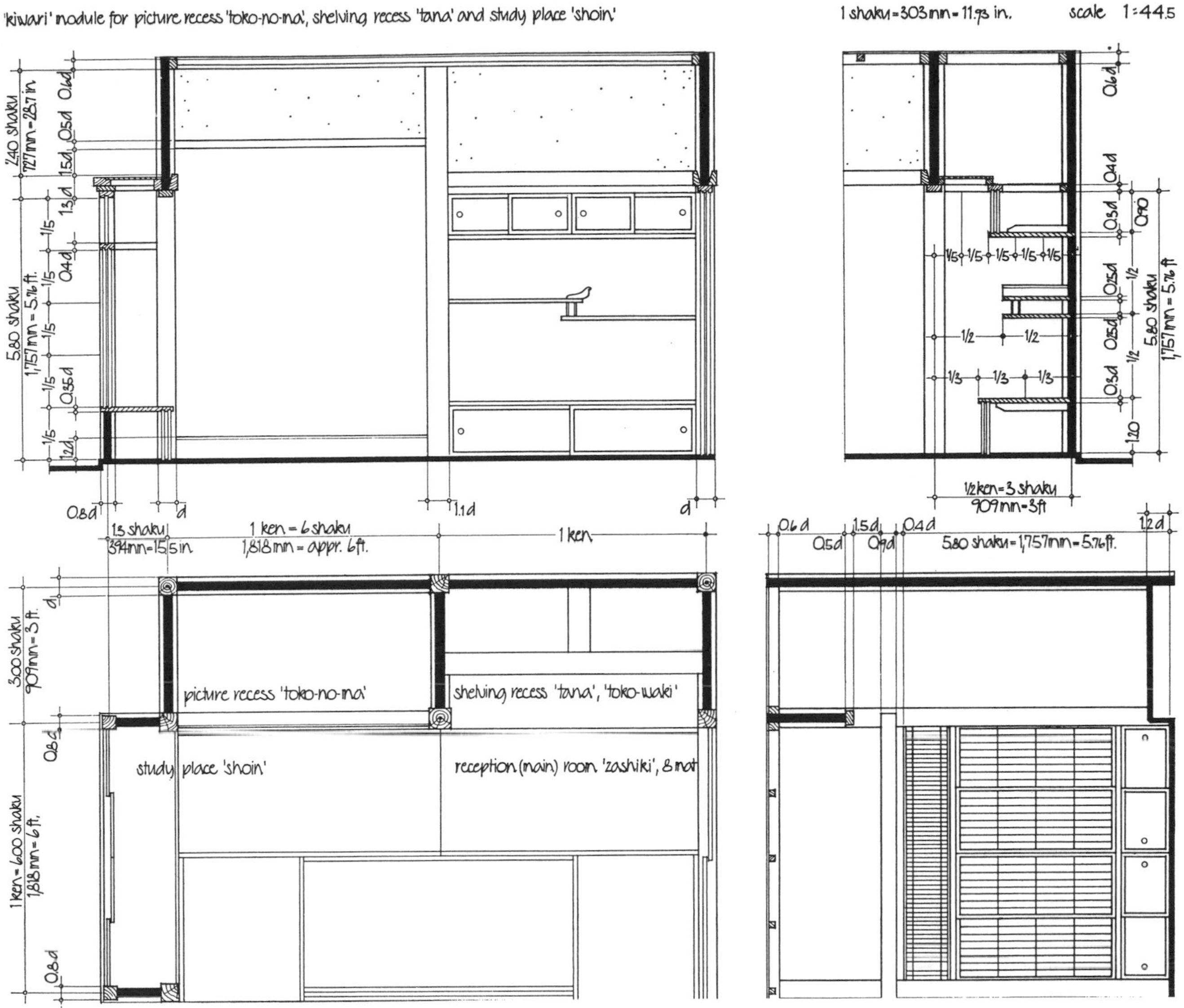

FIGURE 8: The modular order of the picture recess, *tokonoma*.

The ceiling parts, then, are arranged so that they correspond with the position of the columns. That is to say, a ceiling rod is centered above each column whereas the other rods are evenly distributed in between on an average interval of ¼ *ken* = 1.5 *shaku*. The drawings show that, even though the column centers themselves are exactly placed upon the *ken* grid, three or even more different intervals may result, which differences, however, are hardly noticeable.

Here, then, the great problem of standardization is revealed: discrepancy between clear distance and center-to-center distance. Since the Japanese house is based entirely on handicraft, this discrepancy can easily be adjusted, but modern standardization requires an order that integrates both the clear distance and the center-to-center distance into a common system. Only if the thickness of structural members or partition elements follow the same modular order as is set up by the structural center-to-center distances, will the clear width also become a modular measurement.

Though the standard sizes of all wood sections in residential construction are generally determined by the most economical cut of the standard timber of 4 *sun* (121 mm. = 4.8 in.), certain ratios and proportions have been directly adopted from the *kiwari* of the warrior residence, where the module was predominantly based on visual-geometric, i.e., aesthetic, principles.

This visual-aesthetic meaning of *kiwari* can still be observed in the proportions setup for picture recess, *tokonoma*; shelving recess, *tana*; and study place, *shoin*—elements that are all organizationally, spiritually, and historically interrelated and have maintained their decorative function. Again, the basic module for the dimensioning of the wood members is the standard column section (d).

d = 4 *sun* (121 mm. = 4.8 in.)

Recess column, *toko-bashira*:
for dressed column the facia *menuchi* without bevelings = 1.1 d
for round log the entire diameter = 1.0 d

Threshold, *toko-gamachi*:
thickness = 0.8–1.0 d width = 1.0 d
height above floor = 1.0–1.2 d

Crossbeam, *otoshi-gake*:
thickness = 0.5 d width = 0.7–0.8 d
elevation from top of frieze rail = 1.5–3.0 d

Polished facia at the lower part of round recess column, *takenokomen*:
height = 2.5–3.0 d

Ceiling ledge, *tenjō-mawaribuchi*:
thickness = 0.6 d width = 0.5 d

Baseboard of upper cabinet, *fukurodana-ita* (*fukuro to-tana*):
thickness = 0.3–0.35 d width = 3⁄5 of recess depth
distance from frieze rail = 9.3–9.5 *sun* (appr. 285 mm.= 11.4 in.)

Cover board of lower cabinet, *jibukuro-ita* (*ji-ita*):
thickness = 0.3–0.35 d width = 2⁄3 of recess depth
height above floor = 12.0 *sun* (364 mm.= 14.3 in.)

Board of displaced shelves, *chigaidana-ita*:
thickness = 0.2–0.25 d width = ½ recess depth
clear distance between upper and lower shelves = 1 d

Support between shelves, *cbizuka*:
square section = 1.5–1.7 x thickness of shelf boards, *chigaidana-ita*, or = 0.4 d
beveling = 1⁄7 of section

Cornice of upper shelves board, *fude-kaeshi*:
thickness = 1.5–2.0 x thickness of shelf boards, *chigaidana-ita*
projection = 1.0–1.5 x thickness of shelf boards

Reading bay post, *shoin-bashira*:
square section = 0.7–0.8 d

Table board (sill), *shoin-jiita*:
thickness = 0.35 d width = about 1.3 *shaku* (394 mm. = 15.5in.)
height from floor = 1⁄5 of standard door height

Intermediate cross piece, *chū-gamoi*:
thickness = 0.4 d width = 0.8 (facia *menuchi*)
distance from upper track = 1⁄5 of standard door height

Sliding panel, *shoin-shōji*:
height = ⅗ of standard door height
Exterior cornice, *daiwa*:
thickness = 0.5 of *shoin* post; width = 1.2 of *shoin* post
projection= ¼ of width

In the awareness that the inherited standardization basically would be suitable for industrial mass production, an attempt was made after World War II to unify the locally varying standards of measure and to establish the prerequisite for production of residences on a broad industrial basis, as was intended for social housing projects. In these new standards, distinction was made between one- and two-story houses and between two major climatic areas in Japan, resulting in standard sizes for four different types.

However, neither were the proposed measurements adopted nor did the industrialization in social housing become reality. This outcome could be expected with good reason. The inherited problems of Japanese standardization, previously described, cannot be solved by the mere introduction of a few new measurements; furthermore, since labor is cheap in Japan, machine-production afforded little economical advantage, at least not in the existing socio-economic state; and, finally, with constructional standardization being based entirely on handicraft, a shift to machine production would create additional problems requiring entirely new solutions.

Yet, aside from these technical-practical reasons, the real crux of the matter is that this house has meant a realistic architectural solution only for the society of the past. Except for inherited basic constructional defects, the Japanese house had reached a level of perfection that did not demand improvement if considered from the standpoint of living modes and requirements of the past. However, the word "perfection" implies not only the quality of being superb, but also the state of being completed and finished; and indeed the development of Japanese residential architecture has long since come to a standstill; its culmination is over. New technical impediments such as electricity, furniture, glass, metal, radio, etc. adopted from the West have degraded the quality and standard of the traditional Japanese residence; gradual Westernization of living manners has rendered inadequate what formerly was spatially convenient; and dissolution of the traditional family system has removed the philosophical basis that underlies the Japanese house. Once again it is apparent that the traditional dwelling belongs to the past, and that not only spatial requirements of contemporary living in Japan, but also measures and standards of her contemporary residential architecture are in dire need of radical change.

2 system of plan layout

floor mat

The floor mat, called *tatami,* is a tightly packed stiff rice-straw mat, 1.5–2.0 *sun* (45–60 mm. = 1.8–2.4 in.) thick and approximately 3 x 6 feet (910 x 1,820 mm.) in size. It is one of the most distinct and instructive features in the Japanese house, although the most misinterpreted. Since its first appearance it has remained in a state of metamorphosis, while both absorbing and exerting influence.

Originally only a portable floor cover to accommodate two men sitting (or else one sleeping), in time the *tatami* transmuted into the floor itself. Consequently, being subjected to the structural system of the room enclosure, it lost its direct and originally sole dependence on human scale. Yet, on the other hand, because its size is governed by the amount of clearance between columns, it could not function as a constructional measure unit either, because, for the framing of roof or floor, only the column distances from center to center are important. However, once the mat size was standardized, it did determine column distances in one part of Japan by regulating the open width between columns. Yet, what controls all further proportions is the resulting column distance center to center, and no longer the *tatami* size. In another part of Japan *tatami* remained strictly subjugated to structural standard distances where by mats of various sizes must be used in one and the same room. And, furthermore, there are distinct local differences in average mat sizes—even differences according to the type of building in one and the same city.

Nevertheless, the *tatami,* or, to use an alternate reading for the ideograph, the *jō*, became the standard for designating room size, e.g. a room of *3 jō, 4½ jō, 6 jō* etc. The adoption of this rather large standard of measurement (about 900 x 1,800 mm. or 3 x 6 ft.) automatically limited the number of possible room sizes. In the particular instance of the ceiling, the number of *tatami* even determines proportion, but it is important to note that the *tatami* has never, not even fictitiously, functioned as a module of any kind in the Japanese house, as is most frequently assumed.

Being closely related to structure, the *tatami* distinctly reflects the structural order and, stressed by the dark tape binding (usually black) at its long side, shows a pattern that appears both constructional and ornamental. Usually, the mat joints align with column centers, but sometimes not. Here, the discrepancy between center distance and clear width, a problem of modern standardization, clearly reveals itself.

As a fabric that should equally facilitate walking, sitting, and sleeping, the *tatami* demanded both stiffness and resiliency. Limited to the use of natural materials, this demand could be met only by accepting a fabric with high porosity, i.e., with a consistency impractical and unhygienic for a floor, because as such it is susceptible to accumulation of dust and penetration of humidity from the damp ground. It does facilitate ventilation. This summertime advantage, however, is a wintertime nuisance. Having originated as an implement to serve a particular way of life, once it had emerged in the present form, it began to counterinfluence the manners of living of its users.

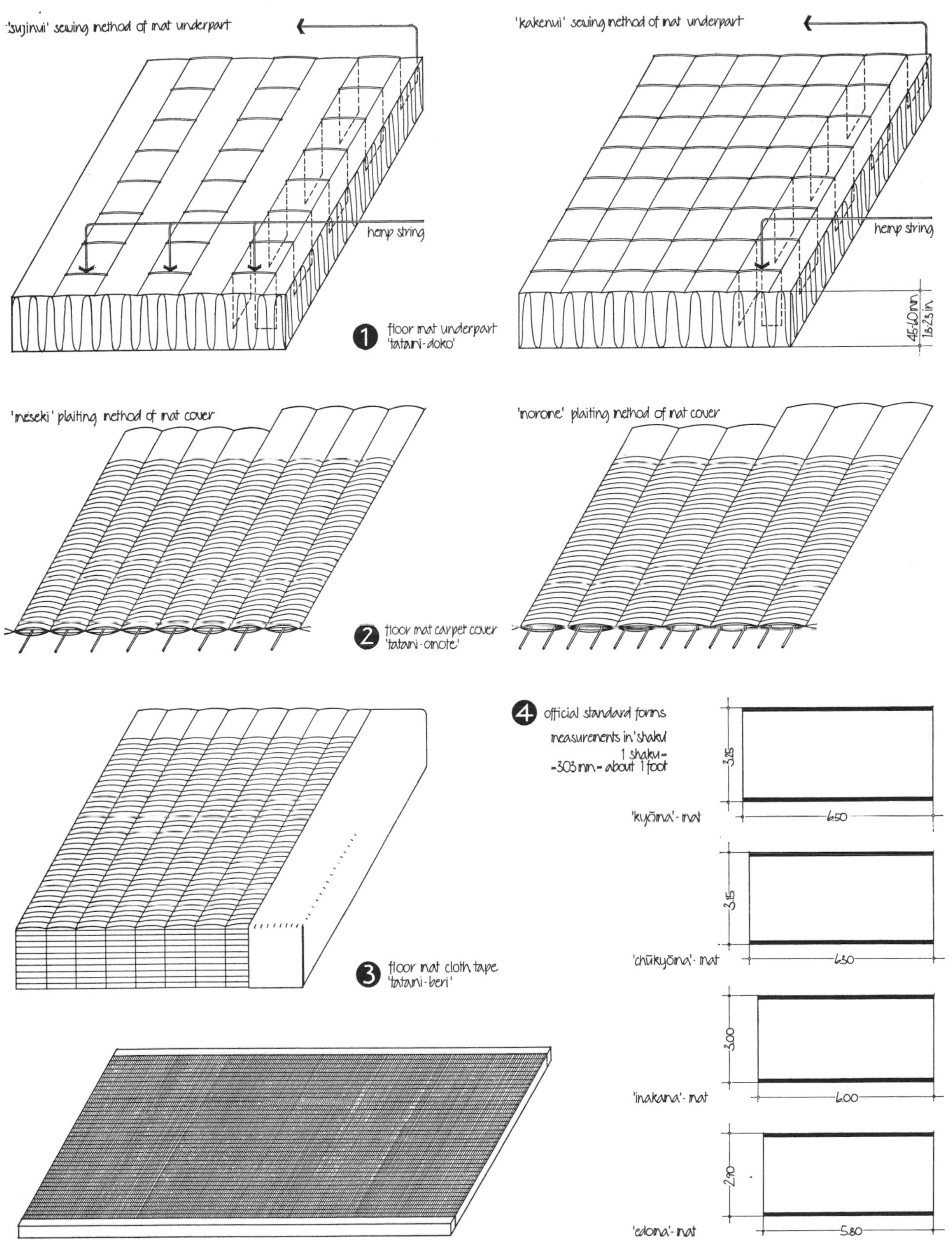

FIGURE 9: Construction details and standard sizes of the *tatami*.

With the mat a fabric of the Japanese home has evolved that constitutes an important junction where many opposing movements have met, have been moderated, and have been coordinated. The *tatami,* as distinct as it is for the Japanese house, is not distinct in itself. It functions as moderator and unifier of architectural contrast sand thus is, in its nature, the product of a compromise between human and structural scale, between vertical and horizontal order, and between climatic and habitual demands. As such it fulfills the demands of none of them completely, and consequently is manifold in its meaning. This indistinctness of the nature of the *tatami* also explains the frequent misinterpretations it is subject to.

The word *tatami* stems from *tatamu,* meaning to fold, to pile up; for the early form of the object, as depicted in early scroll paintings illustrating the *Kojiki* and *Manyōshū,* was but a thin skin cover or a grass mat that could be easily folded. It might also be possible that several layers, one upon the other, were used simultaneously. In the Kamakura period (1185–1336) thickly knit straw mats, called *tsuka-nami,* appeared for the first time in the residences of the nobility. Yet, they did not cover the whole surface but were carried to a desired place. The size of this mat, as is evident in picture scrolls, corresponds to a space occupied by two men sitting, and was already fairly standardized. At the beginning of the Muromachi period (1393–1573) the entire floor was covered for the first time. Thus *tatami* had become floor itself. The spreading of the *shoin* style markedly helped its propagation, but economic circumstances prevented general use among the people before the 18th century.

The three main constituent parts of the *tatami* are:

toko (floor), thick straw underpart
omote (surface), thin reed cover
fuchi or *heri* (edge), cloth tape binding

The multitude of existing "standard" sizes of *tatami* proves more than anything else the inadequacy of *tatami* as a module. However, official standardization lists only four main sizes:

kyōma-tatami 65 x 32.5 *sun* (1,970 x 985 mm. = 78 x 39 in.)
chūkyōma-tatami 63 x 31.5 *sun* (1,909 x 955 m. = 75.6 x 37.8 in.)
inakama-tatami 60 x 30 *sun* (1,818 x 909 mm. = 72 x 36 in.)
edo-tatami 58 x 29 *sun* (1,757 x 879 mm. = 69.6 x 34.8 in.)

kyō-ma method

It is generally assumed that the *ken* in *kyō-ma* measurement is a definite length of 6.5 *shaku (*1,970 mm. = 6.5 ft.) as the *ken* in *inaka-ma* measurement is a definite length of 6 *shaku* (1,818 mm. = 6.0 ft.). Yet, this assumption holds true only for the period prior to the end of the 18th century, when the floor mat, *tatami,* was not yet in common use among the lower classes and also did not yet cover the entire floor area.

When there after the mat became indispensable, it also became a commercial article just as other goods had done before that time and, as such, required an exact size. This fixation of size also was necessary because it was customary for tenants and even house owners to take the mats along with them when moving to another residence. Naturally, the mats had to fit in the new domicile as well. Finally, the tearooms (*sukiya* architecture) also demanded a single-mat format because the mats were frequently rearranged according to the season or to a particular occasion. It is obvious, therefore, that the mat had to be of universal size; *tatami* was standardized. That is to say, when the mat became the covering for the entire floor area, its standard size in return controlled the intercolumniation.

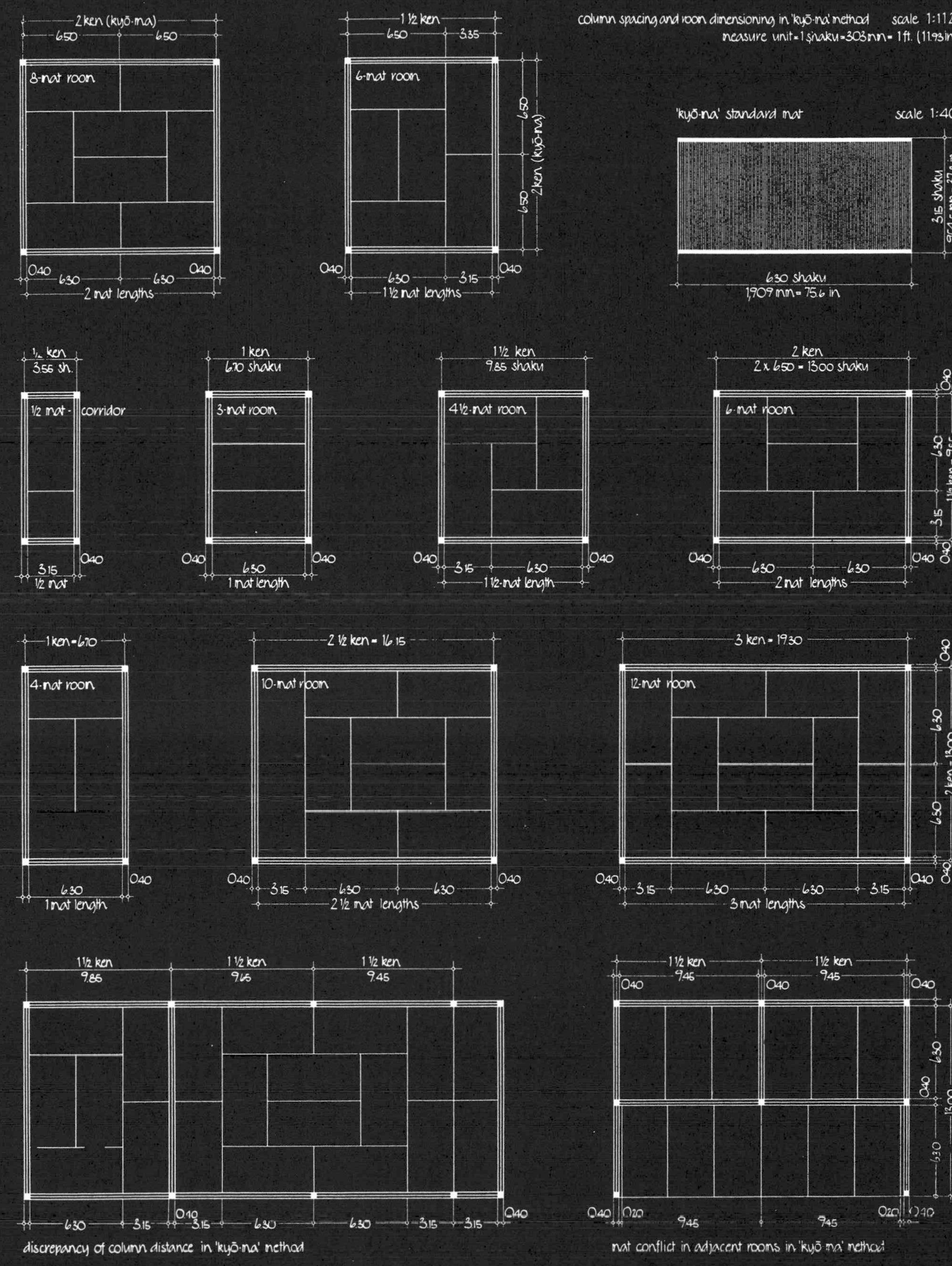

FIGURE 10: The *kyō-ma* method of design.

Thus, it seems appropriate to consider *kyō-ma* from this time on no longer a measurement or a measure system with definite units, but rather a method of designing and a method for deciding exact column distance. As consistent as this method is in itself, the resulting constructional distances are no longer consistently multiples or fractions of the former *ken* of 6.5 *shaku,* but also show in one and the same structure deviations that forbid the identification of *ken* in *kyō-ma* measurement as a fixed length. Rather the *ken* in *kyō-ma* again regained its original meaning as a column interval, a distance, however, measured from face to face of two columns instead of from center to center.

The mat size for the *kyō-ma* system was derived from the mat dimensions in room sizes most frequently used. These were rooms of 6 or 8 mats with a long side column center distance of 2 *ken* in *kyō-ma* measurement (2 x 6.5 = 13.0 *shaku).* With a standard column section of 0.4 *shaku* (4 *sun* = 121 mm. = 4.8 in.) the resulting length of the standard mat became:

13.0–0.4 = 12.6 *shaku* (clear width of 2 *ken* in *kyō-ma*)
1 mat length = 12.6/2 = 6.3 *shaku*
Standard mat, *kyō-ma* system: 6.3 x 3.15 *shaku* (1,909 x 954.5 mm.
= 75.6 x 37.8 in.)

Prefabrication of the standard mat and its consistent use for all different-sized rooms then brought about a deviation from the previous strict use of multiples or fractions of the *ken* of 6.5 *shaku.* Standardization of constructional center distance had finally given way to standardization of intercolumniate clearance.

It is evident that the post center distances correspond to the former *kyō-ma* measurement only in the 6- or 8-mat rooms, i.e., rooms with length of 2 *ken,* while all others show slight differences.

Center-to-center column distances, *ken,* in the *kyō-ma* method:

Room width =			
	1 mat	(6.30 + 0.40) ÷ 1	= 6.70 *shaku*
	1½ mats	(9.45 + 0.40) ÷ 1.5	= 6.57 *shaku*
	2 mats	(12.60 + 0.40) ÷ 2	= 6.50 *shaku* (this is the original *ken* in *kyō-ma* measurement)
	2½ mats	(15.75 + 0.40) ÷ 2.5	= 6.46 *shaku*
	3 mats	(18.90 + 0.40) ÷ 3	= 6.43 *shaku*
	4 mats	(25.20 + 0.40) ÷ 4	= 6.40 *shaku*

With standardization of column clearance, the entire constructional measuring that always relates to center of structural member is no longer consistent. But, as the technique of construction is handicraft, slight variations are not a problem as they would be with machine craft and can be resolved without additional labor or material.

Difficulties, however, still arise in determining the standard measurements necessary for prefabrication of sliding panels between the columns. In fact, in spite of standardization of clear room width, discrepancies in intercolumn distance do occur in certain cases (as is evident in the illustration of *kyō-ma* method of design). Accordingly, sliding elements for wall openings are prefabricated only for the most common cases and frequently are manufactured separately for each house, very clearly demonstrating that even standardization of clear room width does not necessarily guarantee simple standardization of intercolumniate panels.

Another problem is the discrepancy that results when two smaller rooms are backed up to one larger room. In practice, this problem is solved by one of two methods. Either the mats of the two small rooms determine the outside walls and the difference appearing in the large room is compensated by additional wood boards; or the mats of the large room determine the outside walls, requiring special sizes for the mats of the two small rooms.

The *kyō-ma* method, then, constitutes design of constructional members around the standardized unit of the room interior, the mat, *tatami.* The disadvantages for systematic measuring and designing of the structure are obvious. Nevertheless, the fact that the *kyō-ma* method is still being used, even predominantly so (contrary to the opinion of many writers), does prove that the economical advantage gained by standardizing interior units, and the generally larger room sizes, must have outweighed all the other defects. That these defects can be overcome only by handicraft methods is as obvious as is the fact that contemporary architecture based on machine-craft production cannot work on such a basis.

inaka-ma method

Contrary to the inconsistent column distance in the *kyō-ma* method, intercolumniation in the *inaka-ma* method is strictly based on a square grid of 1 *ken* (6 *shaku),* and is not dependent on interior mat or panel size. Consequently, all constructional distances are either a fraction or a multiple of *6 shaku.* However, as the unit ½ *ken* (3 *shaku),* functionally speaking, is slightly too small for minimum spaces such as the veranda, corridor, bath, and toilet, frequently the direct ratio to *ken* is unhesitatingly deserted and instead, distances like 3.5 or 4 *shaku* are used.

Abolishment of the grid system in such a decisive matter as minimum spaces is interesting, since standardization in terms of length should begin with the finding of a common denominator for minimum rooms, which would then be the largest common measure. The larger rooms, then, should be subjected to the order of the smaller ones and not vice versa. It appears that the *ken* of 6 *shaku* is a standard of material economy and practicality rather than one of spatial adequacy, and is abandoned each time utilitarian demands are endangered. This also explains the distinct preference for the *kyō-ma* measurement (not as method but as a larger *ken* unit), for the resulting room sizes are considered more appropriate than those of the *ken* of 6 *shaku.*

From the viewpoint of contemporary architecture with its standardization, such conscious tolerance toward a self-imposed order is significant. For it shows that even the most unique standardization that architecture has produced still does not completely fulfill all the demands of structure, function, economy, and aesthetics. Certainly a larger *shaku* unit could solve the problem to a certain degree, but it is certain then that other disadvantages will arise. It demonstrates that requirements of man, material, and technique are oftentimes opposed to each other and that the standard establishes the optimum of compromise between them. It contradicts the opinion that economical construction necessarily satisfies utilitarian requirements or that perfect compliance with these requirements produces beauty.

Evidently, the Japanese builder-architect, the carpenter, followed this compromising nature of modular design, if not consciously, then instinctively. Though he based his plan essentially upon the *ken* grid, his unique mastership of both design technique and building construction qualified him to know precisely in which cases he had to deviate from the modular grid.

While in the *kyō-ma* method there is only one standard mat, the dimensions of which do not correspond with the on-center constructional distance, in the *inaka-ma* method, several standard mat sizes exist: the norm mat being 3 x 6 *shaku* (909 x 1,818 mm.

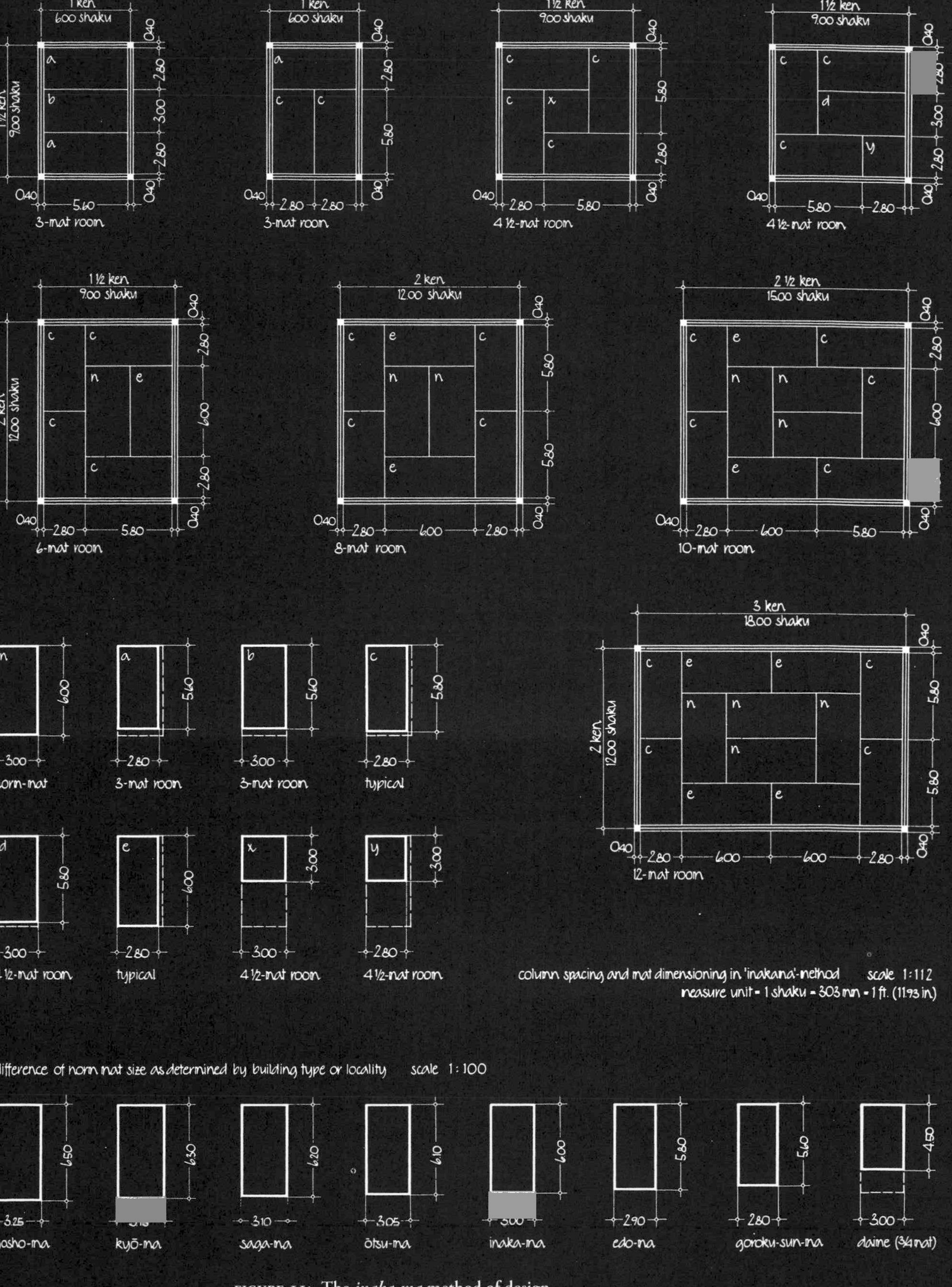

FIGURE 11: The *inaka-ma* method of design.

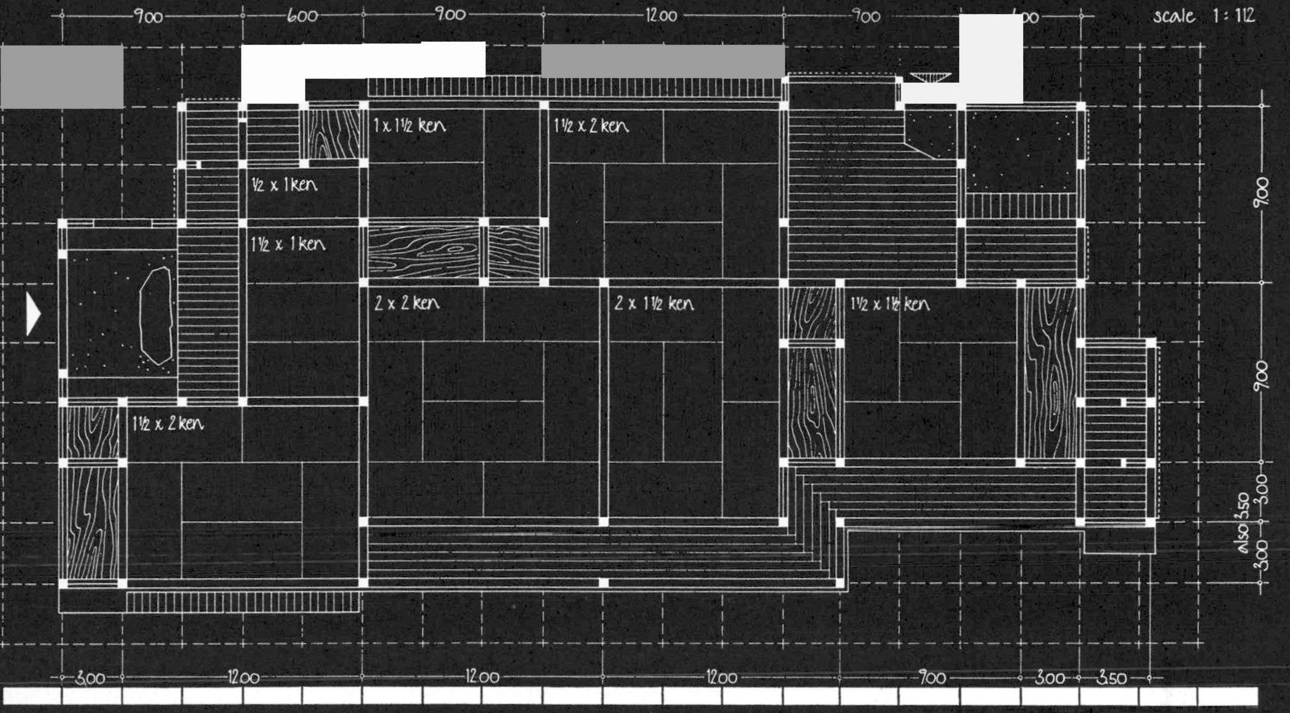

scale 1 : 112

1 x 1½ ken
1½ x 2 ken
½ x 1 ken
1½ x 1 ken
2 x 2 ken
2 x 1½ ken
1½ x 1½ ken
1½ x 2 ken

1 design in 'inaka-ma'-method: column spacing on grid pattern with columns placed on grid center
module for grid pattern - 3.00 shaku - 910 mm - 3.0 ft

measure unit - 1 shaku - 303 mm - 1 ft (11.93 in)
total floor area - 32.75 tsubo - 108.2 sq.m. - 1,165.2 sq.ft

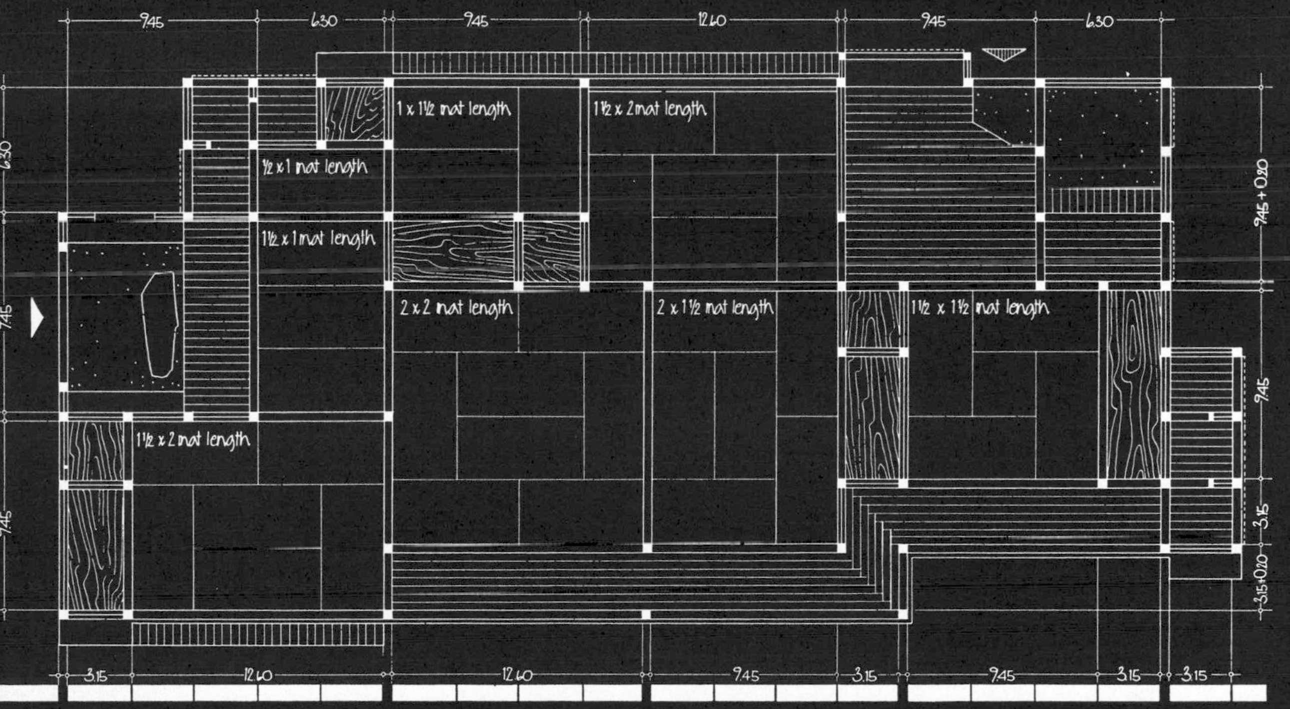

1 x 1½ mat length
1½ x 2 mat length
½ x 1 mat length
1½ x 1 mat length
2 x 2 mat length
2 x 1½ mat length
1½ x 1½ mat length
1½ x 2 mat length

2 design in 'kyō-ma'-method: column spacing according standardized clear width of mat covered space
module for clear width - 3.15 shaku - 955 mm - 3.15 ft

measure unit - 1 shaku - 303 mm - 1 ft (11.93 in)
total floor area - 32.75 tsubo - 128.1 sq.m. - 1,378.7 sq.ft

FIGURE 12: A comparison of the *kyō-ma* and *inaka-ma* methods of design.

= 3 x 6 ft.) whose dimensions are derived directly from center-to center column distance, and several variational types that are smaller in order to compensate for differences at the outside wall. As the column width in the ordinary dwelling is always 4 *sun* (121 mm. = 4.8 in.), the deviation of the variational types from the norm mat is ½ column width or 2 *sun* (60 mm. = 2.4 in.), i.e., the length is reduced to 5.80 *shaku* and the width to 2.80 *shaku.*

The illustration of *inaka-ma* method shows that no less than five variational mat types, (a) to (e), are necessary in addition to the norm mat (n), in order to accurately cover any floor space without additional members. Among the five variational types, two sizes only, (a) and (b), are used in the 3-mat room, a space comparatively rare in the ordinary house. Another type (d) appears only when the 4½-mat room is arranged in the unusual manner of the half mat on the outside. That is to say, only two variational mat types, (c) and (e), are usually required in addition to the norm mat (n). These three mat sizes, then, (n), (c), and (e), are standardized and are usually kept in stock.

Yet, in another area of Japan where the *inaka-ma* method is applied, the norm mat (n) measures not 3.00 x 6.00 *shaku,* but 5.80 x 2.90 *shaku.* No additional standard mats are in use. Consequently, for rooms of 3, 4, and 4½ mats, special sizes smaller than the norm mat are needed. Also, the 6-mat room still requires, in addition to the norm mat, a special size, while the 8-mat room is covered solely by the norm mats. If the room exceeds a width of 2 *ken* (3,636 mm. = 12 ft.), the spaces left between the mat edges and the partition are filled with small wood boards.

The *inaka-ma* method, then, constitutes design on a square grid system of 1 *ken* (6 *shaku),* in which the center line of construction or partition corresponds with the grid line. The mat, *tatami,* being an element of clear room width, is unconditionally subordinated to this system. Even with set standard mat sizes, the present practice of the matmaker is to take the measurements of the completed house framework before delivering the single mat units. In spite of all standardization, then, differences and inaccuracies owing to handicraft technique and irregularity of natural fabric are inevitable, and require special handling.

Design itself, however, in the *inaka-ma* method is an easy arranging of standardized space units on the *ken* grid, and in essence is no different from contemporary modular design. Yet, in the Japanese residence, even though the manual design is limited only to the floor plan in scale 1:100 or 1:50, the actual modular coordination is far more comprehensive than in contemporary design. It penetrates the detail and system, the material and the spiritual substance of building and, in a century-long process, has co-ordinated the market size and the production of fabric. Deviations from this elaborate system are easily accomplished in the handicraft system of the time, but would not be so easily done under the machine-conditioned standardization of the industrial society.

planimetric-functional space

To the architect, the compliance with man's physical requirements in architectural space is a matter of two-dimensional (planimetric) design. As the roof provides protection and adequate spatial height—as a rule beyond that of physical necessity—the space of functional efficiency is reduced to a two-dimensional one in the horizontal plane. Organization of horizontal planimetric space, and not volumetric space, is, therefore, decisive for the functional quality of building, and it is not against the nature of space in architecture to approach functional space, be it for analysis or design, on a two-dimensional basis.

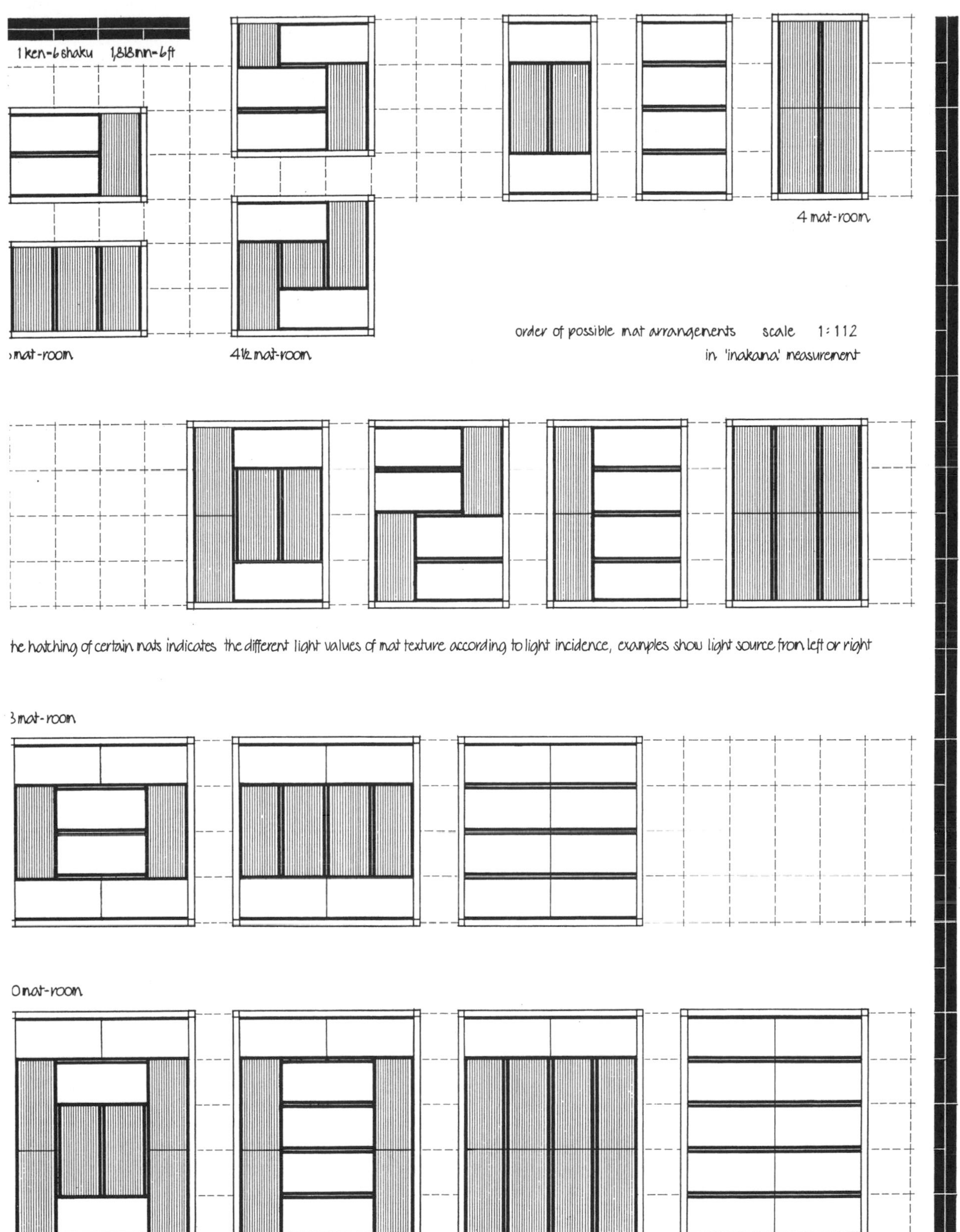

FIGURE 13: *Tatami* arrangements of standard rooms.

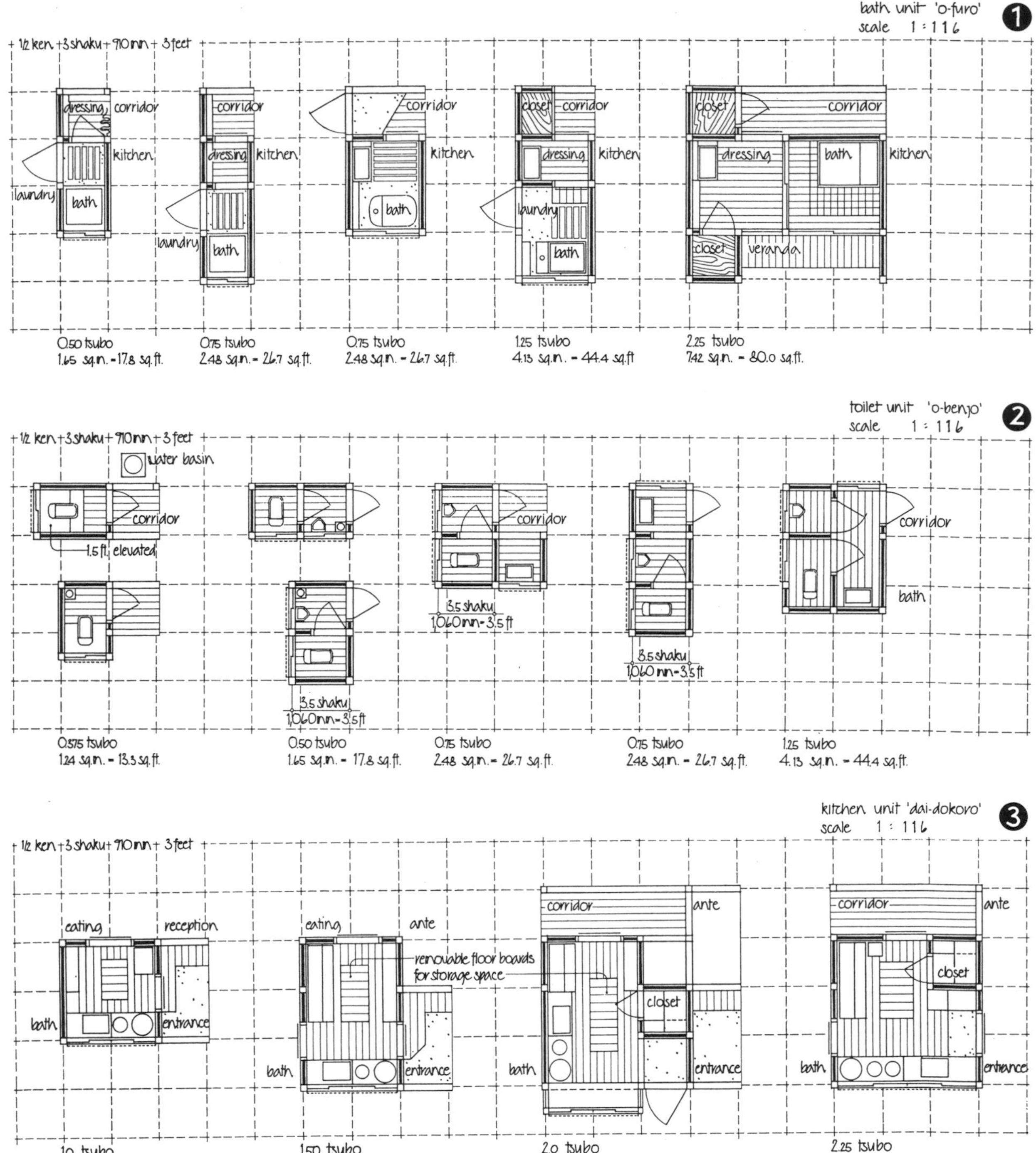

FIGURE 14: Floor plans of standard room units.

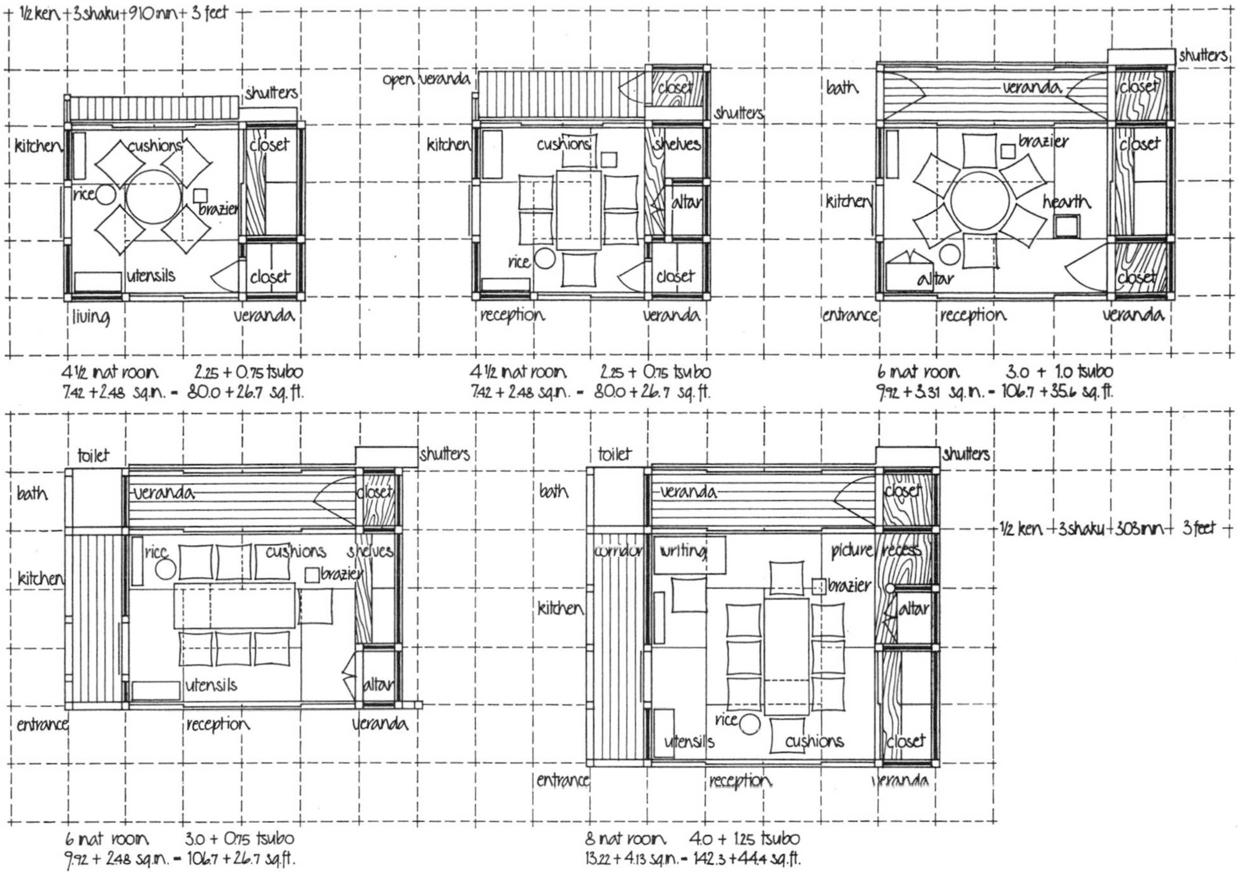

+ 1/2 ken + 3 shaku + 910 mm + 3 feet +

shutters
kitchen
cushions
closet
rice
brazier
utensils
closet
living
veranda

4 1/2 mat room 2.25 + 0.75 tsubo
7.42 + 2.48 sq.m. = 80.0 + 26.7 sq.ft.

open veranda
closet
shutters
kitchen
cushions
shelves
altar
rice
closet
reception
veranda

4 1/2 mat room 2.25 + 0.75 tsubo
7.42 + 2.48 sq.m. = 80.0 + 26.7 sq.ft.

shutters
bath
veranda
closet
brazier
closet
kitchen
hearth
altar
closet
entrance
reception
veranda

6 mat room 3.0 + 1.0 tsubo
9.92 + 3.31 sq.m. = 106.7 + 35.6 sq.ft.

toilet
shutters
bath
veranda
closet
kitchen
rice
cushions
shelves
brazier
utensils
altar
entrance
reception
veranda

6 mat room 3.0 + 0.75 tsubo
9.92 + 2.48 sq.m. = 106.7 + 26.7 sq.ft.

toilet
shutters
bath
veranda
closet
+ 1/2 ken + 3 shaku + 303 mm + 3 feet +
corridor
writing
picture
recess
brazier
kitchen
altar
rice
utensils
cushions
closet
entrance
reception
veranda

8 mat room 4.0 + 1.25 tsubo
13.22 + 4.13 sq.m. = 142.3 + 44.4 sq.ft.

dining room 'cha-no-ma', 'shoku-do' ❹
scale 1 : 116

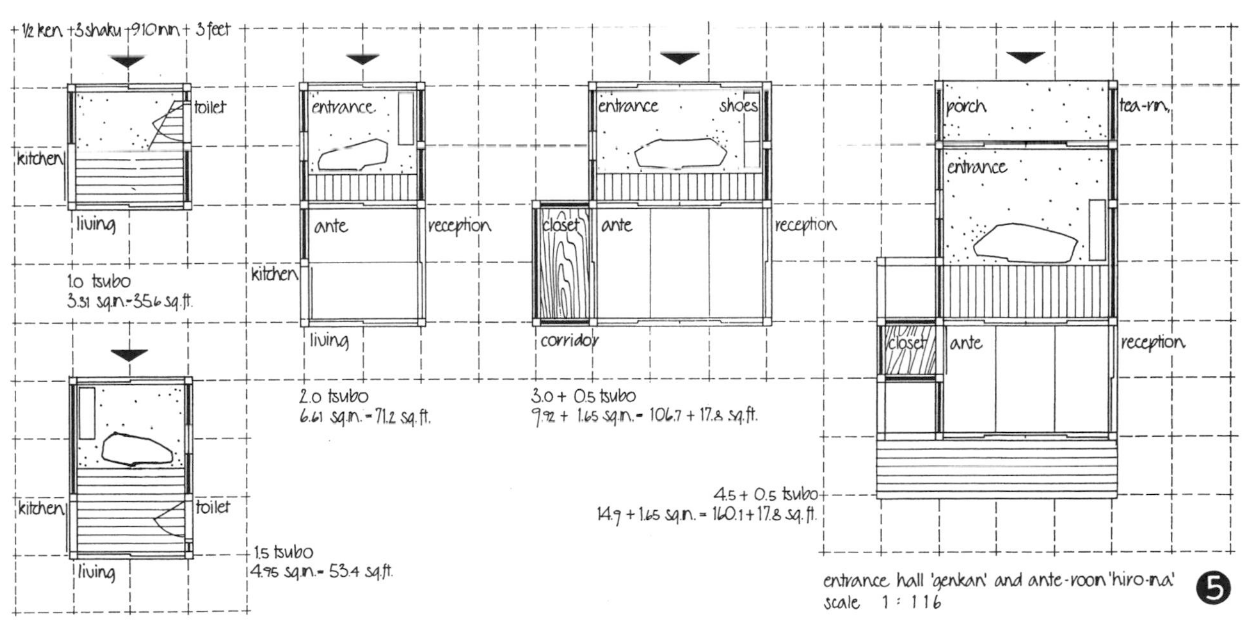

FIGURE 14 (continued): Floor plans of standard room units.

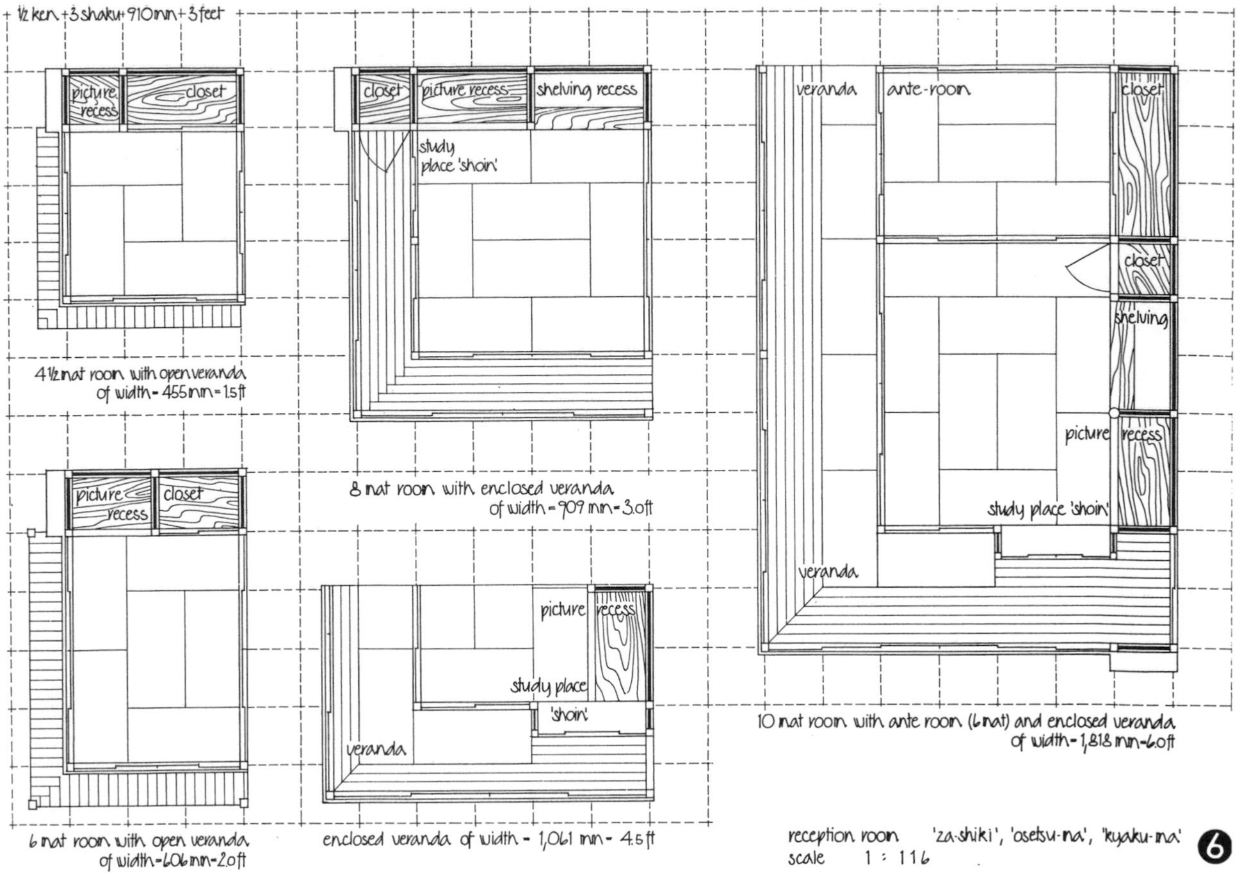

½ ken = 3 shaku = 910 mm = 3 feet

picture recess
closet

4½ mat room with open veranda
of width = 455 mm = 1.5 ft

closet
picture recess
shelving recess
study place 'shoin'

8 mat room with enclosed veranda
of width = 909 mm = 3.0 ft

veranda
ante-room
closet
closet
shelving
picture recess
study place 'shoin'
veranda

10 mat room with ante room (6 mat) and enclosed veranda
of width = 1,818 mm = 6.0 ft

picture recess
closet

6 mat room with open veranda
of width = 606 mm = 2.0 ft

picture recess
study place
'shoin'
veranda

enclosed veranda of width = 1,061 mm = 4.5 ft

reception room 'za-shiki', 'osetsu-ma', 'kyaku-ma' 6
scale 1 : 116

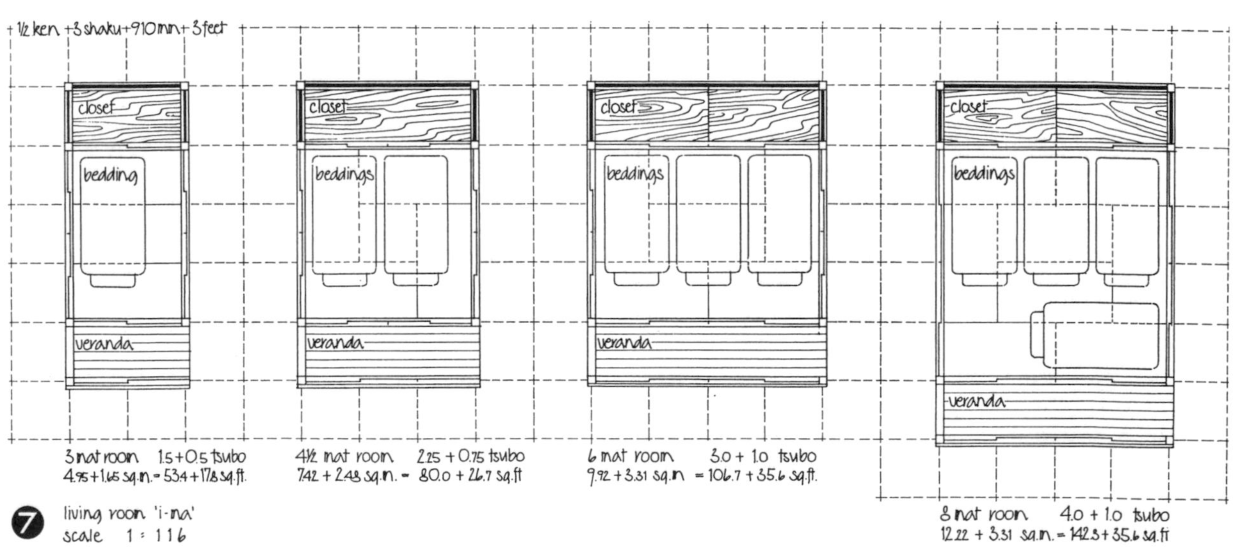

FIGURE 14 (continued): Floor plans of standard room units.

The organization of functional space, as it is traditionally done by the Japanese family itself is but the arranging of standardized spatial units on a two-dimensional grid, using the mat as the ordering unit. It is primarily concerned with establishment of a simple circulation pattern and is influenced by considerations of site relationship, orientation to compass, and possible separation of "official" space from all "private" space, as has been described earlier. While utilitarian spaces such as bath, toilet, and kitchen, of course, are distinct in purpose and form, the physical similarity of all living spaces has given rise to the erroneous belief that the function of the individual Japanese living space is undefined and therefore alterable at will. The fact, however, is that each room has a distinct name relating to its major purpose, and that its use, though multiple, is well defined.

The smallest houses, of course, combine various functions in one or two rooms. Similar to Western practice, the larger the house is, the more distinct is the use of individual living space. Room designations, however, are difficult to translate into Western languages, for there are no equivalent words to describe rooms of double or triple function, nor are the Japanese designations distinct enough in themselves. Instead, at best the names permit only a clue to the original purpose of the room but hardly explain any later use. These names were traditionally maintained despite the fact that room usage changed and even varied from place to place—all adding to the difficulties in finding descriptive names for each room.

3 examples of floor plans

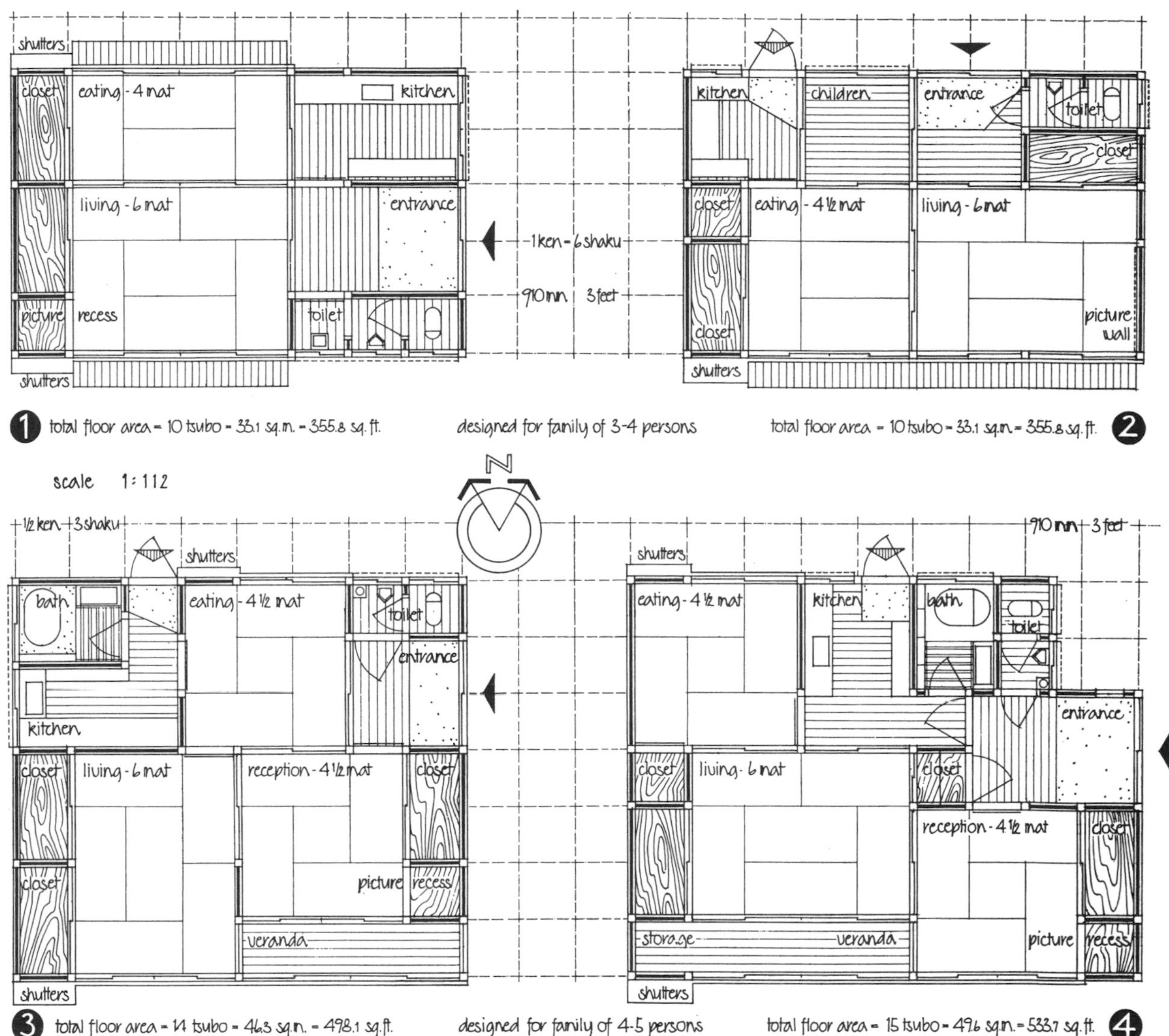

FIGURE 15: Select examples of typical residences.

distinctions

Japanese residential design is distinct in many ways. The distinctions are interrelated very intimately with the mode of living, as architectural design always encompasses the total range of factors that comprehend human living both physically and spiritually. Yet, the distinctions of the mere technique of design are striking and important enough to justify particular mention. For they show that even the method of design itself can produce characteristics in architecture.

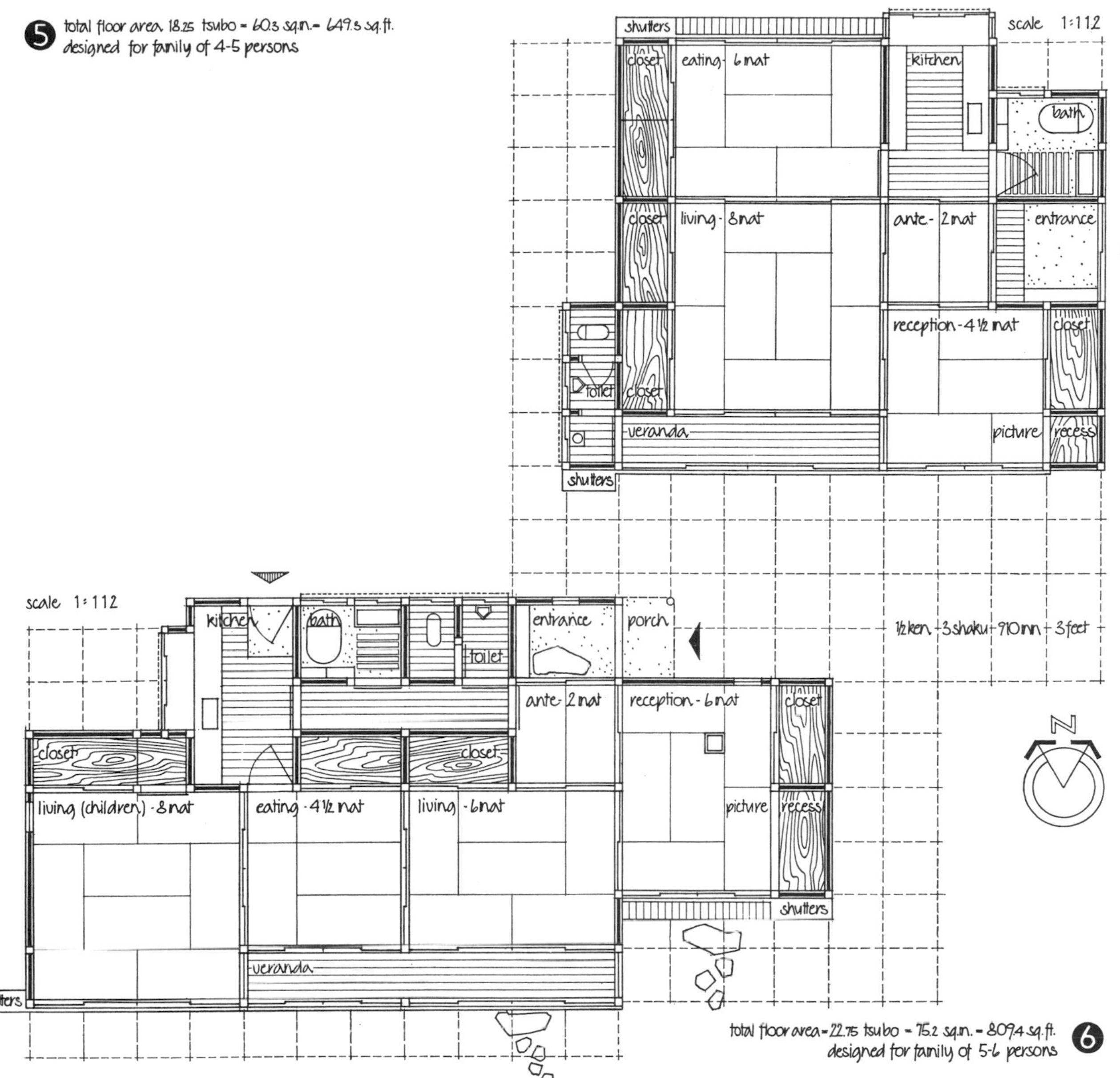

FIGURE 15 (continued): Select examples of typical residences.

Design on the grid basis, no doubt, has been instrumental in producing a strictly rectangular plan. Yet, the rectangle is indeed the logical geometry of floor area, as it is the only form which allows free addition of individual room units that in tum result in another rectangular shape, at the same time providing the basis for a most economical and simple construction. Indeed, to deviate from the rectangular pattern requires sound and valid reason, and the Japanese "designer," though in certain instances departing from the exact *ken* grid pattern of 6 *shaku* (1,818 mm. = 6 ft.), even occasionally using curved forms, apparently never did find any reason to search for another form in the ground plan other than the rectangular.

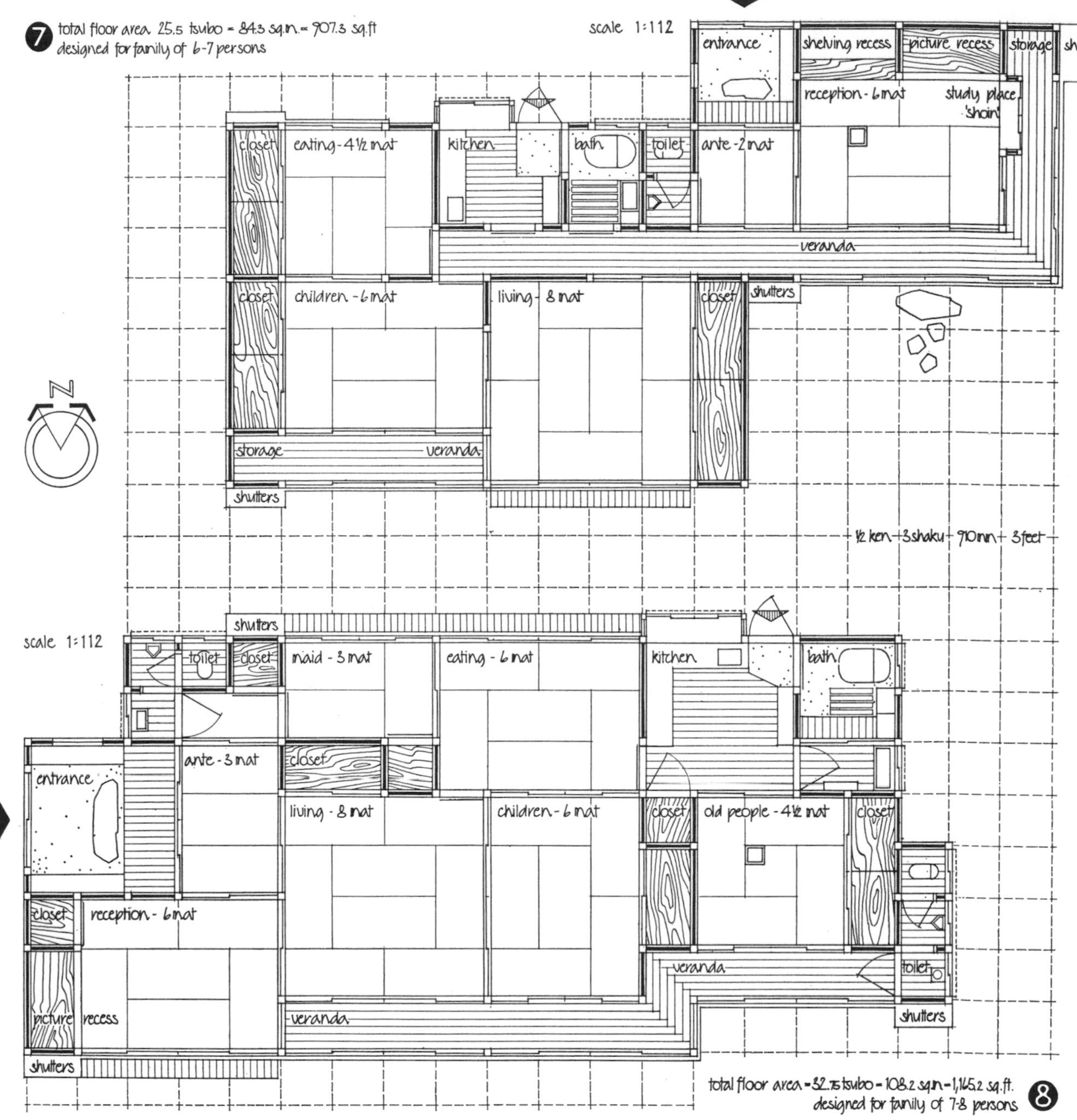

FIGURE 15 (continued): Select examples of typical residences.

Thus, standardized room units are shifted as easily as they are connected along the grid system of the *ken,* which in turn facilitates design pattern of steplike, staggered room units for which Japanese building is noted; because each of the units, being tied to the grid, never loses its cohesiveness with other units in spite of total freedom of placement. On the other hand, the structural system undoubtedly has also contributed to making the "casualness" of room disposition possible. The roof load is transmitted

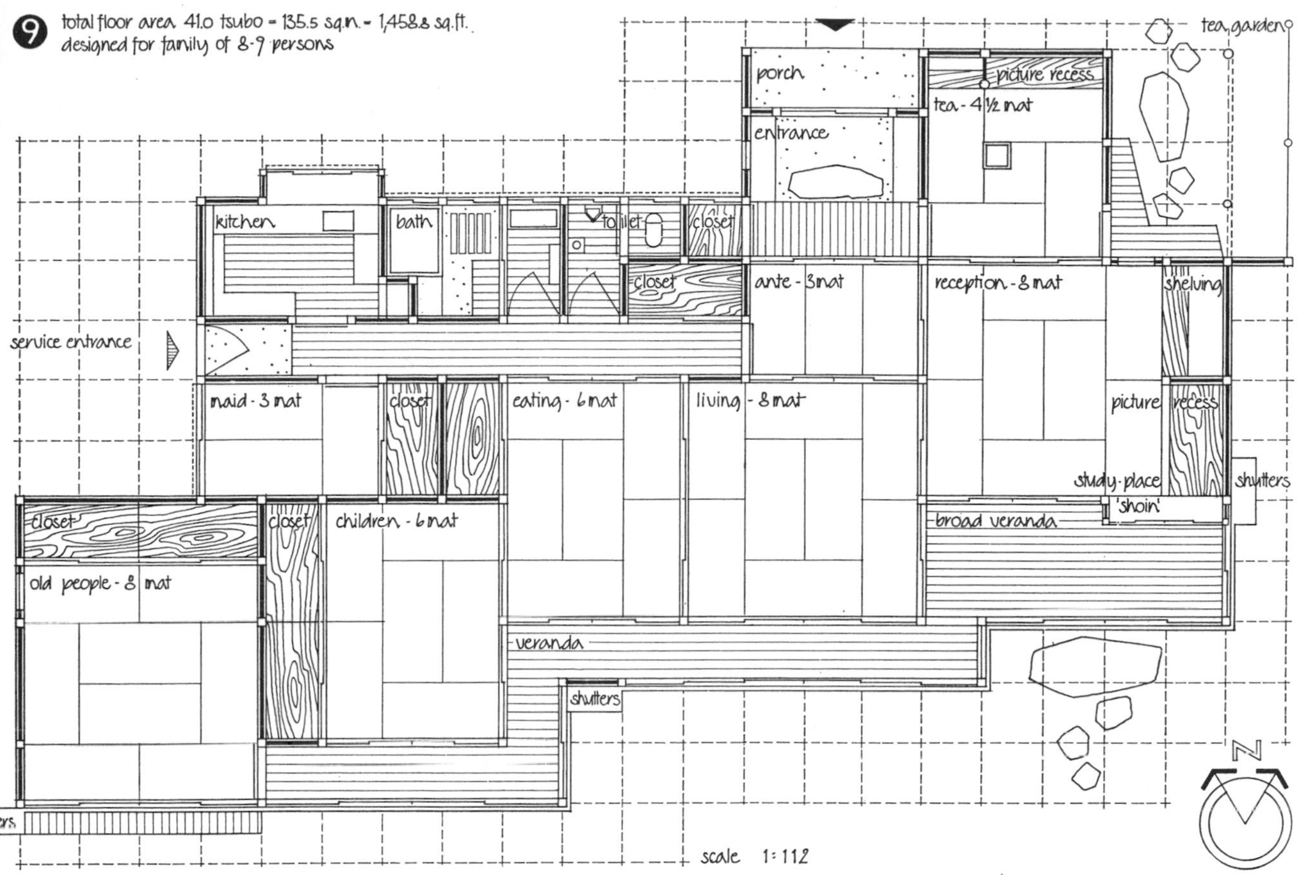

FIGURE 15 (continued): Select examples of typical residences.

by heavy crossbeams (1 *ken* on center) to strong longitudinal members whose maximum span is 3 *ken* (5,454 mm. = 18 ft.), a distance hardly required in the common house. Moreover, additional supporting beams can be used without disadvantageous visual-constructional consequences because of the suspended ceiling and plenty of constructional height. Thus, placement of supporting columns is done freely and follows room organization rather than constructional necessity.

Room is added to room, and space has become additive, a sequence of single room demarcations without distinct beginning or end, constituting no finality but only a state of organic growth. Design is never really completed, nor is the construction of the house itself. With an increase in either children or wealth, another unit is simply added as long as any space on the lot remains; and the house, like its design, becomes dynamic.

Problems in circulation do not arise as they do in the West, for as a rule the room is provided with a veranda-like corridor at the outside or may serve as a corridor itself. Though as time progresses some houses may finally cover the whole site and may reach considerable length, corridors in the Western sense, i.e., as mere means of circulation, are actually not necessary. Here again, a particular mode of living effected a distinct method of design, which in turn, then, enabled a continuous organic growth of building that could not be so simply achieved under the different conditions of Western living and building.

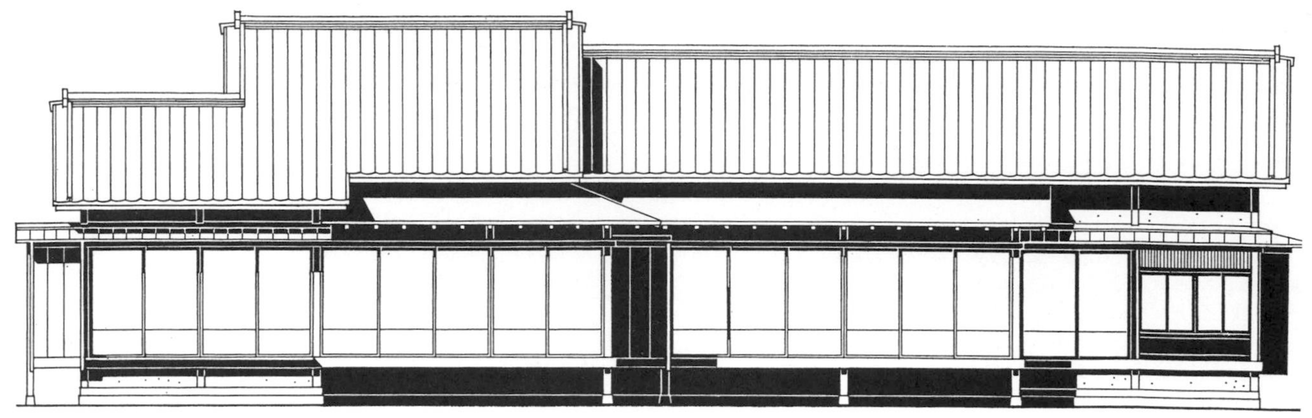

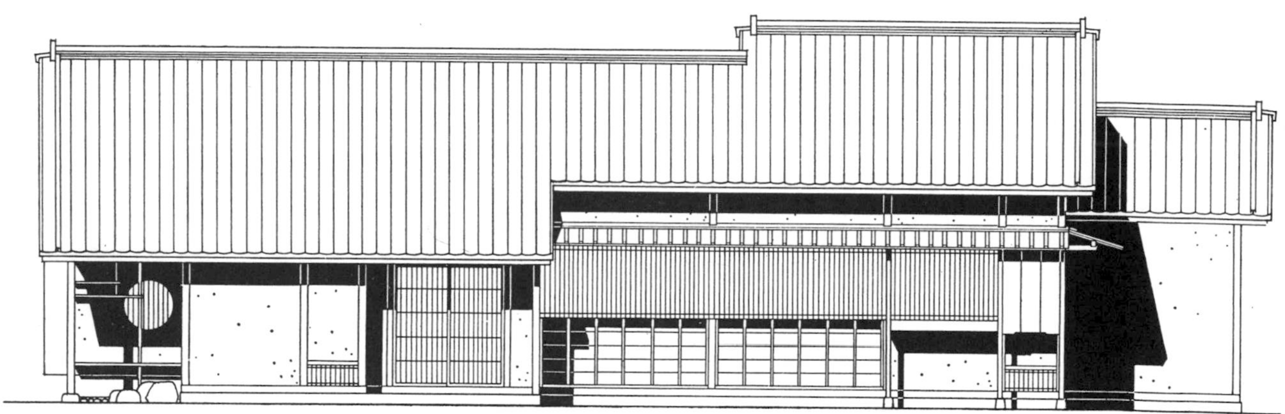

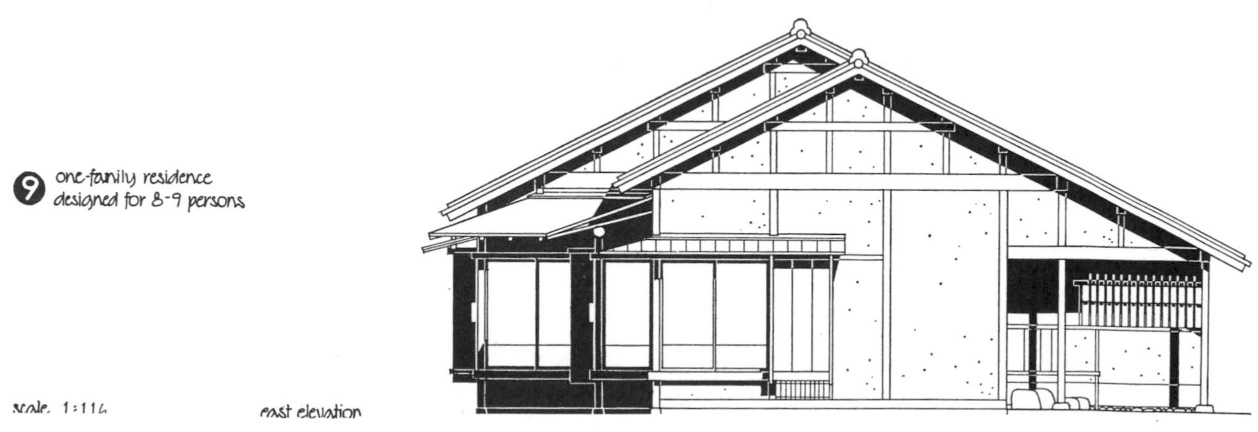

FIGURE 15 (continued): Select examples of typical residences.

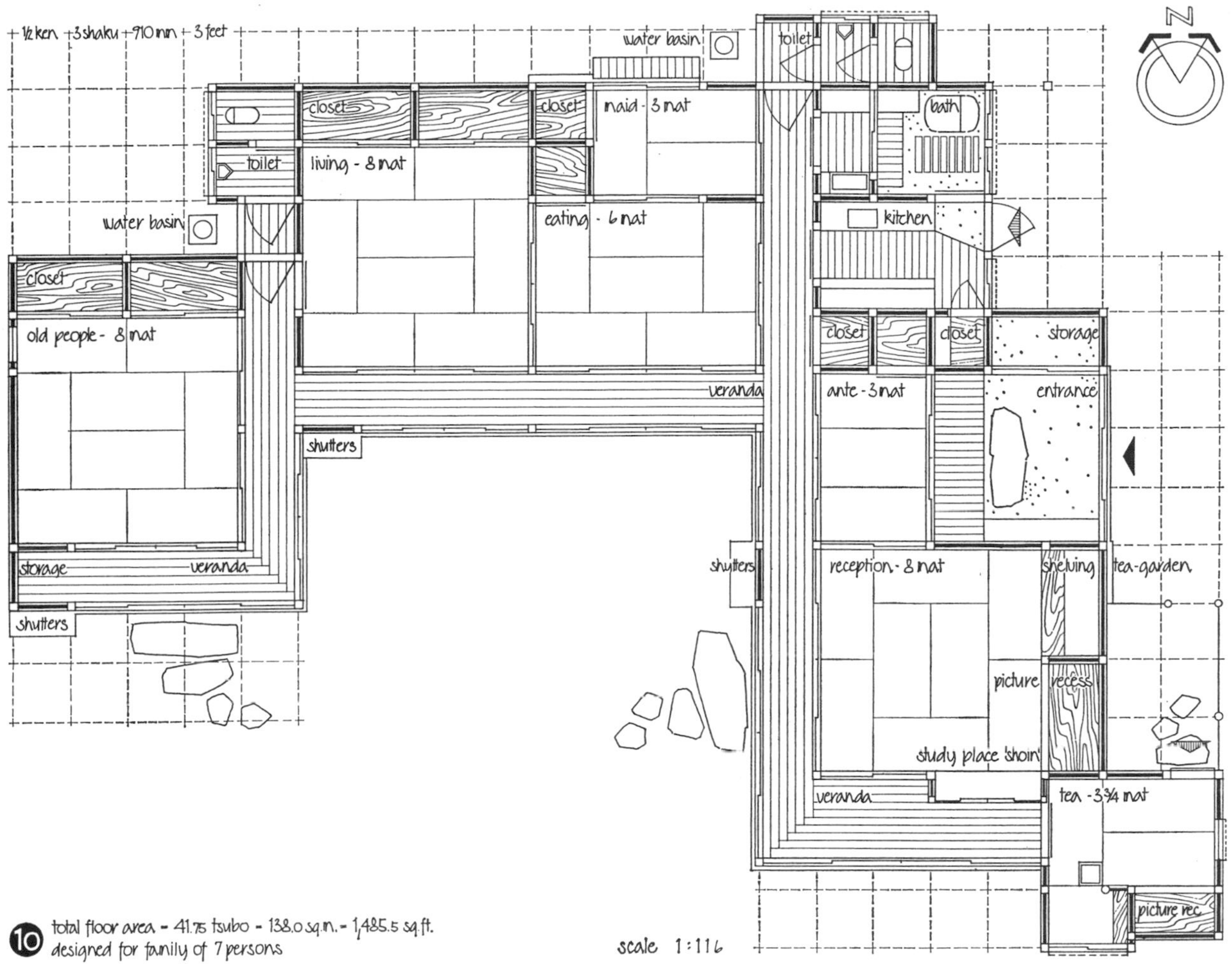

FIGURE 15 (continued): Select examples of typical residences.

The same factors actually also allow the steplike dislocation of adjoining rooms because there are no corridors to demand a linear lineup of adjoining rooms. This steplike pattern is used as long as the site permits and is very much liked because it also affords the opportunity of seeing the outside of one's own house from the inside. This no doubt was a factor that in many cases determined the layout of more extensive houses. But of more architectural importance is the fact that it creates exterior spaces each attached to and marked by two perpendicular outside walls.

This disposition, then, is characteristic of Japanese design: addition of individual spaces with equal value, without particular spatial accentuation, culmination, or finality. Space units, though distinct in themselves, are design-wise not graded into major and minor or into exterior and interior. Rather, the space-marking elements enclose both indoor and outdoor spaces, resulting in a sequence of crisply defined spaces, so different from both the rigid indoor-outdoor separation of traditional Western architecture and the amorphous dissolution of house-garden distinction in contemporary residential architecture.

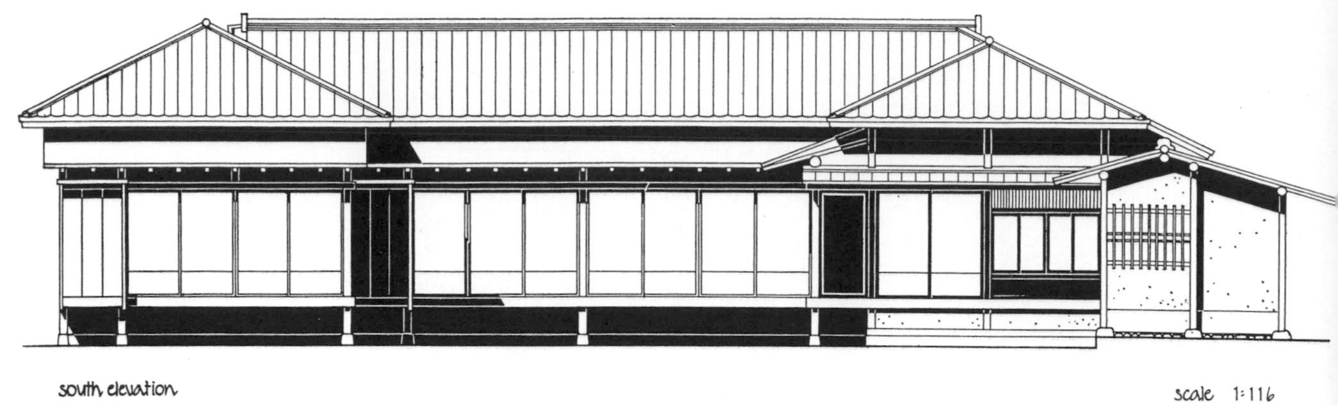

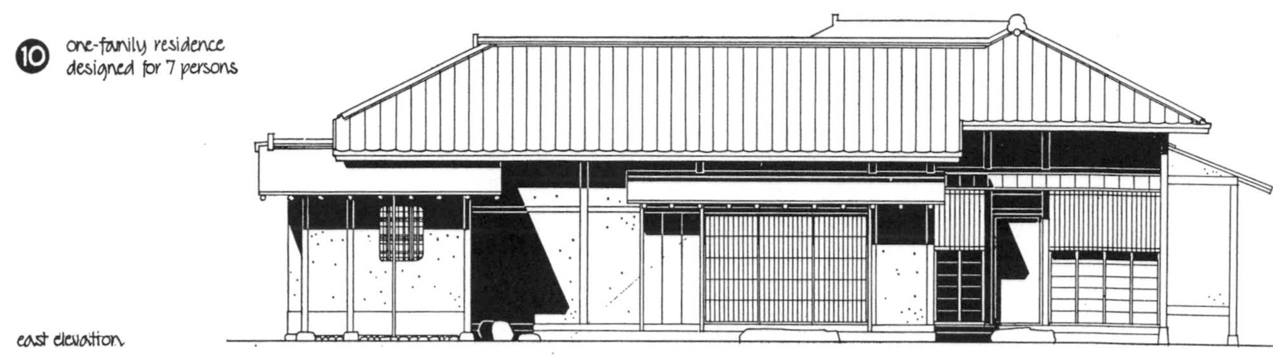

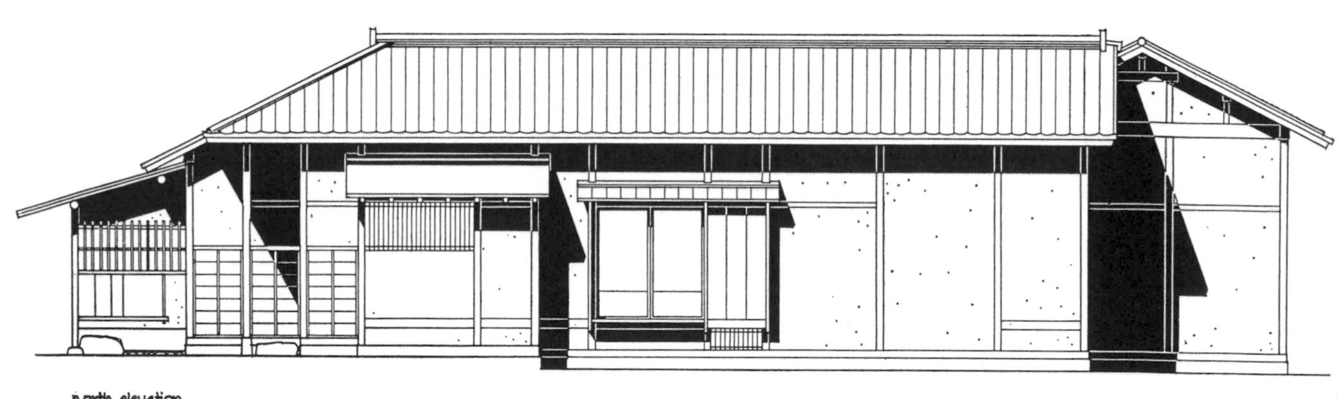

FIGURE 15 (continued): Select examples of typical residences.

superstition

The layout and orientation of the house plan, however, is not entirely done on the basis of practical and logical considerations. Even at the present time, the client usually insists on observance of certain rules in the design that would guarantee the help of the good spirits and would not provoke the antagonism of the evil ones.

Although the carpenter, as architect and builder, usually is familiar with the basics of these rules, the wise man would not take any chances, but would have the plan checked by an expert in this mystic art, by a professional soothsayer, so that the orientation of rooms, the location of important features of the house, and the organization of the total site would not be in contrast to the mysterious instructions handed down from the past.

A compass rose serves as a reference pattern. It is divided into eight major parts corresponding to north, northeast, east, south, southeast, etc.

North	*kan:*	unhappiness (danger)	
Northeast	*gon:*	limitation (stay)	"gate of demon"
East	*shin:*	fear (thunder)	
Southeast	*son:*	modesty	"gate of wind"
South	*ri:*	departure (separation)	
Southwest	*kon:*	obedience (female, earth)	"gate of man"
West	*da:*	joy (pleasure)	
Northwest	*ken:*	heaven (lord, emperor, male)	"gate of heaven"

The intervals between these eight major sectors have each two sectors with names of animals, thus all adding up to twenty-four sectors.

There is no single way of applying this compass rose to the floor plan. The general idea is to superimpose the rose and check the locations of rooms and house features with regard to the meaning implied by the symbols of the rose and elaborated in written instructions that are the basis for the interpretation of the symbols. Usually the rose is centered on the house, but sometimes it is placed on the center of the site. At other times it may be placed on the living room of the head of the house or on the sacred center pillar, *daikoku bashira.* Also, the interpretation of the various symbols with regard to rooms, house features, and site may differ slightly from case to case, but there is fair unanimity regarding the major implications of the mystic meaning of the rose and its instructions.

The northeast-southwest axis with "gate of demon" and "gate of man" as opposites seems to be given prime attention. Toilet or dirt in this axis will bring diseases and misfortune to the inhabitants as will a gate or a storehouse. A firestead in northeast will cause infantile diseases and an extension of the homestead in this direction will bring outright destruction. However, a garden hill in northeast is likely to ward off all the demons and will guarantee good luck, while a well in southwest will assure nothing less than continuous wealth for everyone in the family.

Other instructions concern the configuration of the total floor plan, i.e., the major projections and recesses of the house. Naturally, a simple rectangular plan without such projections or recesses will not be affected by these instructions.

SIDE OF PROJECTION: IMPLICATIONS		SIDE OF RECESS: IMPLICATIONS	
N:	(no mention)	N:	(no mention)
NE:	(no mention)	NE:	(no mention)
E:	favor of superiors, luck	E:	hindrance to fulfillment of hopes
SE:	prosperity in business, assurance of peace	SE:	bad luck

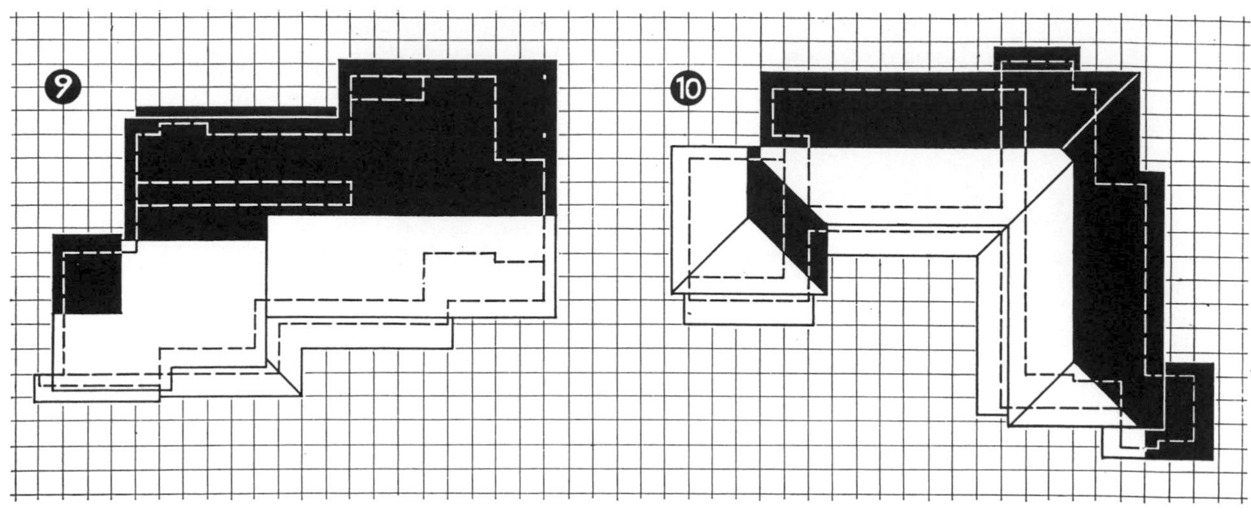

roof plans of designs 9 and 10 — scale 1:280

FIGURE 15 (continued): Select examples of typical residences.

S:	no harm	S:	first wealth, later ruin
SW:	predominance of feminine power, early death of master	SW:	(no mention)
W:	bad luck	W:	prosperity, tenderness of heart
NW:	success in business	NW:	(no mention)

In addition, these instructions specify good and bad locations for wells, Buddha altar, god shelf, toilet, kitchen, and doors. They also concern the garden layout, the appropriate location for rocks and waters, and the arrangement of gates. They may even determine succession of rooms, number and arrangement of mats, and location of the hearth.

Considering the strange interweaving of practical and mystical implications, it seems certain that these rules had come from China. In a land in which directions of winds and water courses are distinct and the climate fairly uniform, and in which the practical always was interlocked with the mystical, it was quite reasonable to set up practical rules for adjusting the house design to the prevailing climate and to lend force to those rules by linking them with consequences of both material and spiritual nature.

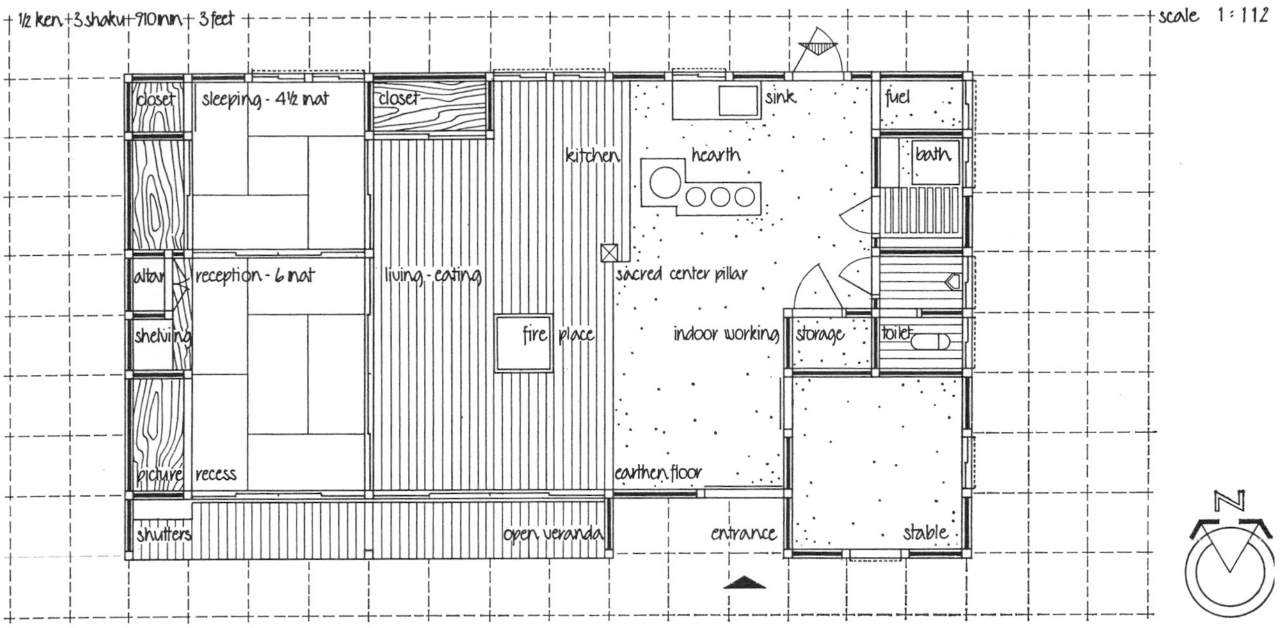

1 floor plan of typical farm house
area with flooring 16.00 tsubo = 52.88 sq.m. = 569.3 sq.ft. area without flooring 11.25 tsubo = 37.2 sq.m. = 400.3 sq.ft.

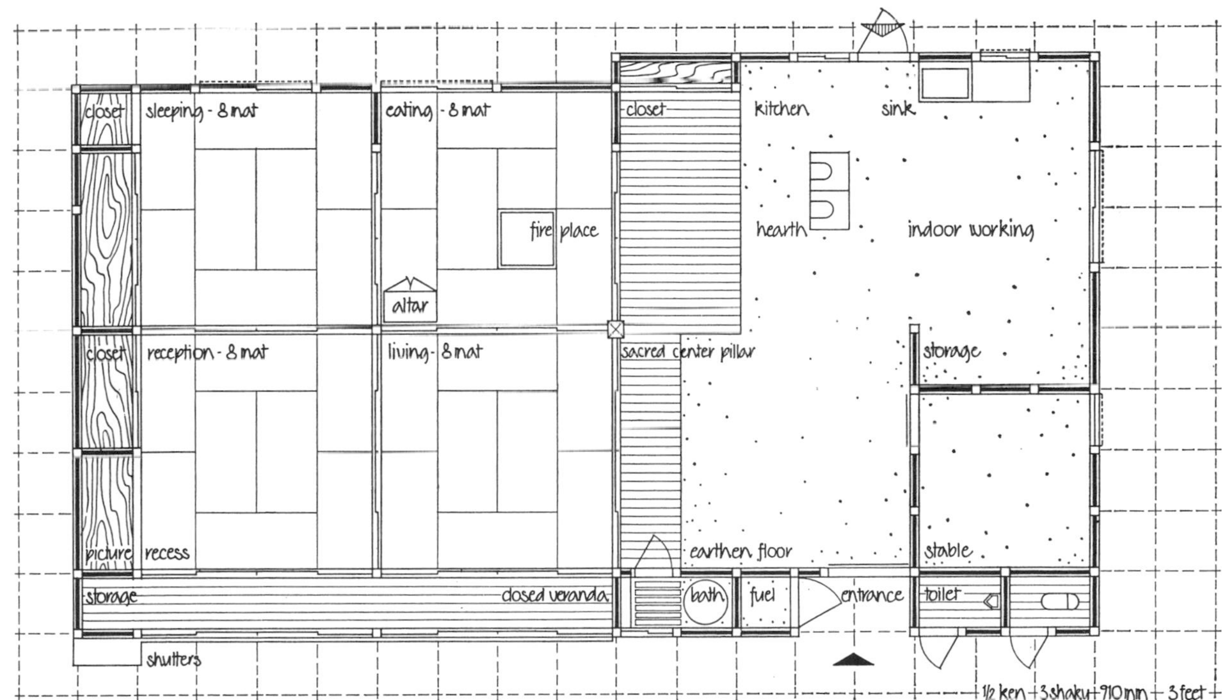

2 floor plan of typical farm house
area with flooring 23.75 tsubo = 78.5 sq.m. = 845.0 sq.ft. area without flooring 15.5 tsubo = 51.2 sq.m. = 551.5 sq.ft. scale 1:112

FIGURE 16: Select examples of typical farmhouses.

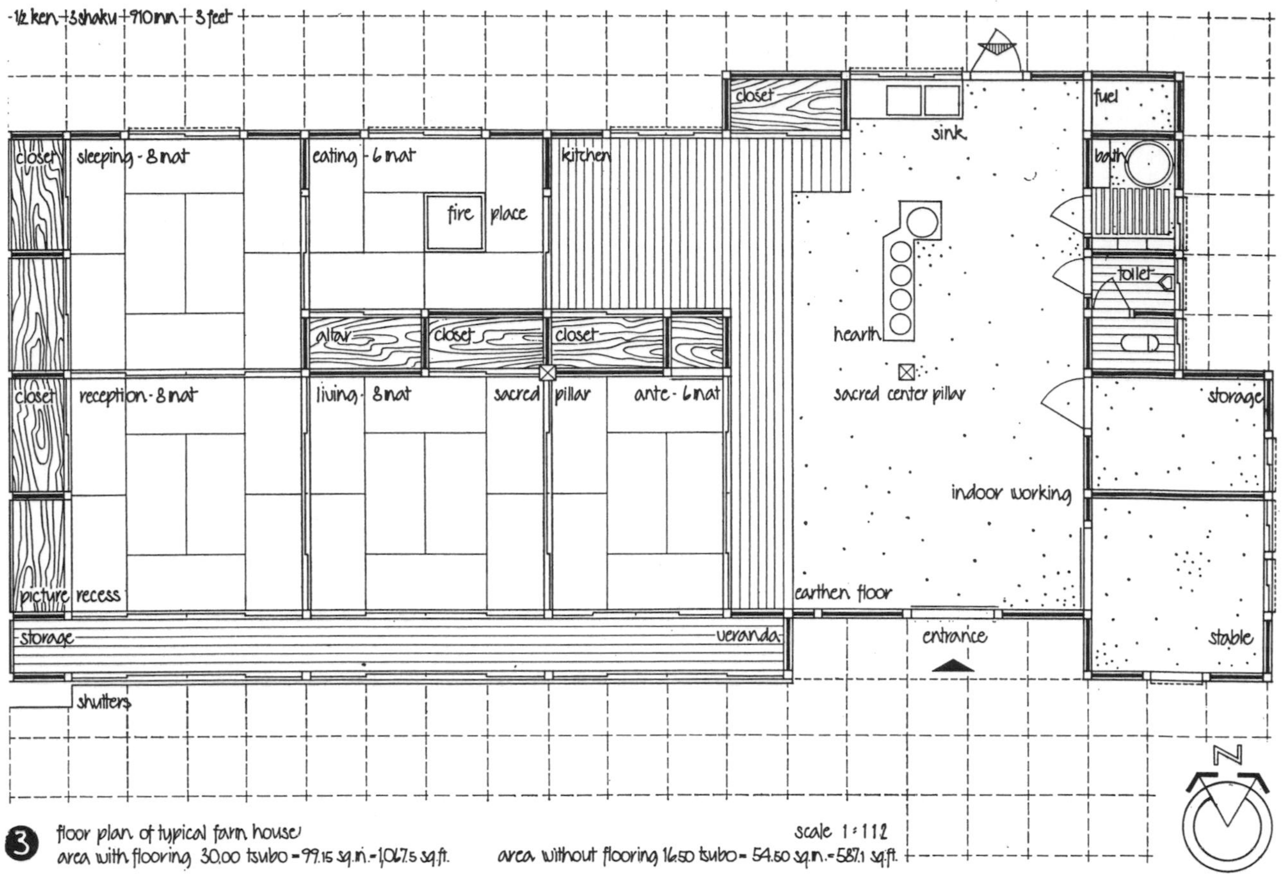

FIGURE 16 (continued): Select examples of typical farmhouses.

It is very likely that Japan adopted these rules developed in China, some of which also apply to Japanese conditions. But among them there were certainly many that needed to be adjusted for Japanese application, and it is possible that in doing so a number of inconsistencies entered the formerly unique compass guide for the house layout.

Since the general observance of these rules is less due to an acknowledgment of their reasonableness than to fear of the unknown and to belief in magic, the rules must properly be called superstitious. On the other hand, although the instructions contain gross and inexplicable contradictions and may obstruct the exploitation of a good design idea, there are many of them that do make sense, especially with regard to the climate. The climatic implication is also evident in the dependence of these rules on the cardinal points of the compass, and, indeed, if considered from the viewpoint of sun exposure, wind direction, bad weatherside, etc., the rules seem to be quite reasonable and helpful.

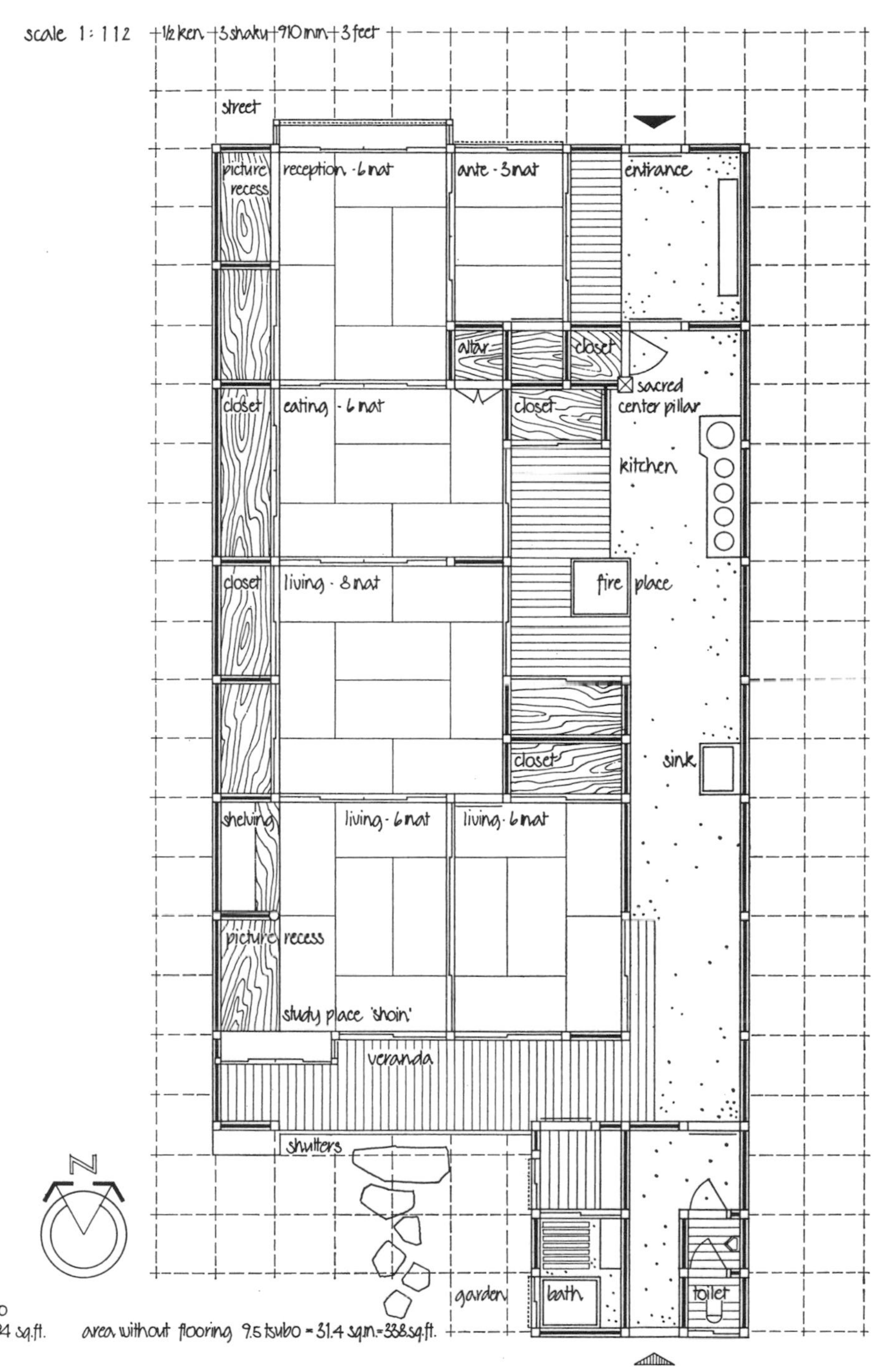

FIGURE 17: Example of typical downtown Kyoto residence (*see also* Figure 18–3).

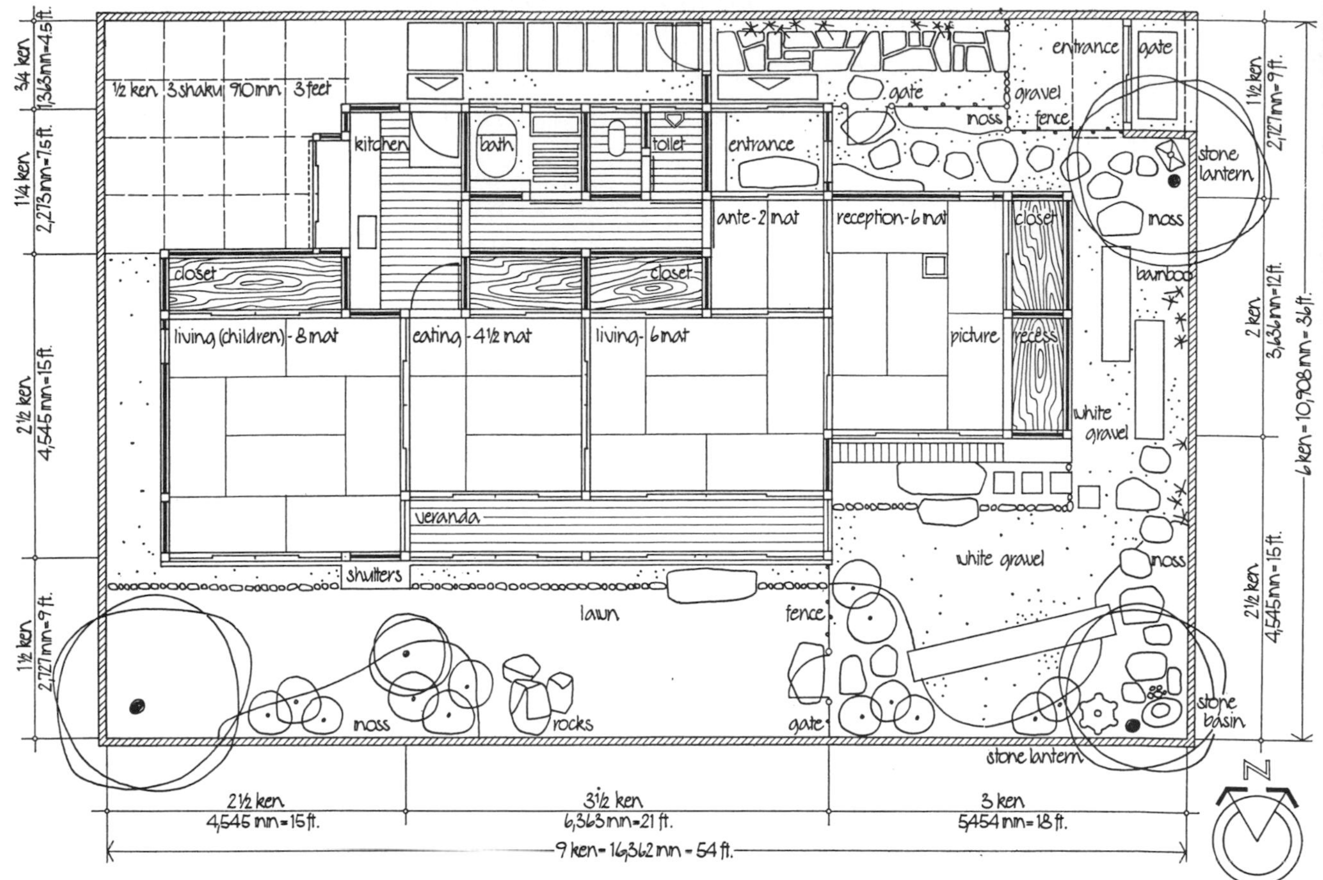

garden design for residence of 22.75 tsubo = 75.2 sq.m = 809.4 sq.ft., building site = 9 x 6 ken = 54 tsubo = 178.5 sq.m = 1,944 sq.ft. scale 1:112

FIGURE 18: Representative examples of house-garden design.

Thus, it rightly can be assumed that the basis of these superstitious rules is the concern with the health of the inhabitants. Their purpose is to give the "designers" of the house a handy rule of thumb, the observance of which would avoid errors in design; and the carpenter manuals suggest that in designing a house, though one need not strictly follow these rules, one should by no means ignore them.

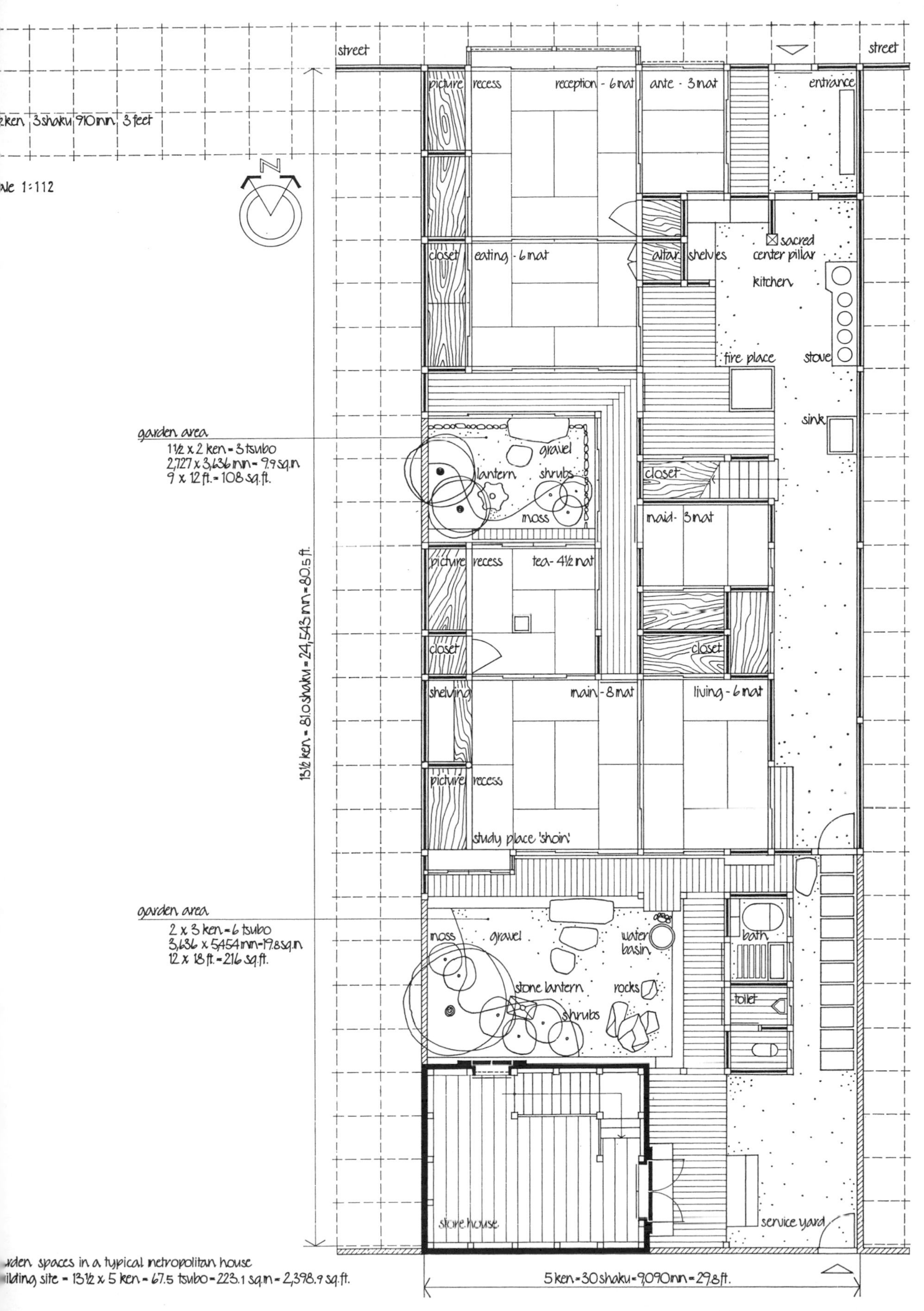

street
street
ken 3shaku 910mm 3feet
ale 1:112
N
picture recess
reception - 6mat
ante - 3mat
entrance
closet
eating - 6mat
altar
shelves
sacred center pillar
kitchen
fire place
stove
sink
garden area
1½ x 2 ken = 3 tsubo
2,727 x 3,636 mm = 9.9 sq.m
9 x 12 ft. = 108 sq.ft.
gravel
lantern
shrubs
moss
closet
maid - 3mat
picture recess
tea - 4½ mat
closet
closet
shelving
main - 8mat
living - 6mat
picture recess
study place 'shoin'
13½ ken = 81.0 shaku = 24,543 mm = 80.5 ft.
garden area
2 x 3 ken = 6 tsubo
3,636 x 5,454 mm = 19.8 sq.m
12 x 18 ft. = 216 sq.ft.
moss
gravel
water basin
stone lantern
rocks
shrubs
bath
toilet
store house
service yard
rden spaces in a typical metropolitan house
ilding site = 13½ x 5 ken = 67.5 tsubo = 223.1 sq.m = 2,398.9 sq.ft.
5 ken = 30 shaku = 9,090 mm = 29.8 ft.

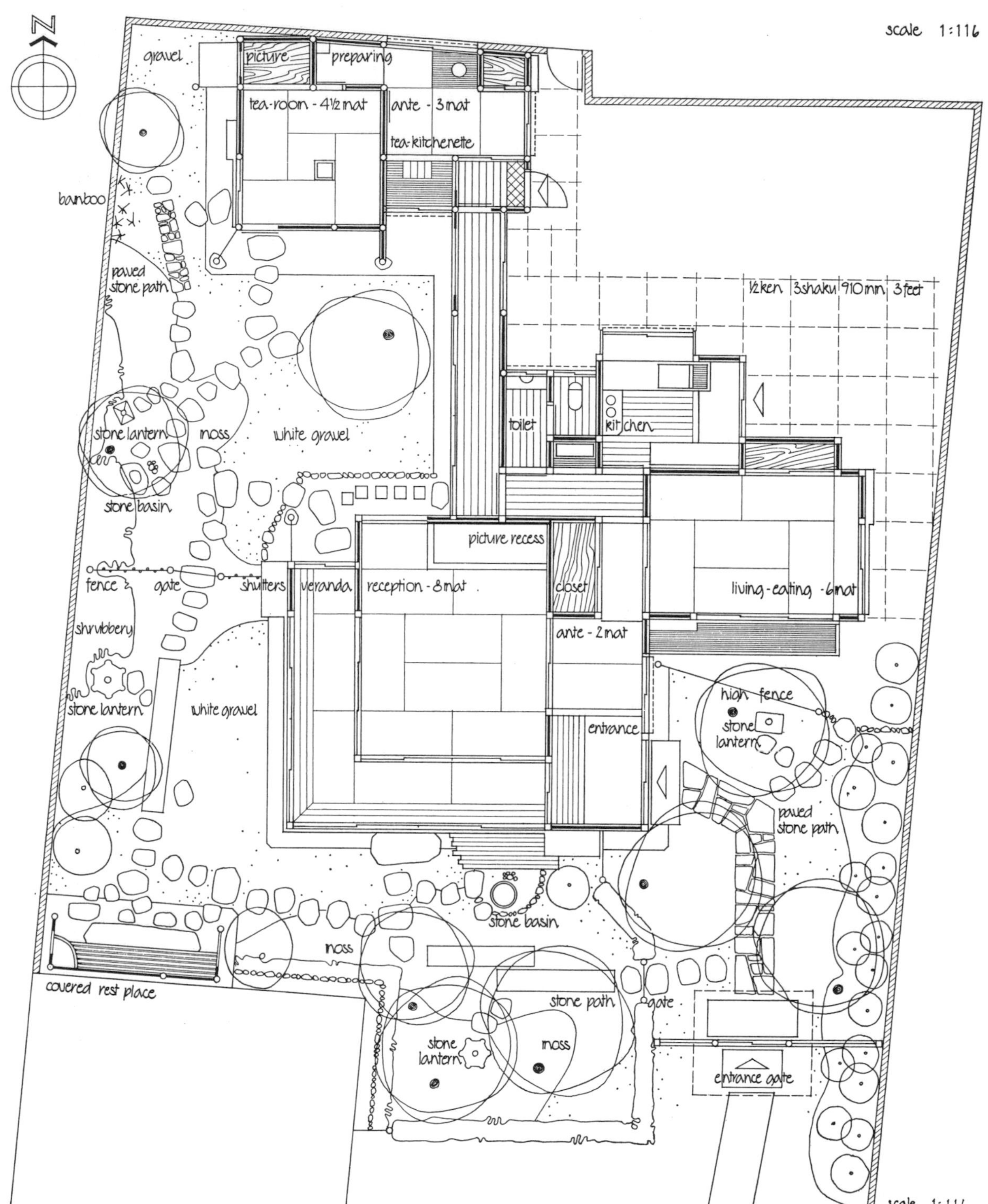

FIGURE 18 (continued): Representative examples of house-garden design.

physique of the tearoom

As much as Zen Buddhism has fostered the ceremonial drinking of tea and has given depth and spiritual esteem to the tea cult, as much has Zen permeated and spiritualized the physique of the tearoom. The first architectural measure toward an independent space for exercising the tea serving was the partitioning of a space called *kakoi* (enclosure) within a main room through portable screens. The name *kakoi* later came to designate those tearooms that are integrated or physically attached to the main house. Partitioned space, thereafter, became enclosed space, and it was Sen-no-Rikyū who created the independent tea hut, *sukiya,* the "abode of fancy." This was usually a detached, hermitage-style structure called *sōan,* available mainly to the wealthy classes. Its forms were so unique that a new architectural style was initiated, the *sukiya* style, but its thorough investigation is beyond the scope of this paper. Instead, the analysis will concern itself only with the spatial and expressional features in the tearoom (*kakoi, cha-shitsu*) that were incorporated into the houses of the common people.

The dimensions of the space for the classic tearoom, as elaborated by Shō-ō, a tea master of the 16th century, are determined by an area covered with 4½ mats, which is a square room of about 2,700 mm. or of 9 ft. width. This size is said to be symbolically linked with the room in which a legendary Buddhist figure welcomed a saint and 84,000 disciples of Buddha as a manifestation that conceptual limitations such as space do not exist for the truly enlightened. Yet, in the world of material reality, the classic 4½-mat tearoom is dimensioned to accommodate not more than five persons. The interior features of the tearoom aim at suggesting the atmosphere of a faraway farmhouse with its remoteness, poverty, humbleness, simplicity, and semidarkness, and many motifs have, therefore, been taken directly from the old farmhouse.

However, what set out as an aestheticism that attempted to uncover the humanistic and artistic values of poverty gradually became an aestheticism of poverty's forms and features alone, to a degree that it no longer had anything in common with the very real and direct poverty of the farmers and general public. Thus, in their wish to manifest solidarity with poverty, the wealthy class engaged the best craftsmen, used the most exquisite material, employed the most elaborate techniques, prepared the most costly tea, served with most precious utensils, and wore the most expensive clothes, thus making the teahouse and tea drinking an elaborate and very costly art a paradoxical attitude, indeed, in an aestheticism that claims to be an appreciation of the values in poverty. Only, when the tearoom was adopted into the houses of the commoners was the discrepancy of the tea's existence solved, and tea became the very humble cognizance of the reward and value of poverty, not only in its physical manifestation as tearoom but also in its symbolic performance as tea serving.

In contrast to the openness of all living rooms in the Japanese house, the tearoom, as created by Sen-no-Rikyū, is a hermitage, enclosed on all four sides by solid clay walls of a particular rough, earthen texture, with no visible attempt to compensate for unevenness in the handicraft technique. The lower part is pasted with gray or white paper, *koshi-bari,* to a height of about 1–1.5 ft. (300–450 mm.). The leaves of old letters are also frequently used to create a feeling of insufficiency. While in the ordinary rooms of the Japanese residence the functions for door, window, and partition are performed as a rule by identical sliding units, *shōji* and *fusuma,* in the tearoom these functions are given separate treatment. There is even a distinction made between the window which provides light and that which permits a limited view to the garden, in case the latter exists at all. For, frequently its function may be fulfilled by the low entry through which the guests crawl while entering from the garden. Also, the entrance, direct from the house interior or indirect from the veranda or the tea kitchenette, is clearly marked by a frameless sliding panel pasted with white opaque paper and is thus in physical contrast to the dark-colored clay wall. Frequently, a third entrance from the house interior is provided, differentiating the entries for tea serving and meal serving. Another difference from the ordinary living room is the use of logs in their natural shape as columns. The frieze rail, *nageshi,* in the tea cult's continuous attempt at simplification, is also absent, as is the clerestory window for ventilation, *ramma.*

The forms of windows vary individually, yet, certain conventional forms that effect a certain uniformity for these wall openings have developed as well. Thus, for the illumination of the room a rectangular window with high sill, *taka-mado,* is used. It is furnished with translucent paper panels and usually receives a bamboo lathwork on the outside, in which case the window is called *renji-mado.* Equally common is the clay-wall window, *shitaji-mado,* which, though not being submitted to formalistic rules, is preferred in a circular shape or as a rectangle with the corners cut off or rounded. It is said that this motif has been taken from the old farmhouse, where ventilation was provided by simply laying bare the bamboo skeleton of the wall from its wall clay. Though the positioning of the windows appears rather free, it again follows certain principles that allow no arbitrary measures. One of them is that the place of the host is effectively illuminated so that the guests can properly observe the host's art of preparing tea. Another is that the recess with the hanging picture scroll receives sufficient light. Frequently the light is tempered by bamboo curtains attached to the windows from the outside, which in the latter part of the tea gathering, are removed, thus creating an entirely different light condition that enriches the experience of "tea."

The presence of the picture recess, *tokonoma,* in the tearoom indicates the strong relationship of "tea" with Zen Buddhism. For the Zen temple itself was but a college room for the monk students, with one wall slightly recessed to contain a Buddha statue or sacred picture, in front of which the monks held their discussions and meditational practices, burning a censer and drinking ceremonial tea. One may still find a censer in the tearoom next to the flower vase—a remnant of the original form of *tokonoma.* For the recess post, *toko-bashira,* a natural stem of irregular form, different from the material of the columns in other rooms, is preferred. The hearth, a square hole of 1.4 x 1.4 (also 1.3 x 1.3) *shaku* (430 x 430 mm. = 16.7 x 16.7 in.) sunk into the floor, is located in a particular relationship to the two entrances and to the picture recess—a consequence of the exacting rules of the tea-serving procedure. Here the water is heated in an iron kettle, which is frequently suspended from the ceiling by an iron chain. The ceiling is much lower than in ordinary rooms; it may have a pattern of bamboo wicker or of interwoven wooden strips and is divided with one part sloped, as if to suggest the underside of a roof or attic space.

This sloped part may have a skylight with a movable cover, as in the kitchen of the old farmhouse, and, with rising or sinking daylight, it is mainly through this window that the room receives the fast-changing light of the rising or sinking sun. Such a control of room illumination, together with the single flower and the picture scroll in the alcove, provides infinite possibilities to adapt the emotional quality of the tearoom either to the weather or to the disposition of the house master, making the architecture of the tearoom not only physically but also psychologically a true image of man himself. To exploit these possibilities, of course, presupposes an awareness of the potential of light in architecture, and in the tearoom it appears as if the Japanese understood very well the importance of light in the art of living.

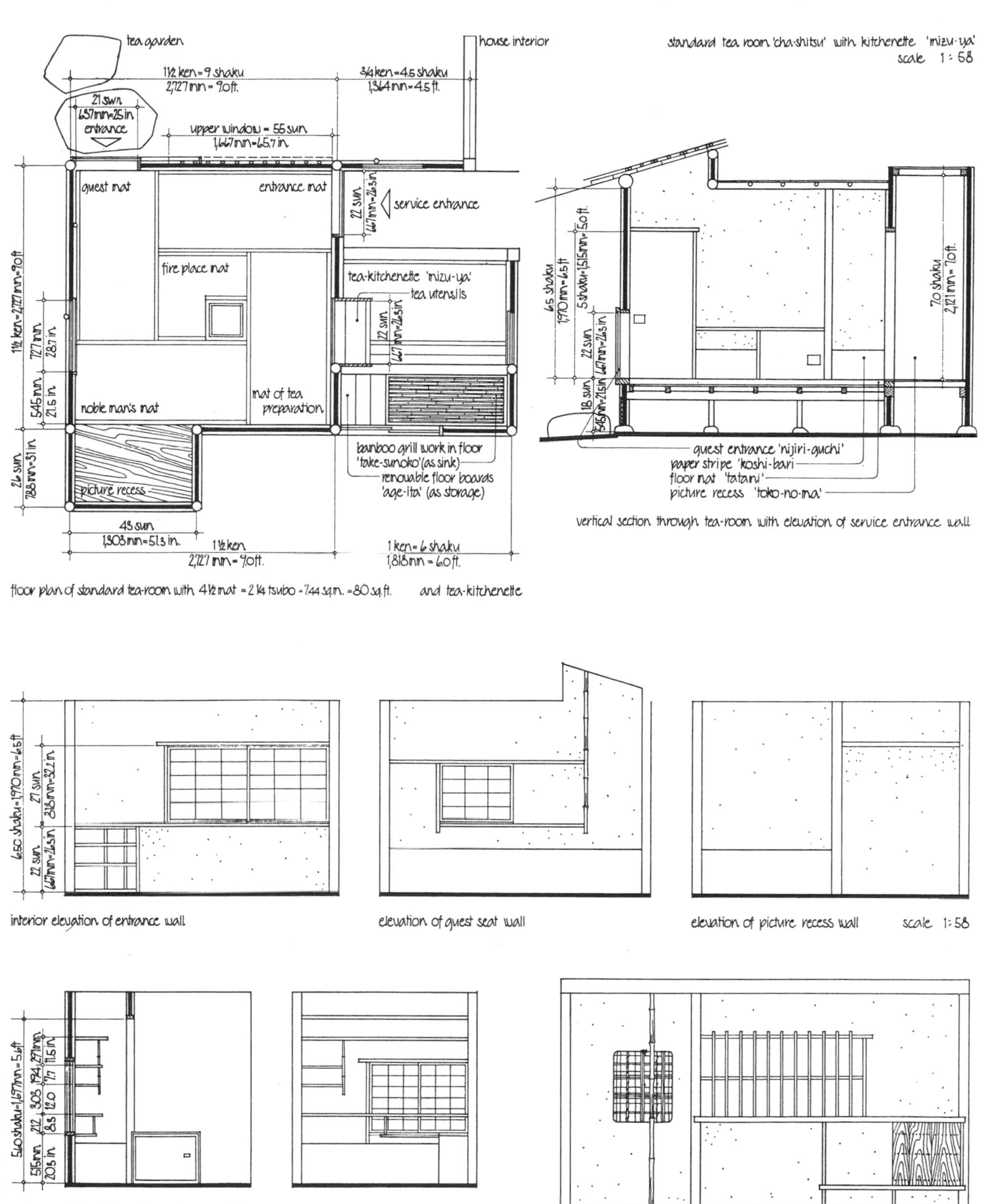

FIGURE 19: Plan of prototype tearoom, *cha-shitsu*, with kitchenette, *mizuya*.

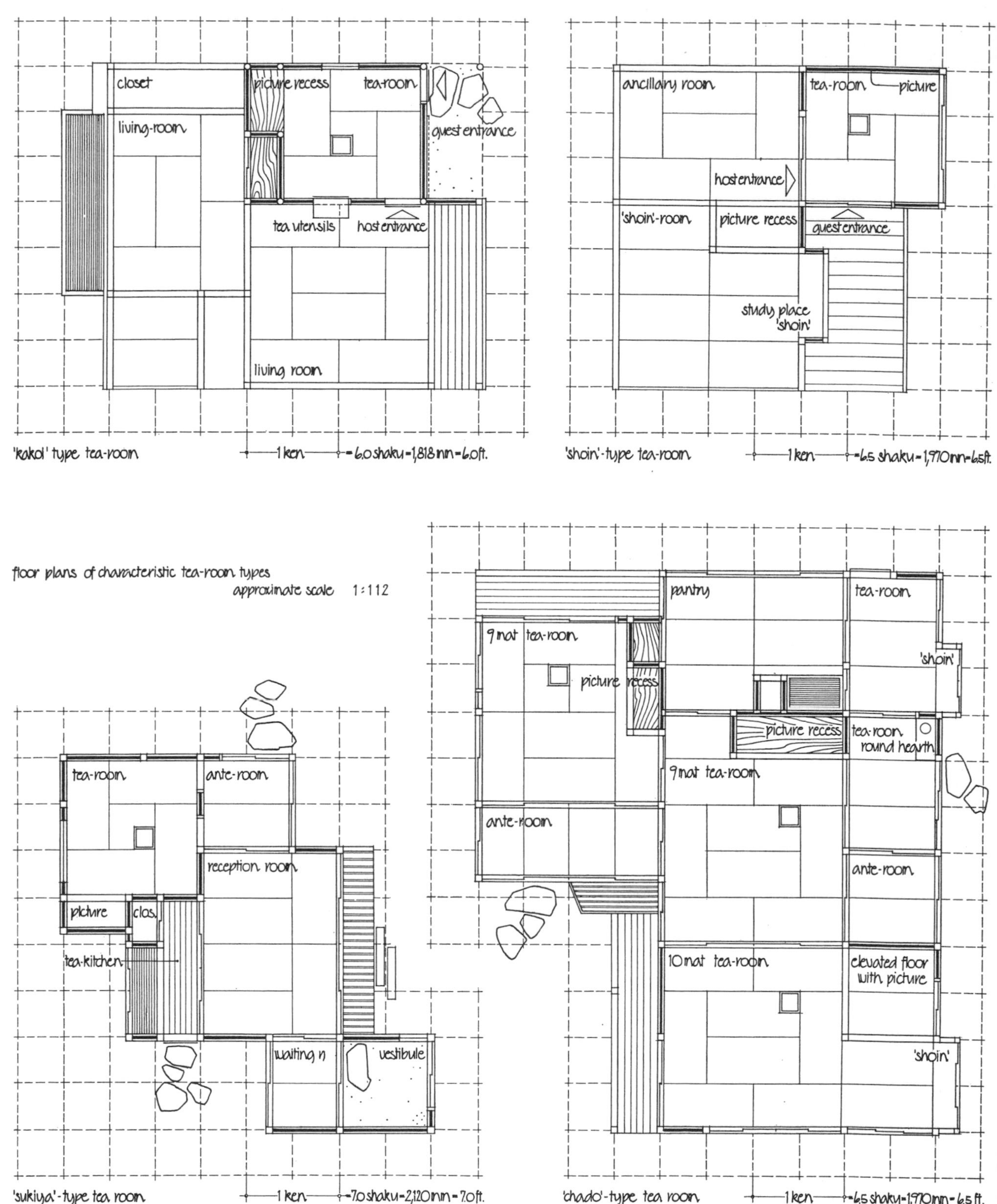

FIGURE 20: Floor-plans of characteristic tearoom types.

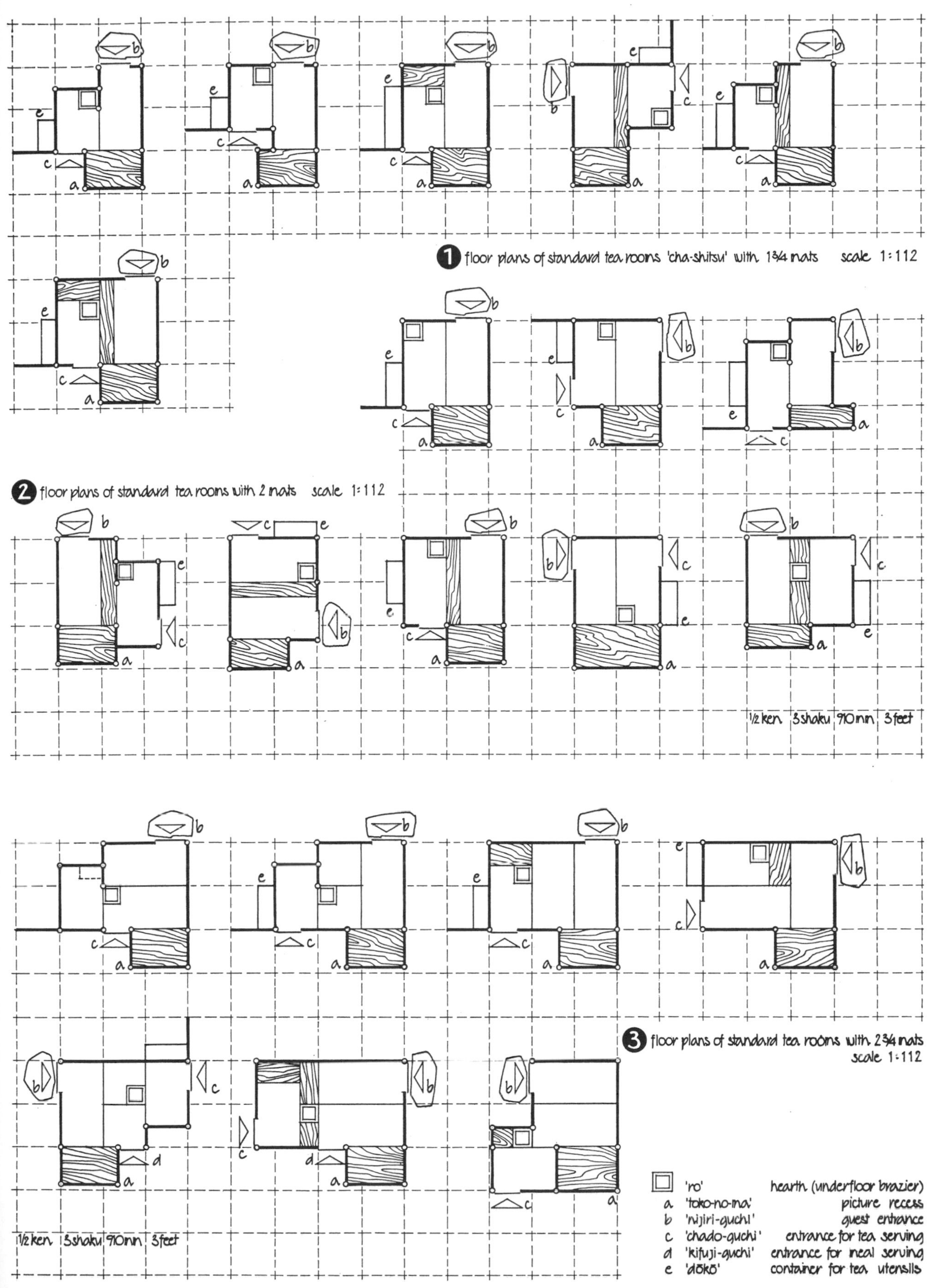

FIGURE 21: Floor-plan diagrams of standard tearooms showing variations in size and arrangement.

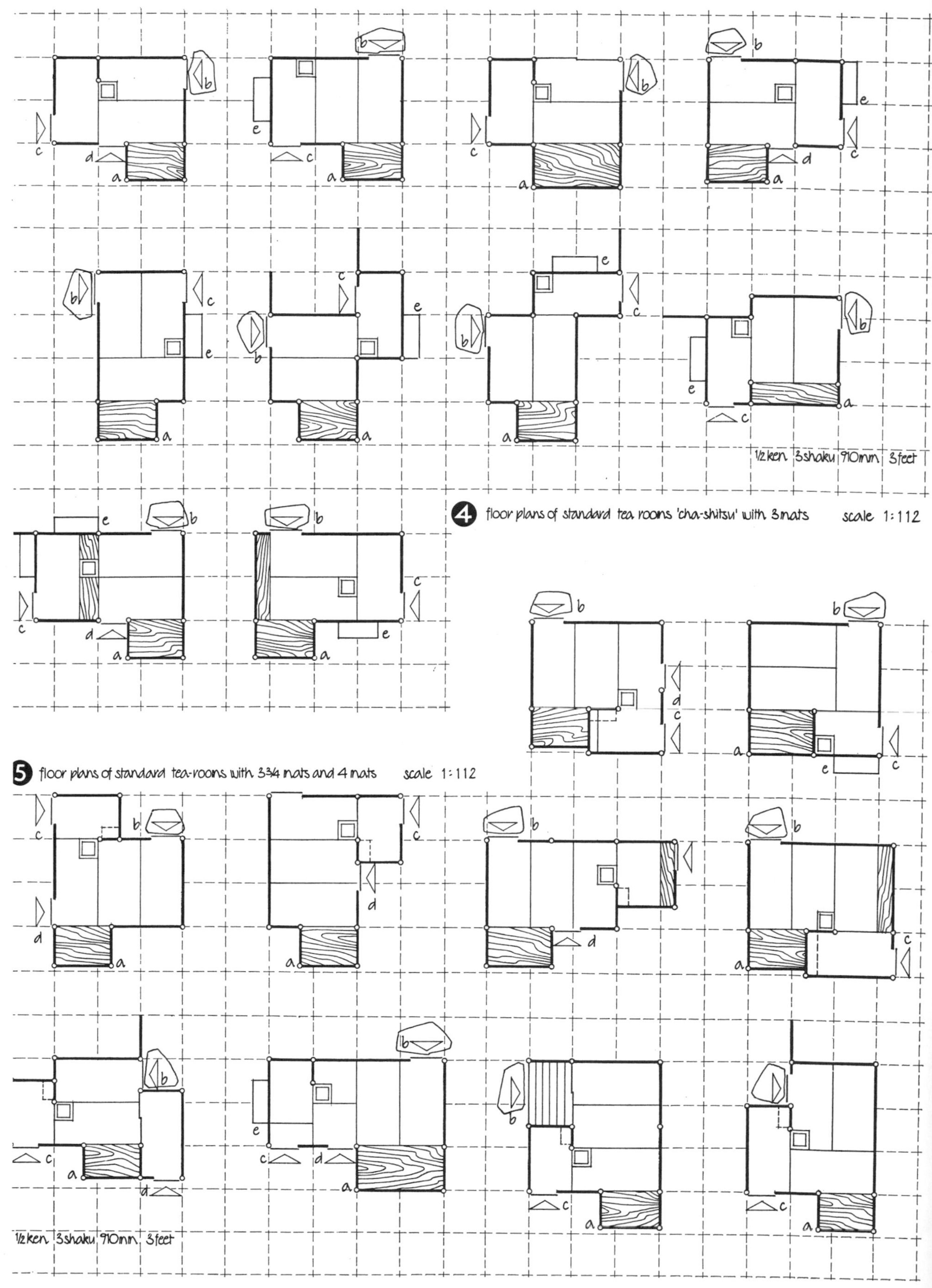

FIGURE 21 (continued): Floor-plan diagrams of standard tearooms showing variations in size and arrangement.

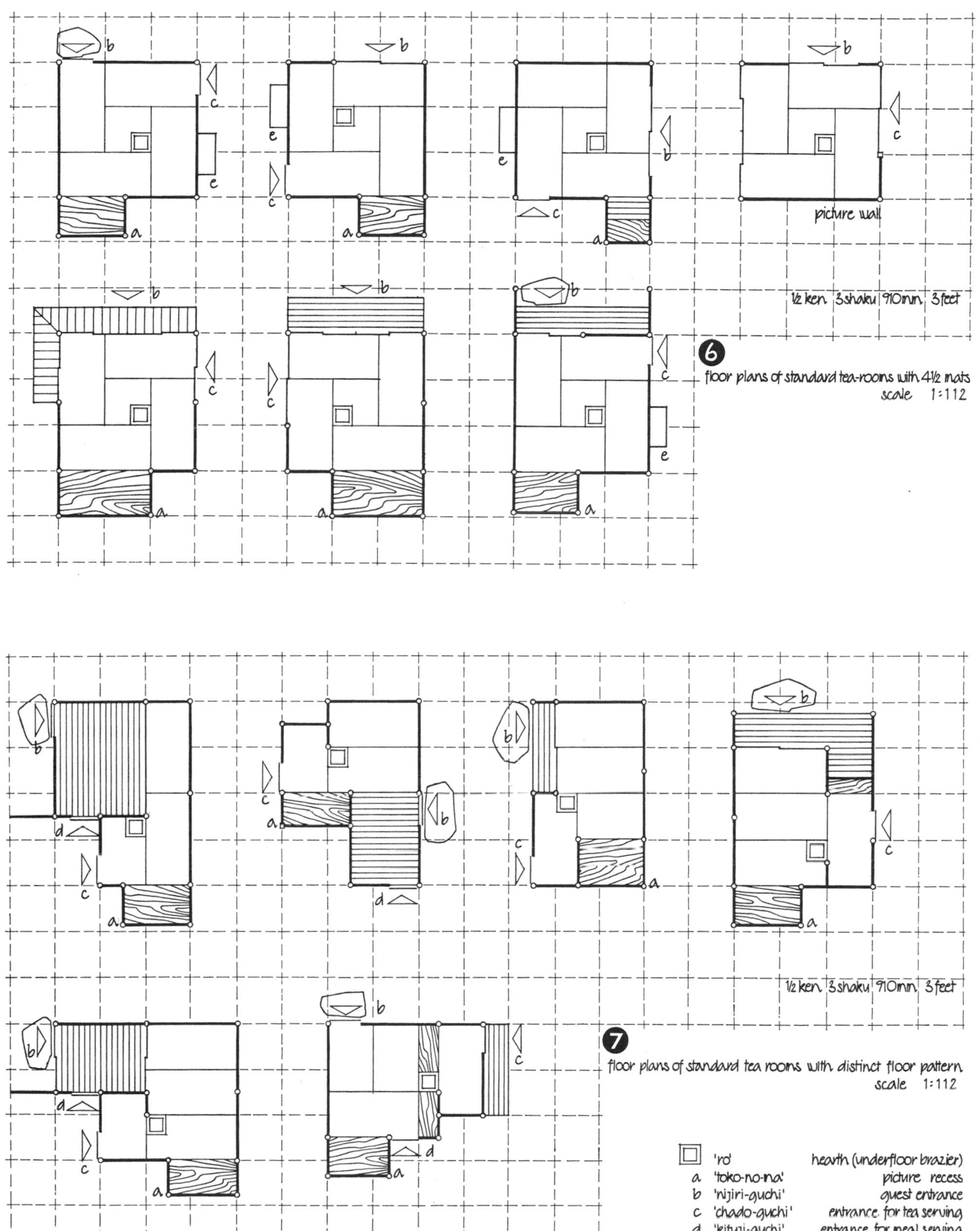

FIGURE 21 (continued): Floor-plan diagrams of standard tearooms showing variations in size and arrangement.

In this role, the spatial character of the tearoom is basically different from that of all the other rooms. The tearoom is a seclusion, boldly isolated from the outside world, be it house interior or garden—a space free from any outside intrusion, both actually and suggestively. It is significant that the rigid enclosure was not created as a defensive measure, such as the defense against weather which caused the isolation of the interior of Western buildings; nor was it an inevitable circumstance brought about by constructional methods. Instead, this solid enclosure was effected by the realization that seclusion in building is essential in order to create a maximum atmosphere of introversion in building.

In the classic tearoom of 4½ mats, the mats are arranged around the half mat in the middle, which contains the hearth. Each mat has its particular name that corresponds with the procedure of tea serving. Thus, the half mat in the middle is called "hearth mat"; the mat in front of the picture recess, i.e., the most honorable seat, is called "mat before the alcove" or "nobleman's mat"; the mat at the guest entrance, where the guests take their seats, is called "guest mat"; the mat upon which the host prepares the tea is the "mat of tea preparation"; and the mat in front of the service entrance from the house interior is called "entrance mat." Smaller rooms have only the "guest mat" and the "mat of tea preparation," the latter then containing the fire place. The variety of room sizes, according to mat numbers, is enlarged by the use of a ¾ mat called *daime,* which is liked very much because it creates an alcove owing to the shorter length of the mat. Even in rooms with only normal mats, this spatial effect of an alcove is purposefully produced by projecting a stub wall 1–2 ft. (300–600 mm.) into the room at the mat joint. This clay wall directly joins the hearth and is terminated with a natural round stem, *naka-bashira,* of frequently irregular shape which has a strong sculptural effect. Through this manipulation, a place for tea preparation of no more than 3 x 4.5 (6) ft. (900 x 1,350 mm.) is spatially, yet not visually, separated, allowing for an arrangement of shelves behind the stub wall without interfering with the simple austerity of the tearoom.

While in ordinary houses the utensils for the tea serving are kept in another room, usually the dining room, *chanoma,* the tea ceremony being prepared in the kitchen, in more extensive houses a particular kitchenette called *mizuya* is provided for this purpose. Its size is not larger than two mats (1,818 x 1,818 mm. = 6 x 6 ft.), yet, it contains all facilities necessary for the preparation of the tea ceremony. One part of its floor along the exterior wall is perforated with a bamboo grill that serves as a sink for cleaning the tea utensils. The wall shelves are designed along both practical and aesthetic lines, and all other features of this room are determined by the same principles as those of the tearoom. It was the exemplary convenience and practicality of this kitchenette that influenced the unhygienic and inconvenient kitchen in old houses to become more efficient and human.

These, then, are the physical components of the tearoom. The motifs were features of the old farmhouse and, to a limited degree, of the primitive city dwelling, complemented by characteristics of the Zen college. Their execution, however, is subjected to the principles that were proclaimed by the tea masters to be the essence of tea feeling and the prerequisite for a profound tea experience. Their psychological implications are infinite; they not only make the tea cult an ever new experience, but they will also respond to the particular state of mind of each individual. While the restrained decoration in the form of a hanging picture scroll, *kakemono,* and a single flower or branch changes according to the season, weather, or disposition, and thus is ever new, the permanent component of the tearoom's physique is also ever new. For it contains many symbolic meanings that may be perceived differently according to the mood of the individual beholder.

Thus, their irregularity and roughness of a natural wood column may suggest poverty in all its humbleness and simpleness. It may also be conceived of as a bold demonstra- tion that form is to be neglected if the spirit behind the matter is to come to the open. Conspicuous and unnatural form may direct attention to itself rather than to inner truth. The same column may convey the notion of something imperfect that engages the imagination to complete it. The experiencing of beauty is not passive beholding but active partaking. Therefore, Zen asserts that perfection of beauty lies in its imperfection, in which the emphasis rests upon the process through which perfection is sought, rather than upon the perfection itself. Symmetry and geometry are to be avoided because they express not only completion and perfection, but also repetition. Again, the frailty of the slender columns may transmit the awareness that all material is perishable. House is only a temporary refuge for the body, as the body is for the soul. Eternal only is the spirit behind the phenomena, and spirit has mastery over matter. The suggestive power of this natural-irregular column, in the subdued light of the intimate tearoom, may even carry one to the desolateness of the rugged mountains, where the life of a daring young pine tree has come to an untimely end because of cold and lack of food among the vastness of rocks, while the singing of the teakettle may be heard as the tremendous howl of the storm that brings the tree's final downfall.

Also, the single flower in the vase in the picture recess is infinite in its spiritual content. Never placed in the center of the alcove, it affirms that nature is asymmetrical, as is life and existence. There is beauty everywhere, but it must be sought and brought out. Simplicity is set against multiplicity; a single flower is apt to reveal its inherent beauty much more clearly than a whole bouquet. Just as two different themes of music may nullify each other's beauty, so too two strong motifs of color, form, or meaning, if not in precise harmony, may nullify each other's aesthetic value. Moreover, the flower is taken from nature. Brought into the realm of architecture, flower becomes architecture, and architecture is made by man, is human. Nature unfolds true beauty if brought into the human sphere. Human interpretation of nature, humanization, produces beauty. Flower may suggest humanity. When primitive man offered the first flower to his maiden, he transcended his existence as a brute subjected to raw drives, and became human. Again, it may reflect mood and temperament of the house master. *Sukiya* is the "abode of fancy" and, as such, is very personal. Shelter is built for man and not man for shelter. Adjustment to temporary psychological disposition is a function of art, and, as such, art must be true to contemporaneous life. And, finally, the lonely flower, brightly shining in the darkness of the room, may appeal very much to one's emotions: sacrifice for beauty. And it appears as if the flower itself were aware of this. For more than in life, it offers its beauty at the time of its death.

Equally, the tearoom, as space, is an infinite, ever changing source for spiritual experience through its manifold symbolic manifestations. Rigidly enclosed, it suggests separateness from the outer world: seclusion. Only in seclusion can the mind free itself from the continuous entanglement with everyday life and its selfish aims and material values, and strive for the spiritual elevation to which all life should serve. It may create a feeling of loneliness—eternal loneliness, different from that which man feels in his longing for something greater and better than himself. Rather, it is the solitariness of an absolute being that arises when the soul leaves the world of space, time, and causation behind. Except for flower and hanging picture scroll that respond to a temporary aesthetic mood, the room conveys a feeling of being vacant and empty. The reality of the room is its void, not its walls, ceiling, and floor, even less its furniture or decoration; and the reality of a teacup is its hollowness, not its material form. Vacuum is all-potent because it grants infinity of use and freedom of movement, both in spirit and material; only in vacuum can the full extent of man's aesthetic emotion unfold, and only through making oneself a vacuum can man's physical and intellectual, moral and spiritual limitations be overcome.

The semidarkness of the tearoom may suggest remoteness and refuge. It tempers all features of the room and blends them into harmony. Sometimes there is a limited view to the garden. But this produces neither glare of light nor a distraction of contemplating mind. Rather, this glimpse of the macrocosm, by symbolically establishing a relation between man's moral proportions and the universe, leads man toward "innerliness," where the true life takes place.

Also, one may be captivated by the spirit of purity and cleanliness prevailing in form, feature, and motif. Cleanliness is not newness, and so everything that might suggest recent acquisition is avoided. Purity of mind and body is the moral quality of man; it is comprehensive and inconspicuous. Cleaning of the room is an art as is the cleaning of the tea utensils.

Simplicity and primitivity of the tearoom may symbolize the "original abode," i.e., *the* human space. Zen asserts that elaborate and sophisticated object forms are likely to obstruct the realization of the subject matter behind the object. Consequently, Zen aims at simplification to the very point where subject and object can no longer be dualistically conceived. In order to uncover the very basis of man's life, representation and performance of dwelling has to be reduced to the barest essentials: the hut and the drink, the tearoom and the tea.

Thus, the physique of the tearoom, both as a whole and in detail, is infinite in its spiritual perception, an immense source for the exercise of art in living. It reveals abundant richness by substantiating humble poverty. To build a simple hut is as much an art as to drink a cup of tea. For true art is perfected only when it ceases to appear as "art"; it is perfection of the artlessness when the innermost sincerity of man's own being asserts itself. To live this life of *wabi* is to free oneself from the continuous enslavement to man's material wants and comforts and to follow the very basic longing of going back to the simple and true, to be one with the universe.

4 structural framework

process

The construction of the Japanese house, both the act and the system, albeit very refined in detail, has in fact never quite left its original primitive stage. When, during the first and second centuries, dwellings with elevated floor, *taka-yuka*, first appeared, Japanese residential architecture not only found one of its distinct constructional-organizational features, but also made its first and last, though major, technical achievement. All fundamental constructional distinctions of the Japanese residence already existed in the *taka-yuka* and no essential change took place thereafter.

While in the constructional system of the earliest "house," the pit dwelling, *tate-ana*, the slanting rafters rose directly from the ground and were themselves the major members forming both the framework and roof, in the system of the dwelling with elevated floor, *taka-yuka*, the vertical columns became the major supporting members. The resistant qualities of this house, however, were less than adequate in bearing horizontal stresses provoked by seasonal typhoons and frequent earthquakes, and in this regard were also inferior to the original pit dwelling construction.

This constructional deficiency of the prototype of the Japanese house has given rise to many a speculation as to the underlying reasons. The most simple, though least convincing, explanation is that the diagonal members of construction were distasteful to the Japanese sense of form. Yet, the foregoing study does not convey the slightest clue that such a visual-sensational concept had ever been instrumental in the formation of architectural features, but rather proves the contrary, a distinct disregard of form. Also, in the case of construction, it seems improbable that during the feudalistic society, when the mass of people hardly had enough to sustain themselves, man would concern himself with formalistic ideas, and even less would intentionally sacrifice security, durability, and economy for a visual effect. This seems all the more certain because, after introduction of the suspended ceiling, diagonal members in the roof construction would have been no longer visible. Moreover, with regard to the wall framework, the carpenter already knew very well how to conceal the constructional members in the upright framework. Instead, all evidence shows that obstacles such as arresting restrictions of the rulers, minute standardization of methods, traditional attitude of the guilds, submissive teaching of Buddhism, stagnating influence of Confucianism, and also, no doubt, historic lack of inventiveness proved to be too strong to overcome.

And it is no contradiction to the aforesaid that in detail Japanese construction displays high elaborateness and a refinement that has reached perfection in method, economy, and form. For constructional detail was the only architectural sphere that neither could be controlled by man or law nor required innate inventiveness for improvement. Indeed, it appears that the very reason for Japan's famous refinement in constructional detail was the immutability of the basic constructional system which directed the handicraftsman's imaginative spirit to detail and provided centuries for gradual empirical improvement. While primitiveness of structural system might at first sight appear

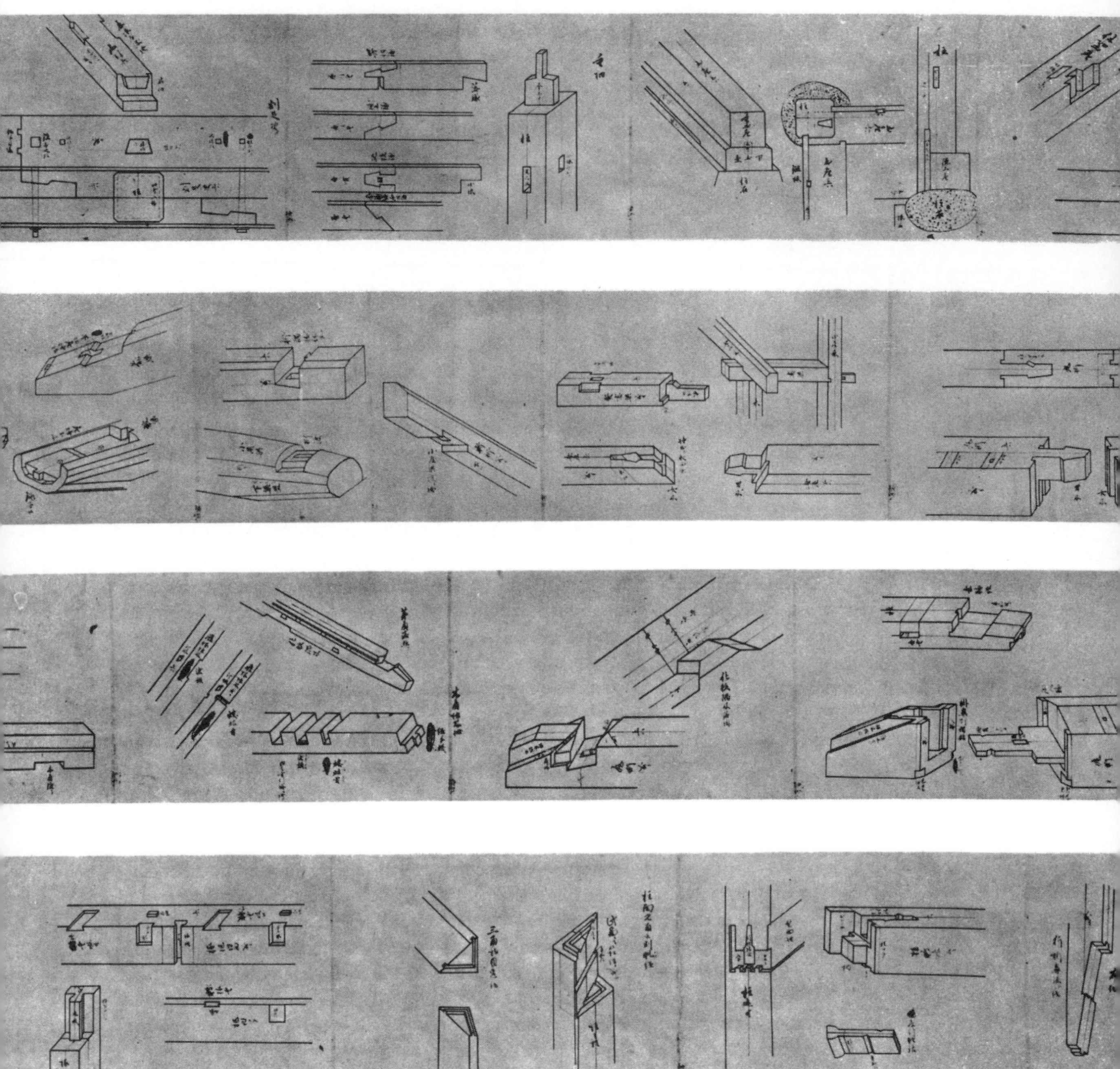

FIGURE 22: Carpenter's scroll (right to left). The scroll, reproduced in total, depicts construction details for residential building.

contradictory to the refinement of constructional detail, it becomes evident that one was only the logical consequence of the other.

Because the structure is a simple post-beam framework without any braces or struts, the wall planes in between those structural members support only themselves and do not require foundations. Only at places of actual structural supports, i.e., at columns,

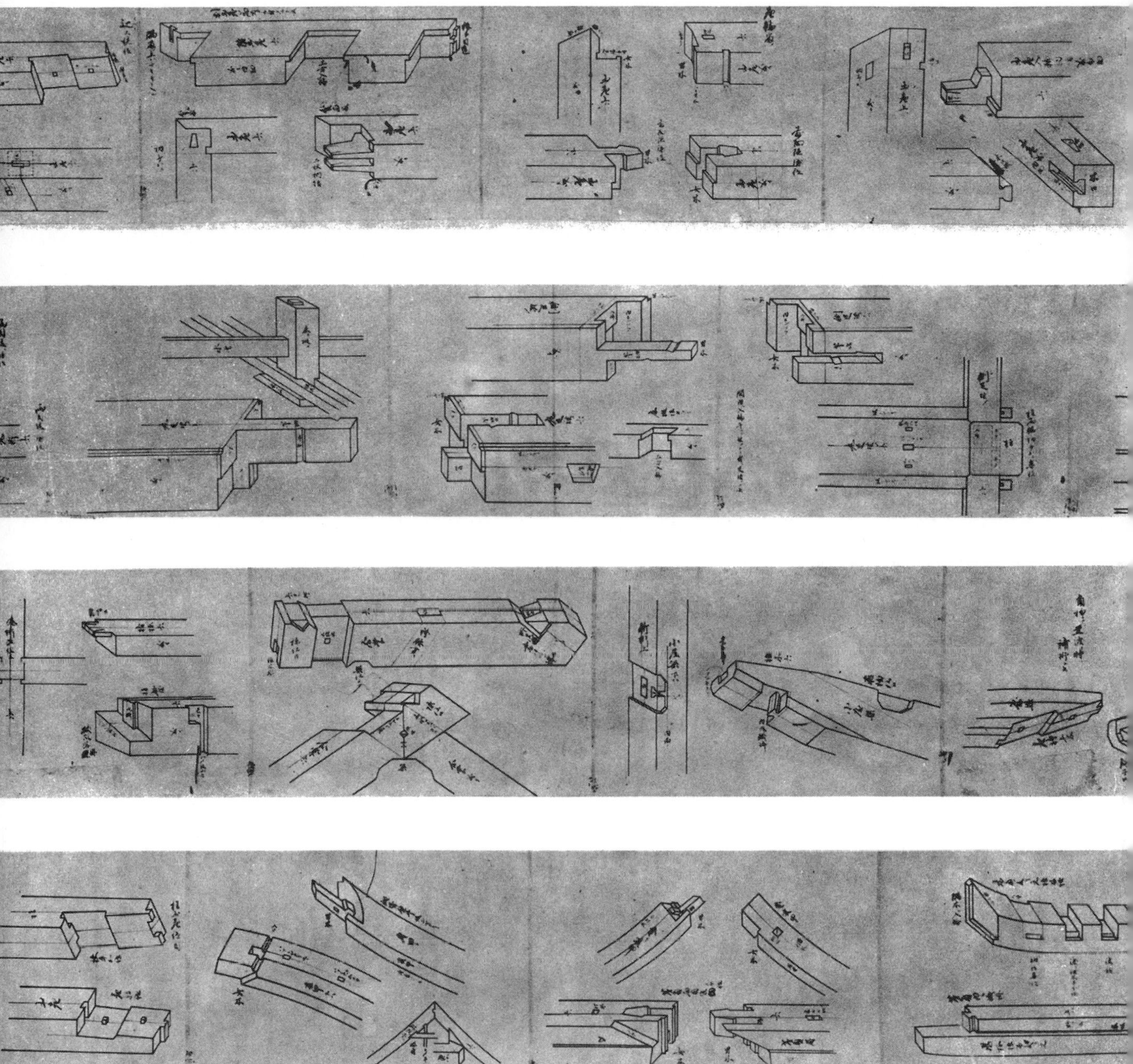

is the groundsill provided with a simple foundation of natural or hewn stone that raises the whole wooden framework above the damp ground. In present construction concrete has largely replaced slab stone.

The upright members, *hashira,* are erected upon the groundsill's frame in standard distances and connected to each other by horizontal tie members. Simultaneously, the floor beam, *ashigatame,* is set in and the top is then held together by eaves beams, thus completing the upright framework which, except for elaborateness of joint detail, lacks any constructional stability.

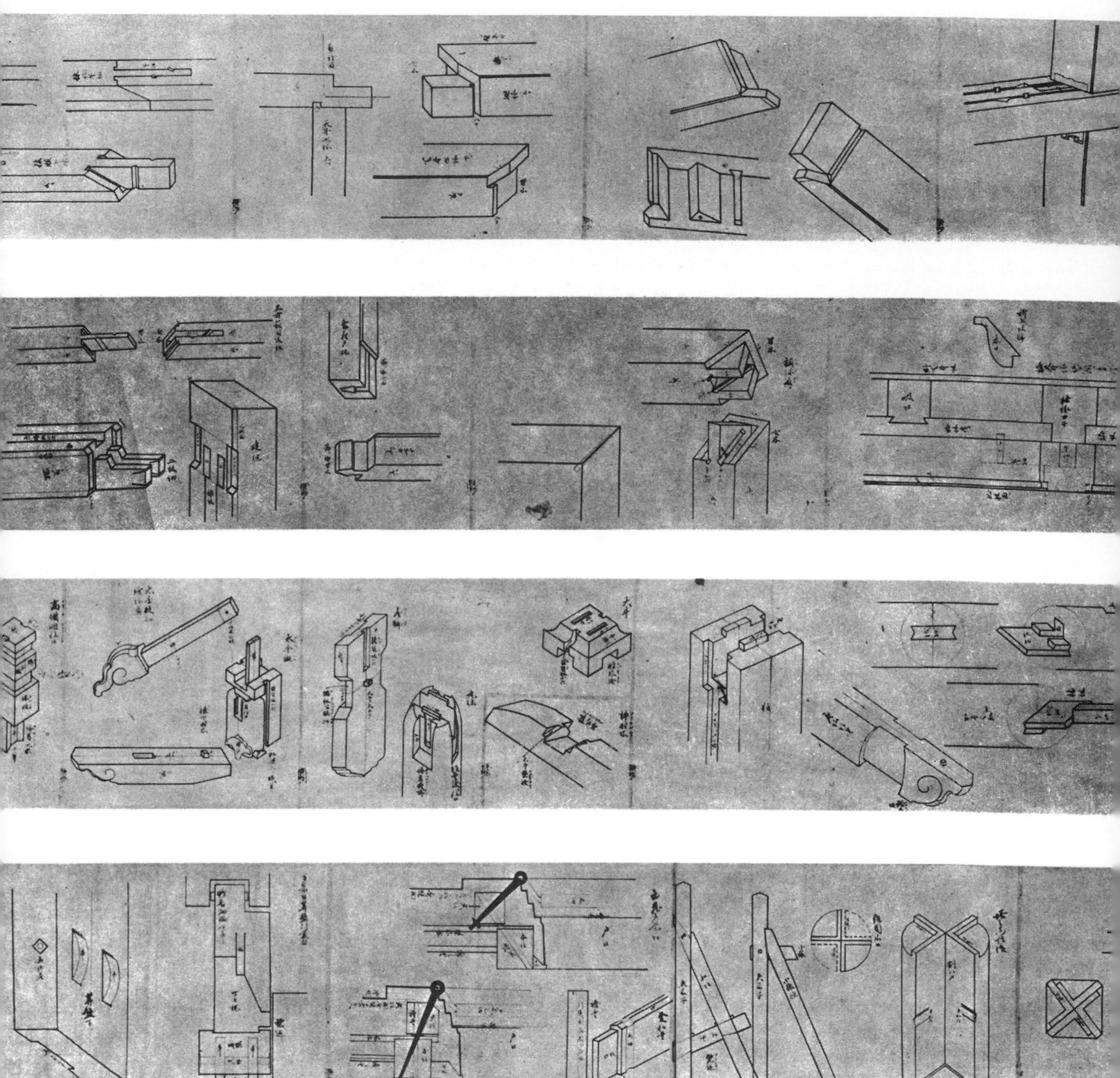

FIGURE 22 (continued): Carpenter's scroll (right to left).

This primitiveness is more obvious in the roof construction. Heavy and untreated logs are simply dropped from eaves beam to center beam, and at their joint in the middle are hardly more than just laid upon each other. Preference for entire trunks, roughly hewn with archlike shape to gain some additional strength, stresses this primeval character. Upon these transverse beams, posts are erected and onto them purlins and rafters are finally laid. Part is put onto part, member upon member, a system of horizontals

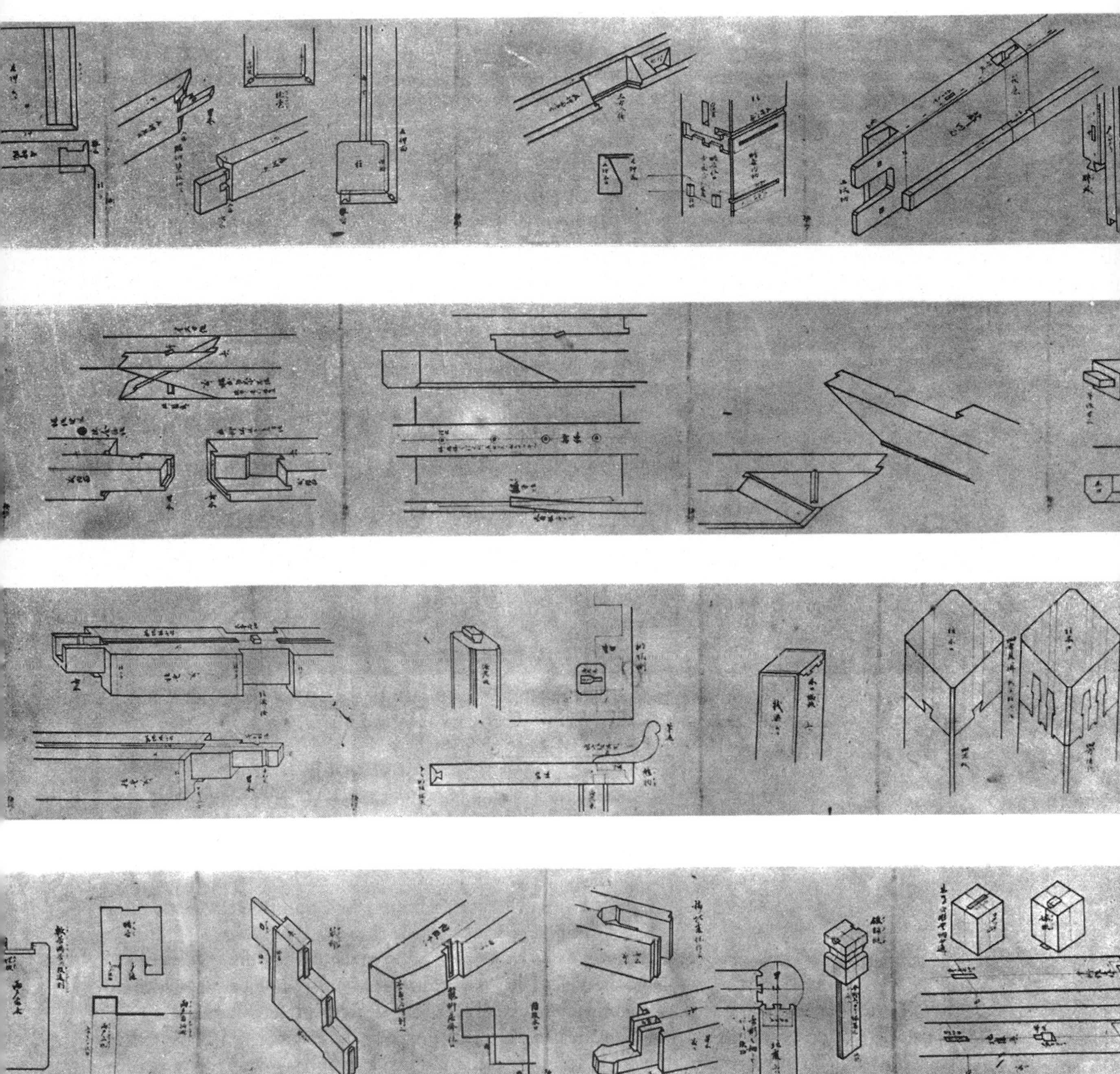

and verticals capable only of sustaining vertical pressure and possessing nothing to resist horizontal stress other than its own weight. Until the advent of Western methods, diagonal ties or struts were not used, or, if known of at all, certainly their structural value in saving material and granting firmness and durability was not realized.

Yet, this form of setting up the framework is surprisingly fast. As the components have previously been dressed, the assemblage itself takes but a few days. With hardly more accomplished than what appears to be circumscription of space by fragile timbers, the roof will already be covered and heavily loaded with tiles that are traditionally

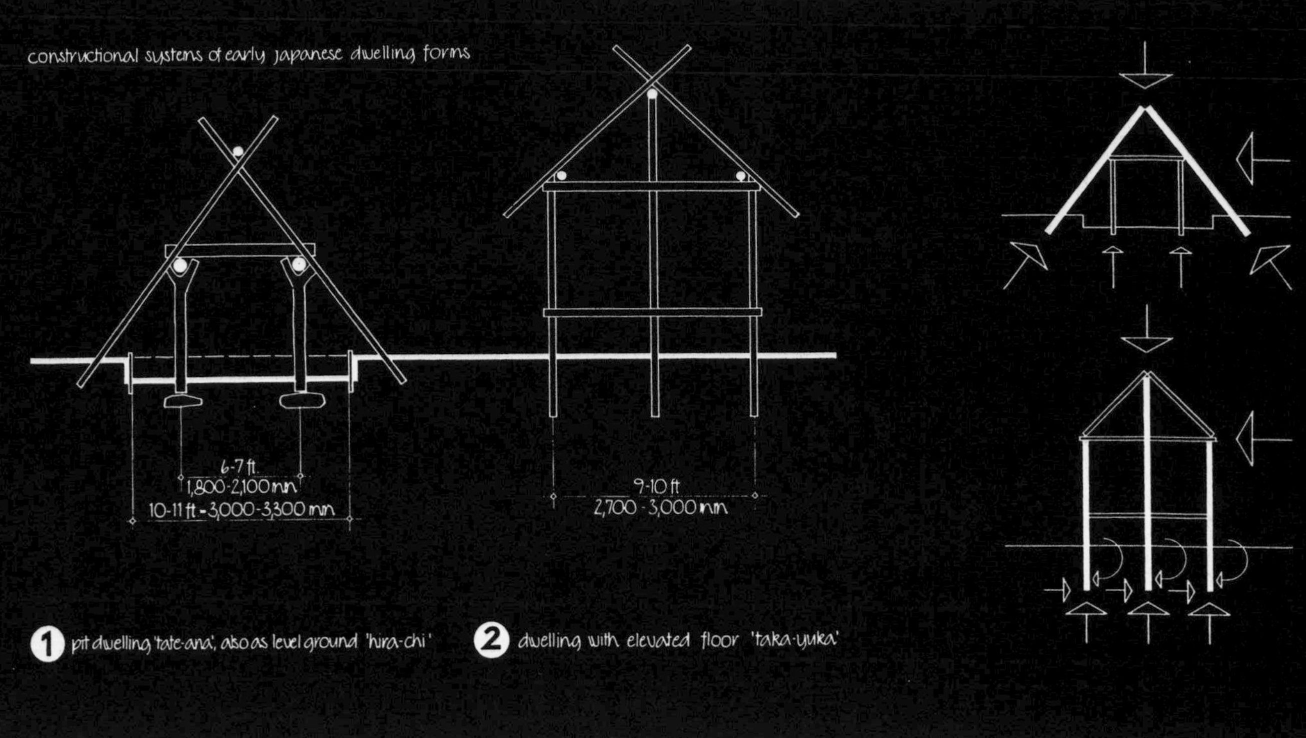

FIGURE 23: Constructional systems of early Japanese dwellings.

embedded in clay or, as is often done today, laid upon latticework. The roof, then, is the first component of the Japanese residence to be completed in the construction process, and it appears as if the preceding work is primarily orientated to achieve that aim in the quickest way possible. Once material and man is protected against the frequent rains, the carpenter can continue his work with more ease and leisure.

This change of pace seems to be almost symbolic of the distinct difference in constructional quality, for the succeeding work displays high elaborateness, structural sense, and sophisticated refinement to a degree comparable to a cabinetmaker's sensitive exactness. Floor boards are laid upon a sleeper-joint construction which is elevated on posts perching on foundation stones; at the top and bottom wooden tracks for sliding panels are fixed between the uprights; the ceiling is suspended from the beams above; clay mixed with chopped straw is applied on both sides of the latticework between the uprights to form the wall; interior elements are minutely joined and set in; and finally the Japanese residence's most unique ingredient, the floor mat, *tatami,* is laid.

Constructional work is done entirely by the master carpenter and his assistants. Yet, the mats, sliding panels, and other interior elements in more recent times are frequently manufactured at different places due to the specialization of trades. While in the West the specialization of the building industry has alienated the architect from many fields in building, in Japan the master carpenter, owing to standardization and limitation of architectural work, still fully masters and controls every phase of residential construction.

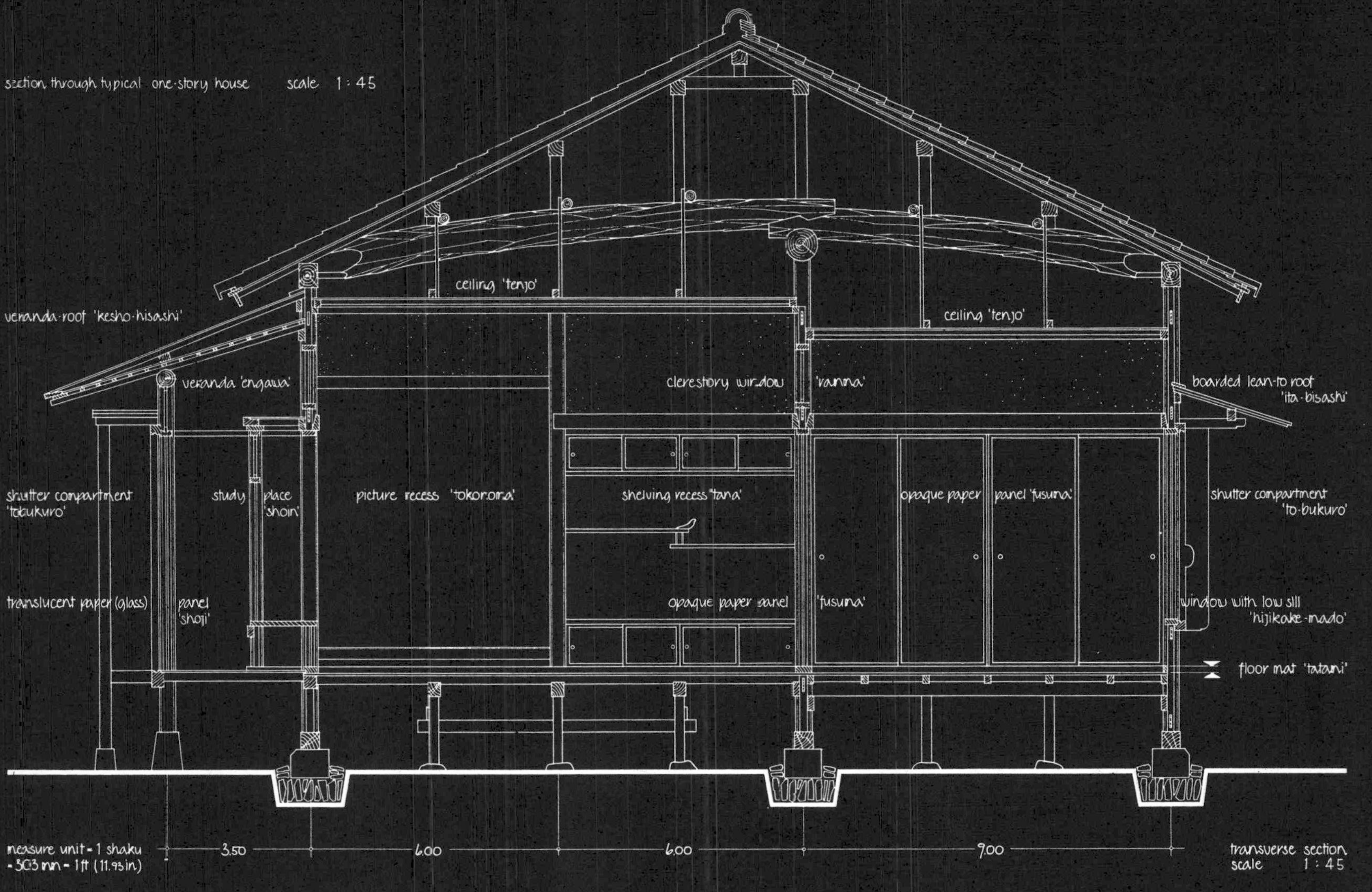

FIGURE 24: Section of typical one-story residence.

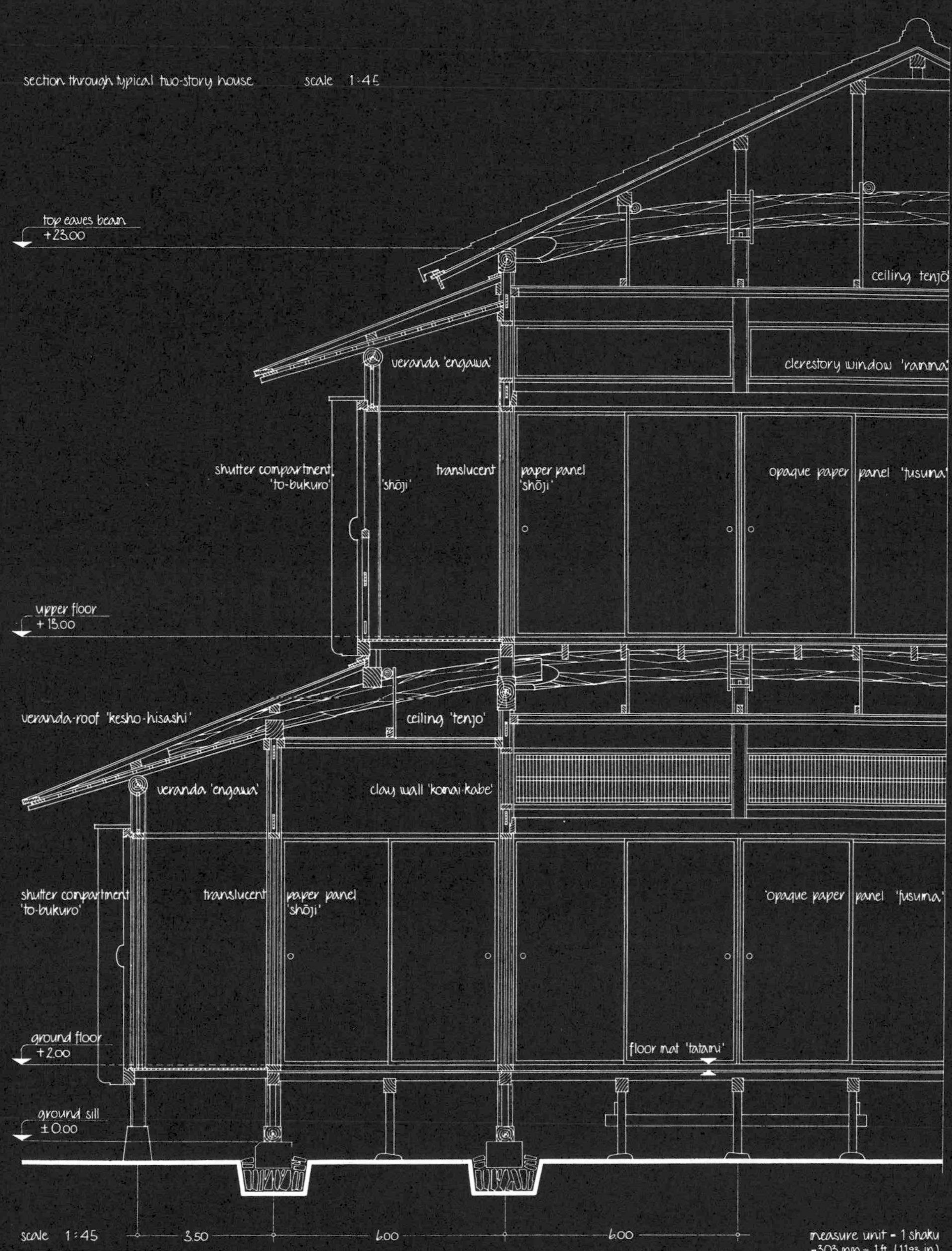

FIGURE 25: Section of typical two-story residence.

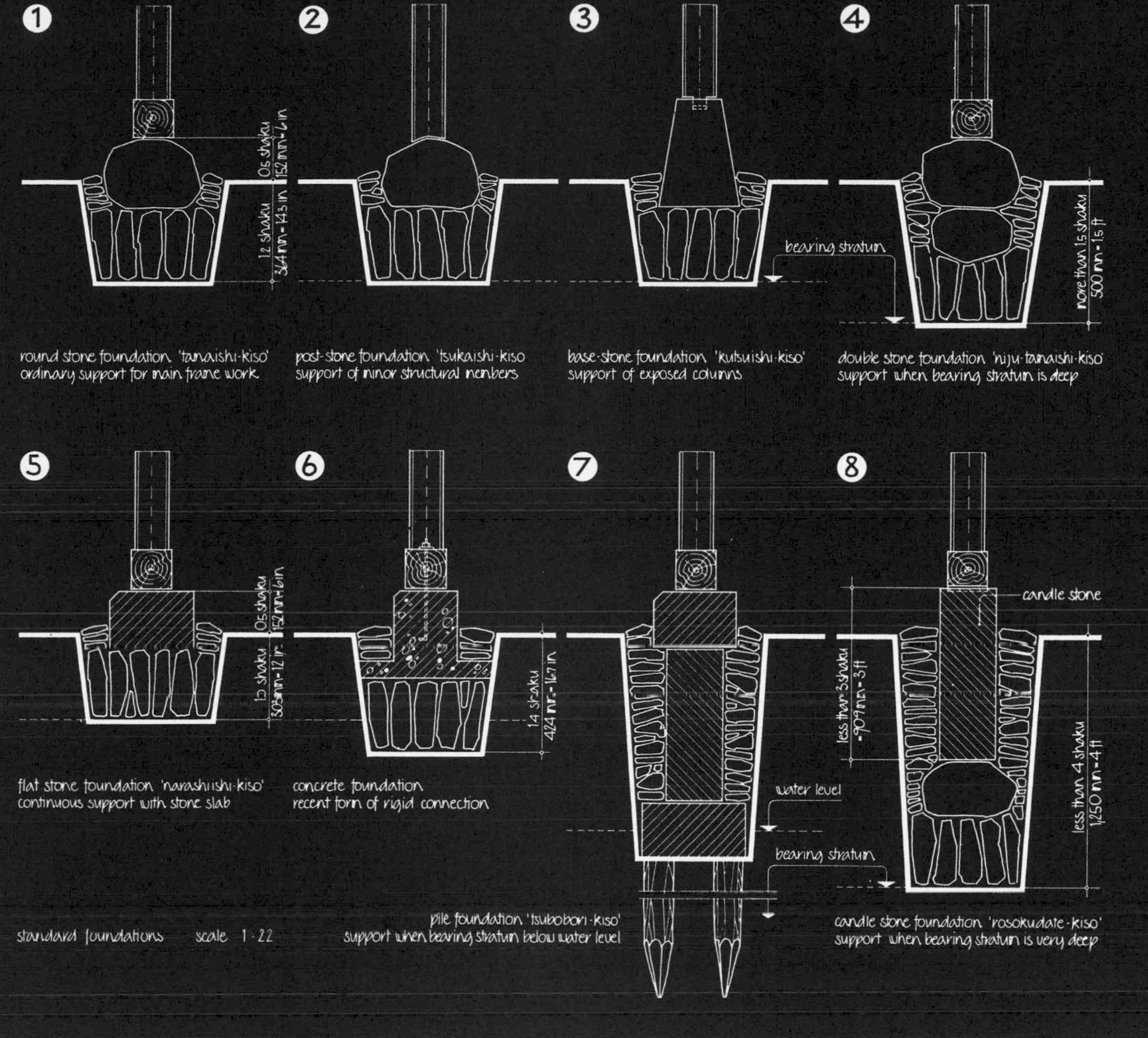

FIGURE 26: Details of typical foundations.

foundation

If there is some truth in the overemphasized architectural saying that the simplest response to a problem is also its most appropriate solution, then, the foundation of the Japanese house seems to prove such theory. For there is hardly anything as simple and logical as the organization of the foundation. As may be expected, the foundation, both in type and performance, is also standardized and classified as to its particular constructional function and as to the varying ground conditions prevailing. Since there is no basement and the floor is elevated about 2½ feet (750 mm.) above ground level, the sole function of the foundation is to keep the wood parts clear from the usually damp ground, rather than to tie construction solidly to the ground. Further, with the wall

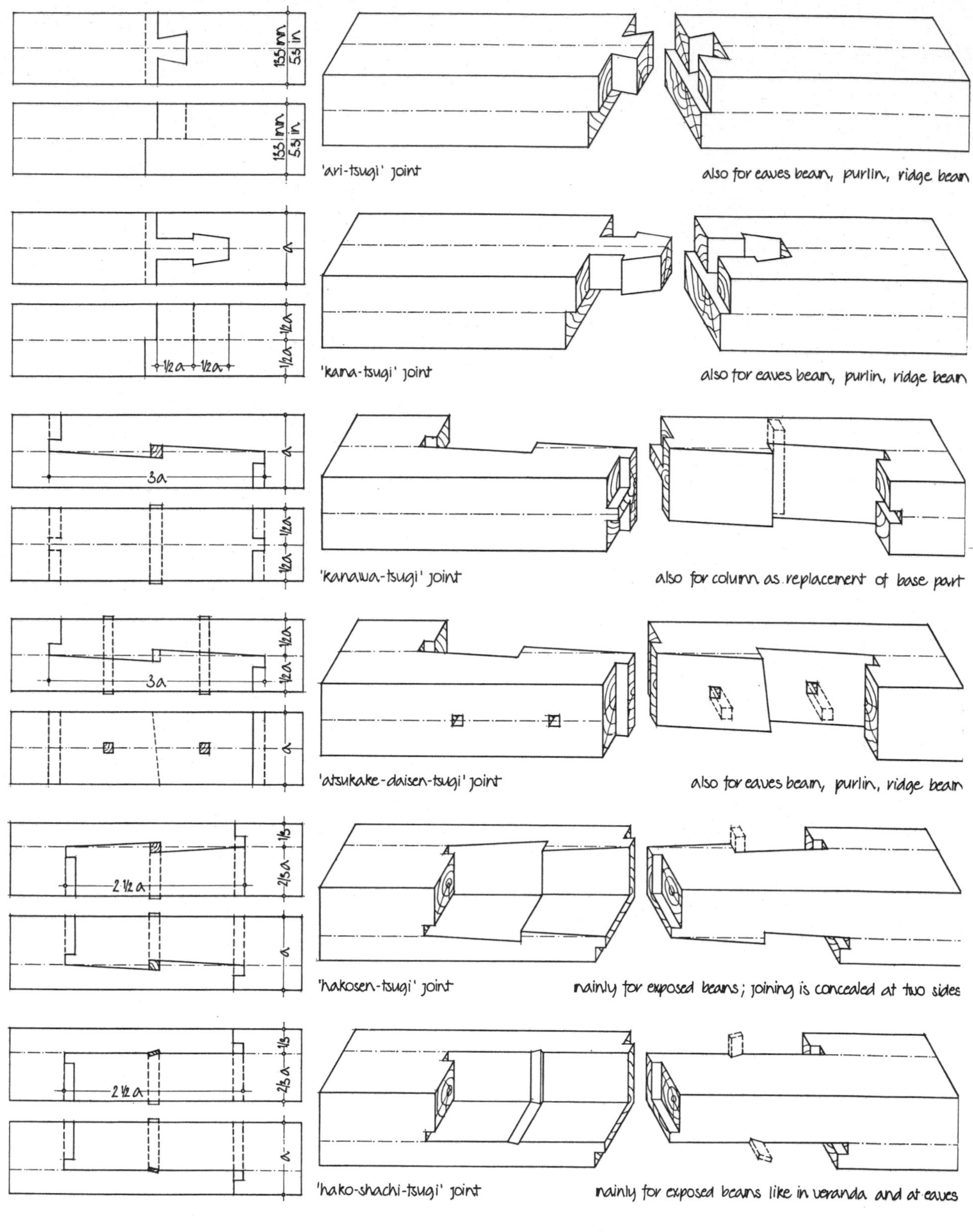

FIGURE 27: Some standard longitudinal joints.

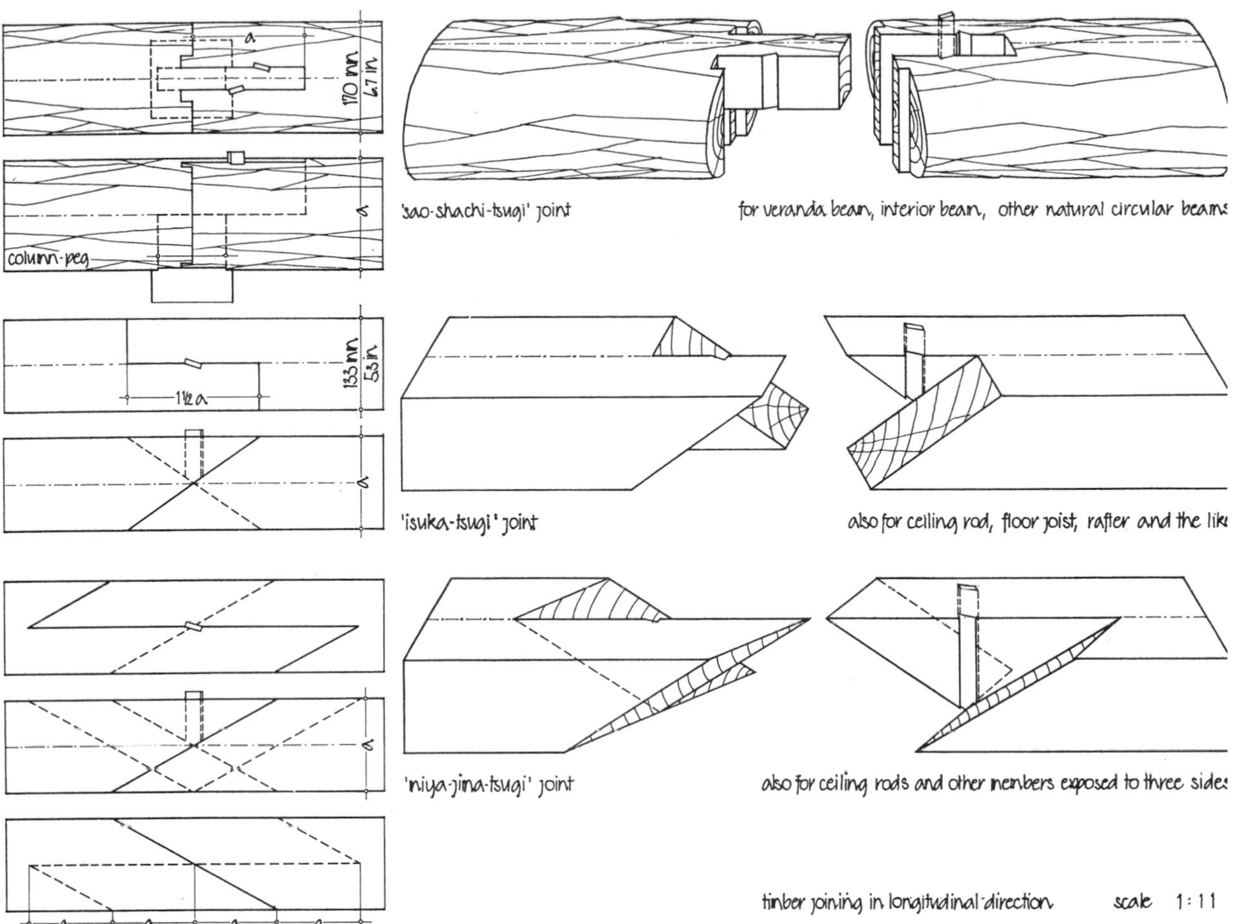

FIGURE 27 (continued): Some standard longitudinal joints.

itself not bearing any weight other than its own, only the structurally bearing members, the columns, are provided with foundations, either directly as in the veranda, porch, or interior, or otherwise via the groundsill.

Thus, the whole structure does not gain any additional stability or firmness from the foundation, but achieves, constructionally, protection of its most important parts and obtains, visually, accentuation of constructional lightness through the egg-shaped stones upon which the column and framework rest. Frequently, in order to prevent not only shelter-seeking animal creatures but also human creatures with less modest intentions from entering all too easily, the foundation facing to the street, or sometimes the entire outside foundation, is closed up by laying a continuous layer of stone slabs, or more recently concrete, underneath the groundsill.

In view of the frequent earthquakes, this loose connection between the foundation stone and framework is doubtlessly very appropriate constructionally, especially for a house with such deficient framework as that of the Japanese. However, the fact that in more recent times the groundsill is tied by strong bolts to the concrete foundation does raise doubt as to whether the Japanese actually were fully aware of the advantage of countering horizontal stress with flexibility rather than rigidity.

wall framework

The appropriateness of using the word "wall" for what vertically encloses space in the Japanese house is generally questioned by scholars, for the wall in the Western sense has in the past achieved the meaning of something solid. On the other hand, contemporary architecture, although attempting to clearly distinguish the wall's supporting elements from its screening elements, as did the Japanese, still uses as a general term "wall," or as specific terms "bearing wall" and "non-bearing wall" (curtain wall), not only for lack of a more appropriate word but also because originally in Western residential architecture wooden structures were based on similar construction principles.

Although the greater portion of the wall's screening members are movable and removable, in the ensemble of space-forming members the solid wall plays an important role, and its functional, proportional, and aesthetical significance is generally underestimated. Not only is the entire section above the upper track for the sliding doors made solid, but there is no house without at least one entire solid clay wall.

The wall framework is composed of conspicuously short members, and joinings of members in longitudinal direction are frequent.The probable reason for this is that wood fabric is floated down small and often shallow rivers from the mountains and is easier to handle in small pieces in the river as well as at the job site. The standard details for joinery are multiple. Some are so elaborate that they weaken the timber unduly, while others are striking in their simplicity.

The framing of the wall once more demonstrates primitiveness in system and refinement in detail. Upon the prepared foundation, the groundsill, *dodai,* is leveled and connected at the corners and junctions with standard methods, special joinery being provided for corners, which remain exposed. Then, the columns, *hashira,* are erected at standard distances and connected with each other by five, or as in the case of door openings, two (three) horizontal tie members, *nuki.* The tie members penetrate the column at standardized vertical distances of about 2 feet. Fastened only by wedges, the tie members function to keep the column upright and to sustain the solid wall, but contribute very little to the stability of the framework.

Therefore, in more recent times, under Western influence, diagonal struts are applied at the corners in the vertical plane, the groundsill plane, and the beam plane. These diagonal members are usually covered up, but in the case of the wall framework, they sometimes are left visible to the outside. This clearly contradicts the widespread opinion that the absence of diagonals would be the result of a formalistic taste.

Although the floor beam, *ashigatame,* is inserted into the column simultaneously with the horizontal tie members, constructionally it is an element of floor construction rather than of framework and therefore is mentioned in context with floor. At their top the columns have pegs by which they are joined to the eaves beam, *nokigeta,* interior beam, *keta,* and veranda beam, *en-geta.* As the latter two are usually round logs, the column head is shaped accordingly. In case the column distance exceeds 1½ *ken* (2,727 mm. = 9 ft.), a hanging post, *tsuri-zuka,* is tied to the beams, holding the upper sliding track, *kamoi,* for the paper panels and receiving the horizontal tie members, *nuki,* which sustain the solid wall. Until this stage the framework is called *jiku-bu* (literally, vertical part).

roof

The roof construction of the Japanese house has been the subject of many controversies, less as to its constructional inadequacy, which in fact cannot be disputed, than to

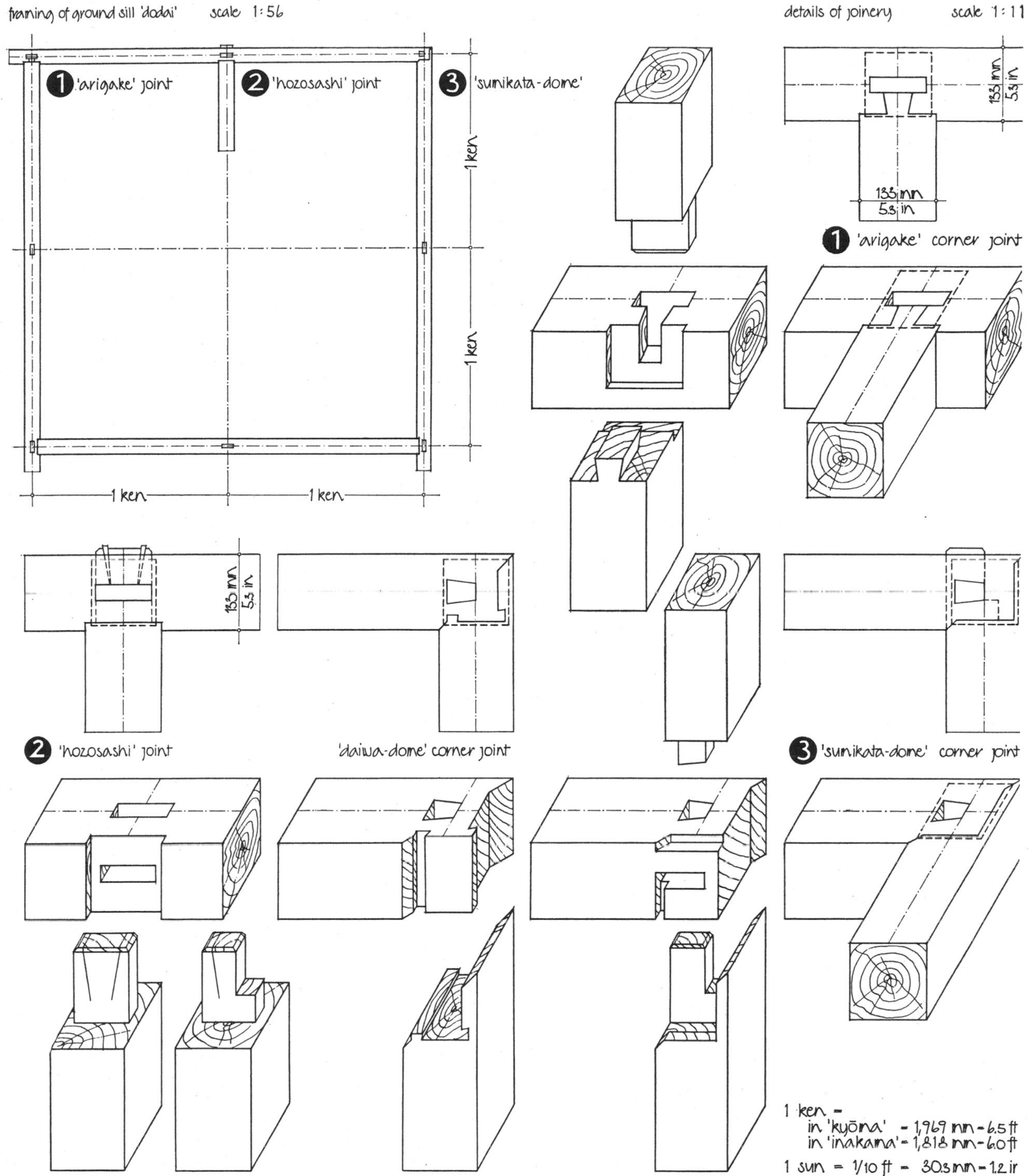

FIGURE 28: Framing of groundsill and joints details.

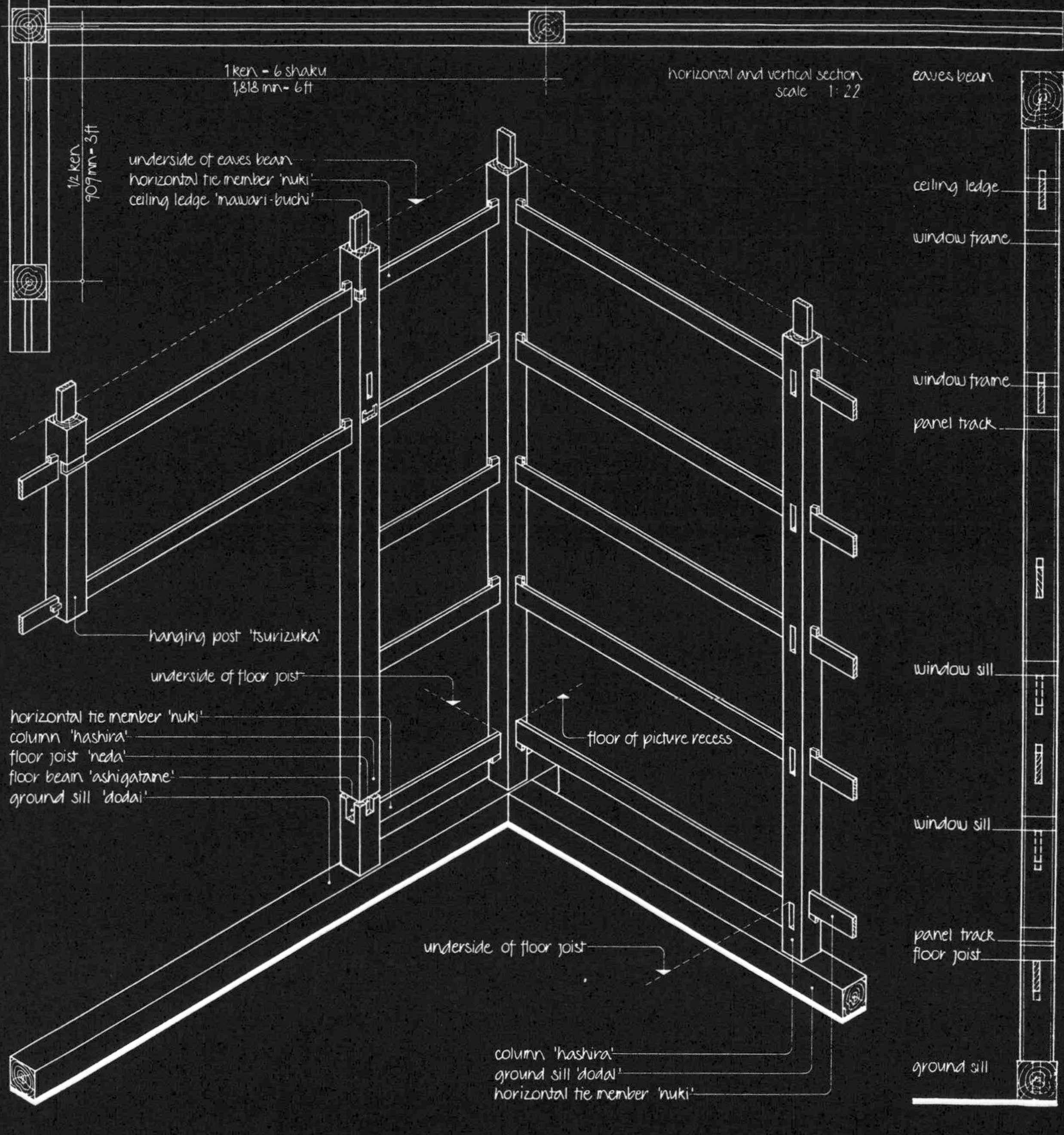

FIGURE 29: Wall framework construction.

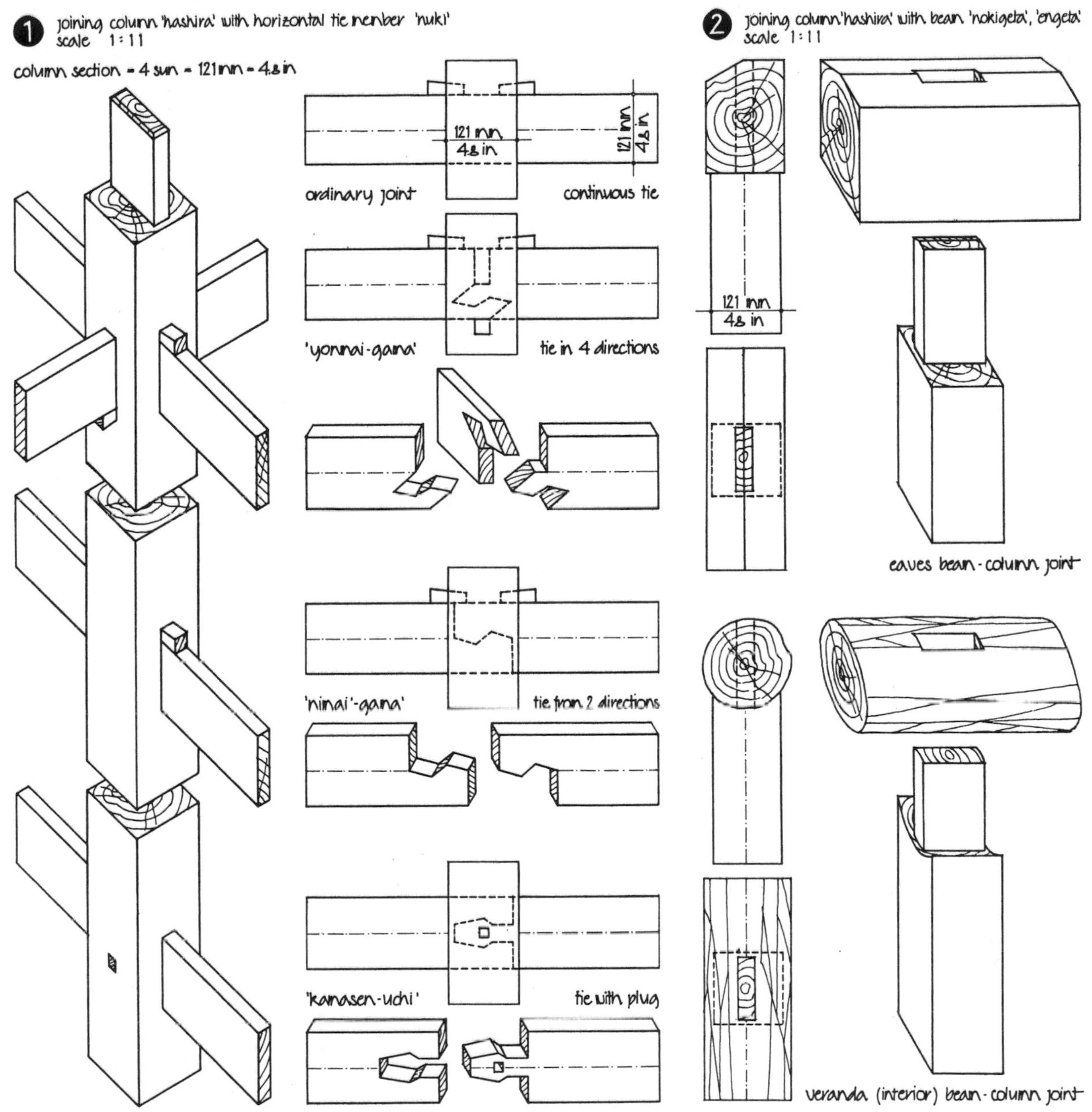

FIGURE 30: Column, beam, and tie joinings.

the factors that were instrumental in preventing its improvement. Though Western influence has taught the structural merits of triangulation, it did not succeed in replacing the heavy, rough-treated trunks that, albeit delicately joined, are simply laid from eaves beam to center beam and carry the entire roof load, equally distributed on their full length. It appears that until the present both tradition and simpleness of method proved to be stronger than did constructional reasoning.

Upon these crossbeams, *hari,* posts, *koya-zuka,* stand in standard distance supporting the purlins, *moya,* and the rafters, *taruki,* above. As the rafters need not be very strong, it is easy to curve the roof slightly. Upon the rafters a layer of butted boards encloses the roof construction and provides support for either the clay or latticework which receives the final tile cover.

Three roof shapes have emerged in the Japanese residential architecture:

kiri-zuma	gabled roof
yose-mune	hipped roof (All carpenter manuals refer to it as *hōgyō,* and call the square pyramidal roof *yose-mune,* while historians seem to have decided just the opposite.)
iri-moya	hipped gable roof

Formally speaking, the hipped gable roof constitutes a combination of the other two simple forms, but it seems probable that this roof was introduced from China as an independent form. On the other hand, its distinct shape strongly resembles the roof of the old farmhouse, which is derived directly from the early pit dwelling, *tate-ana.* Presumably China also took this roof form from its own prehistoric pit dwelling.

While the roof shape itself is hardly characteristic of Japan, certainly the use of separate lean-to roofs, *hisashi,* for the veranda and above all the wall openings is a characteristic feature of the Japanese dwelling. Their lineage goes back to the *shinden*-style mansions of the nobility in the 10th–12th centuries, which were patterned after Chinese model. In these mansions the open, veranda-like rooms attached at all four sides to the enclosed main room, *moya,* yet under one and the same roof, were called *hisashi.* Thereafter, in the process of adding these veranda rooms into the enclosed space, the newly screened-in areas received a separate lean-to roof. Contradictory as the incorporation of a room into the house enclosure and the simultaneous differentiation by separation of roofs appear, it actually was a reasonable and necessary change. For since the separation between outdoors and indoors had moved further to the outside, the heavy rainfalls demanded low roof eaves for protection. It is likely that owing to both the particular roof construction and the fairly steep roof slope, this requirement could not be met with a single roof slope even though the main supporting members still remained inside at the periphery of the main room, the *moya.* Also, such use of a separate roof must have been very practical for the common people, who in early times neither could afford, nor were allowed, to provide a *hisashi* space in the original construction, as this was a distinction of the architecture of the aristocracy. In a word, the lean-to roof was the simplest method of later adding covered space such as veranda, toilet, bath, or the like to an existing house.

Actually, the historical precedence is of less significance than an interesting phenomenon that went with it. Since those two early rooms in Japanese architecture, *moya* and *hisashi,* could be identified by their different roofs, these definitions were gradually attributed to the roof itself. As roof definitions, the terms *moya* and *hisashi* are still used in the traditional houses, while their original usage as room definition has been extinguished by the growth of rooms with more distinct denominations.

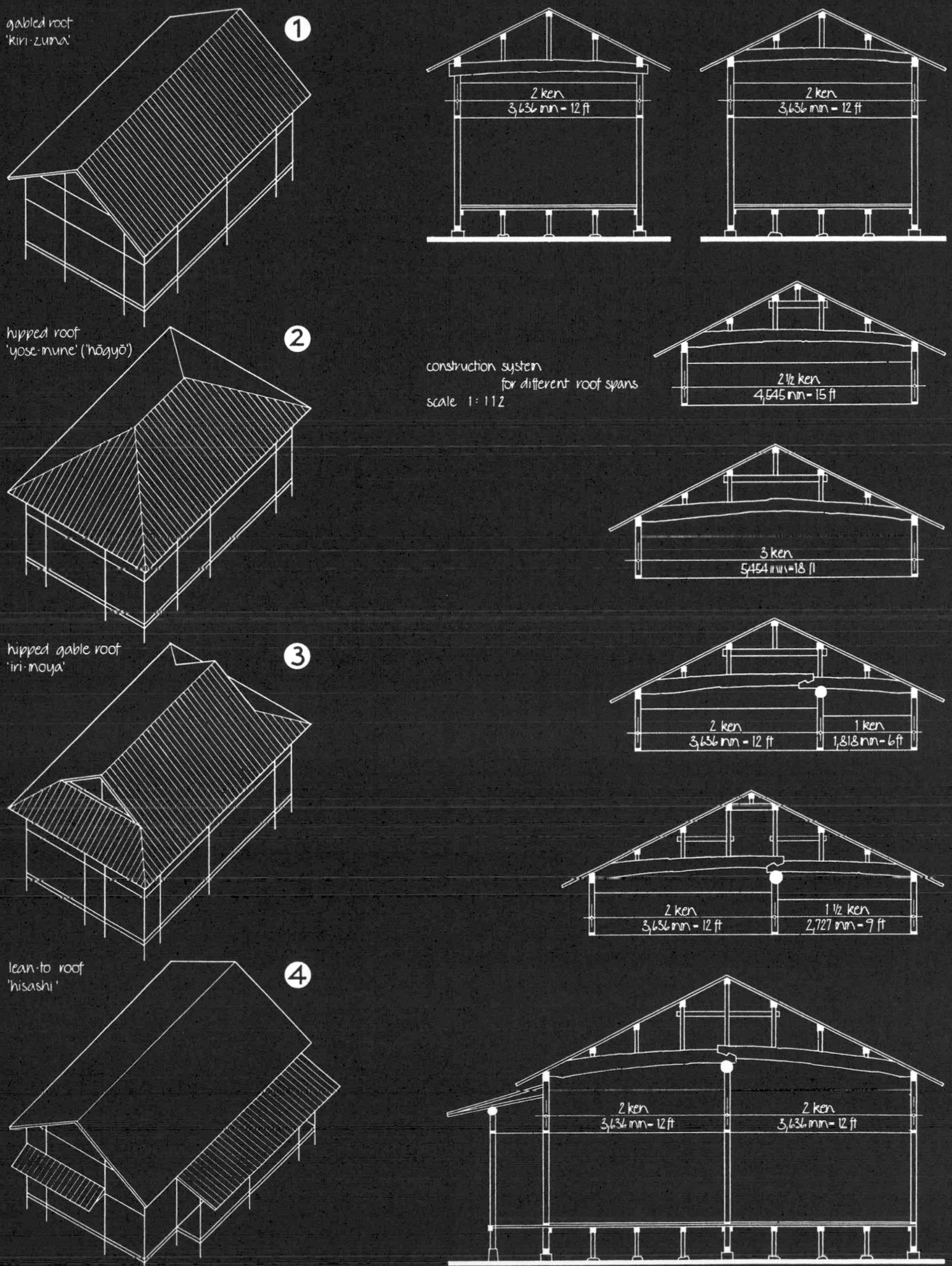

FIGURE 31: Roof types and framing systems for different roof spans.

In this unconscious transfer of designation from room to roof, an important architectural causation is restated: the roof is the most basic requirement for protection against weather, it is the earliest element of man's space designation in architecture (a profound meaning that is still preserved in the German word for "shelter," the "Ob-Dach," i.e., the "roof above"). This twofold use of the word appears to be especially characteristic of Japanese architecture. While in Western architecture solid walls or, in warmer areas, columns of a particular order distinctly create the "indoor" feeling and even do so without necessarily requiring a cover above—a roof—Japanese "indoor" feeling is primarily dependent on the roof. This significance of the roof in Japanese architecture is confirmed by the word for roof itself. For the two Chinese ideographs, *ya-ne,* for the Japanese word for roof mean nothing but "house" (interior) and "root" (source). Roof is the very root of house.

The system of framing the roof skeleton, as defective as it is constructionally, still has many advantages. Within a basic construction system, all different lengths can be spanned with equal-sized members. Naturally, in the case of crossbeams the length may vary according to the depth of the building, but otherwise the size of the building does not affect the stress on any member and consequently does not demand separate dimensioning for each structure. Since the maximum free span is 2½ or 3 *ken* (4,500 or 5,400 mm. = 15 or 18 ft.) such a system allows, without abnormal constructional measures, free room areas of 18 x 18 ft. or 18 mats, an exceptional room size in the ordinary residences. That is to say, this constructional system permits practically any desired column placement for any possible room arrangement without constructional disadvantages. Also, visual problems do not arise because the suspended ceiling conceals the roof construction, which in the process may have become quite complex and unsightly. It is for this reason that in designing a house, both the patron, in arranging rooms, and the carpenter, in placing posts along the *ken* grid, need not pay attention to visual or constructional consequences and, therefore, can design freely.

The early method of tying roof tile to roof skeleton was with clay, a form even now widely preferred in the building of traditional houses because of its simplicity. The rafters are boarded or covered with bark, which provides a base for the roof plaster, a mixture of seasoned clay and chopped straw, in which the tiles are embedded. It seems probable that this simple and appropriate method has survived from a time when tool and technique were not developed far enough to guarantee an exact and even roof plane. For by using clay any unevenness can be leveled and any difference in dimension can be compensated for more easily than by other methods.

Although clay in conjunction with tiles adds rigidity to an otherwise weak framework, the disproportionate increase in the roof load makes the house even more susceptible to collapse in case of horizontal stress. There is no evidence to sustain the belief that the disproportionately heavy weight of the Japanese roof was by its sheer mass meant to resist sudden earthquake shocks or the continuous pressure of seasonal storms. Nor are there any instances other than exceptional ones where top weight has shown constructional merits at the time of strong horizontal stress.

Thus, the practice of placing tiles on lathwork has increased. In this system the rafters are boarded as in the clay-bed method, but instead of applying clay to the boards lathwork is used. This, however, has not proved overly effective in resisting storms. The wind easily grips under the tile, and at times after a typhoon roofs can be seen practically devoid of tile. In this respect, the clay-embedded roofing shows more resistance.

The method used to protect the ridge against rain is quite remarkable. While West-

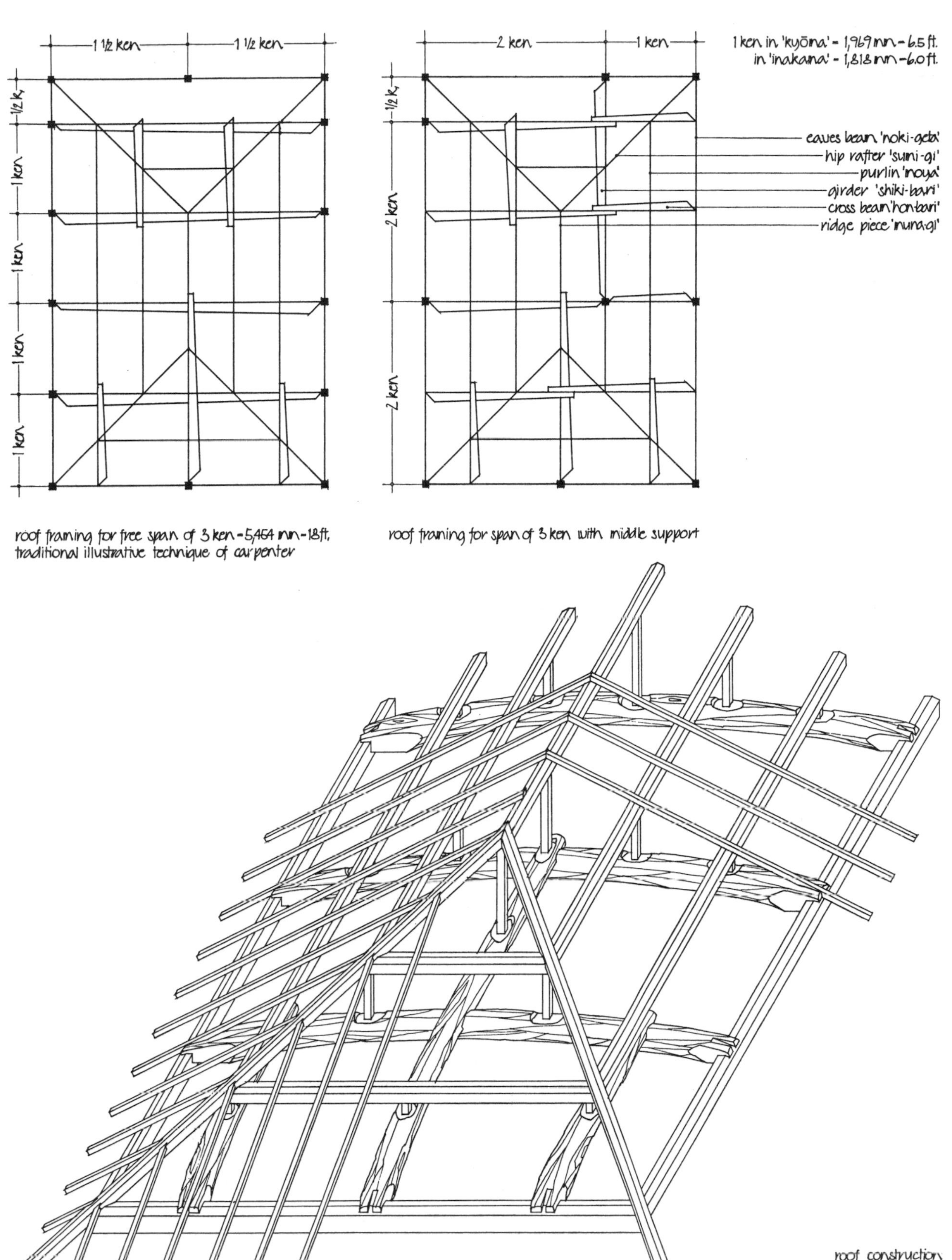

FIGURE 32: Hipped-roof construction.

dimensioning of eaves beam 'nokigeta' according 'kiwari-module: height/width = 1.6/1.1 x column section (= 4 sun) = 4/4.4 sun = 194/133 mm = 7.7/5.25 in

1 scale 1:11

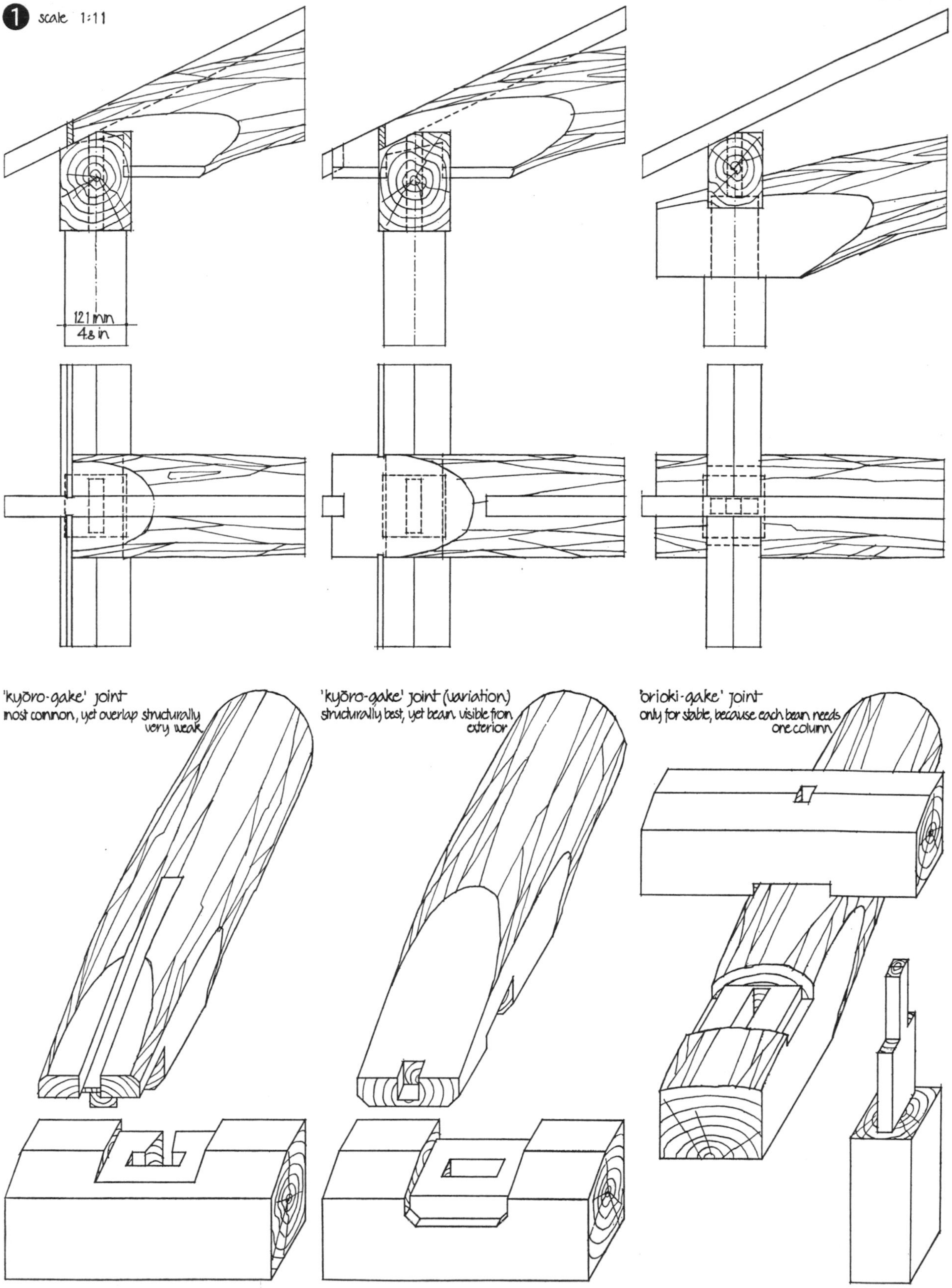

121 mm
4.8 in

'kyōro-gake' joint
most common, yet overlap structurally very weak

'kyōro-gake' joint (variation)
structurally best, yet beam visible from exterior

'orioki-gake' joint
only for stable, because each beam needs one column

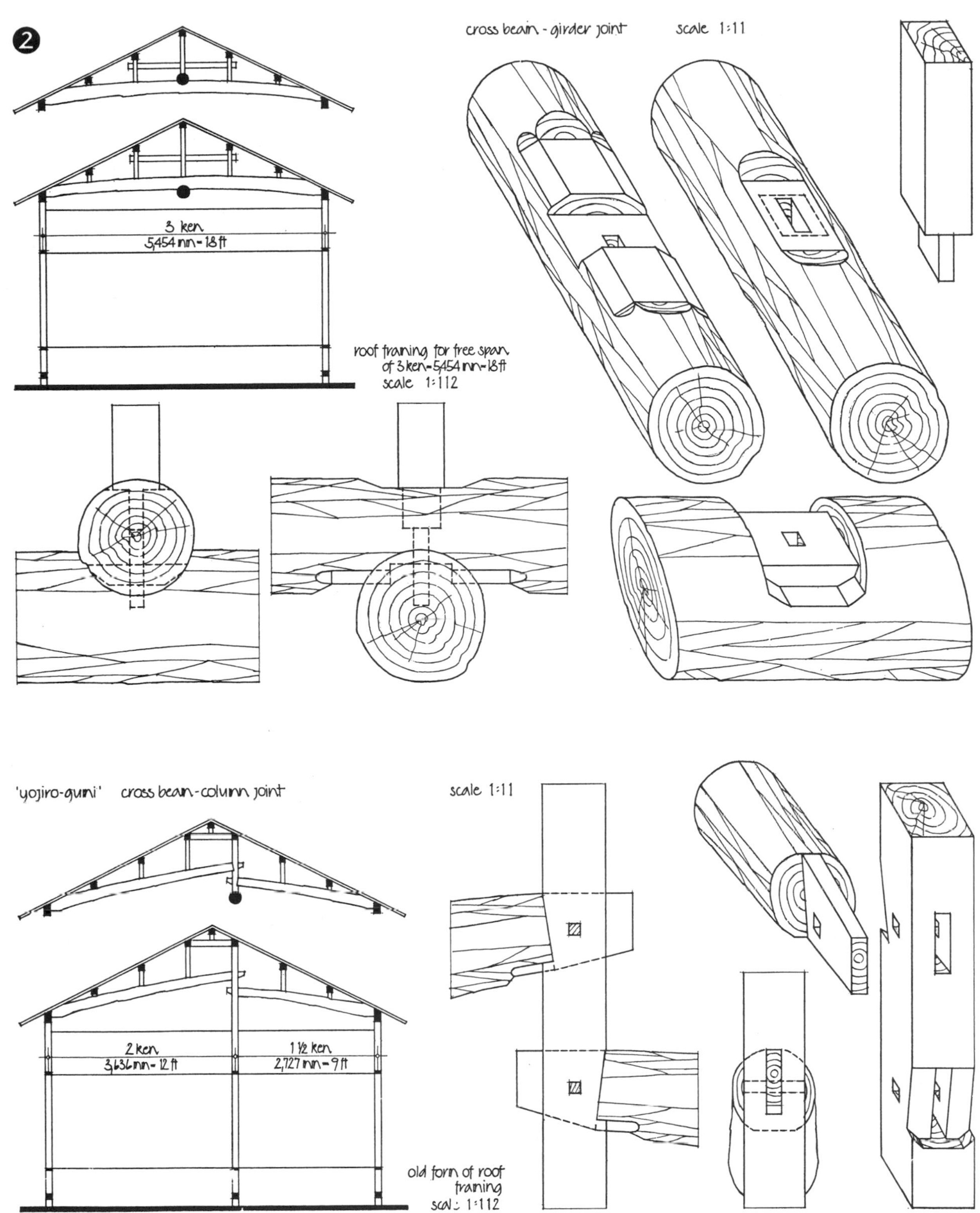

FIGURE 33: Details of roof structure.

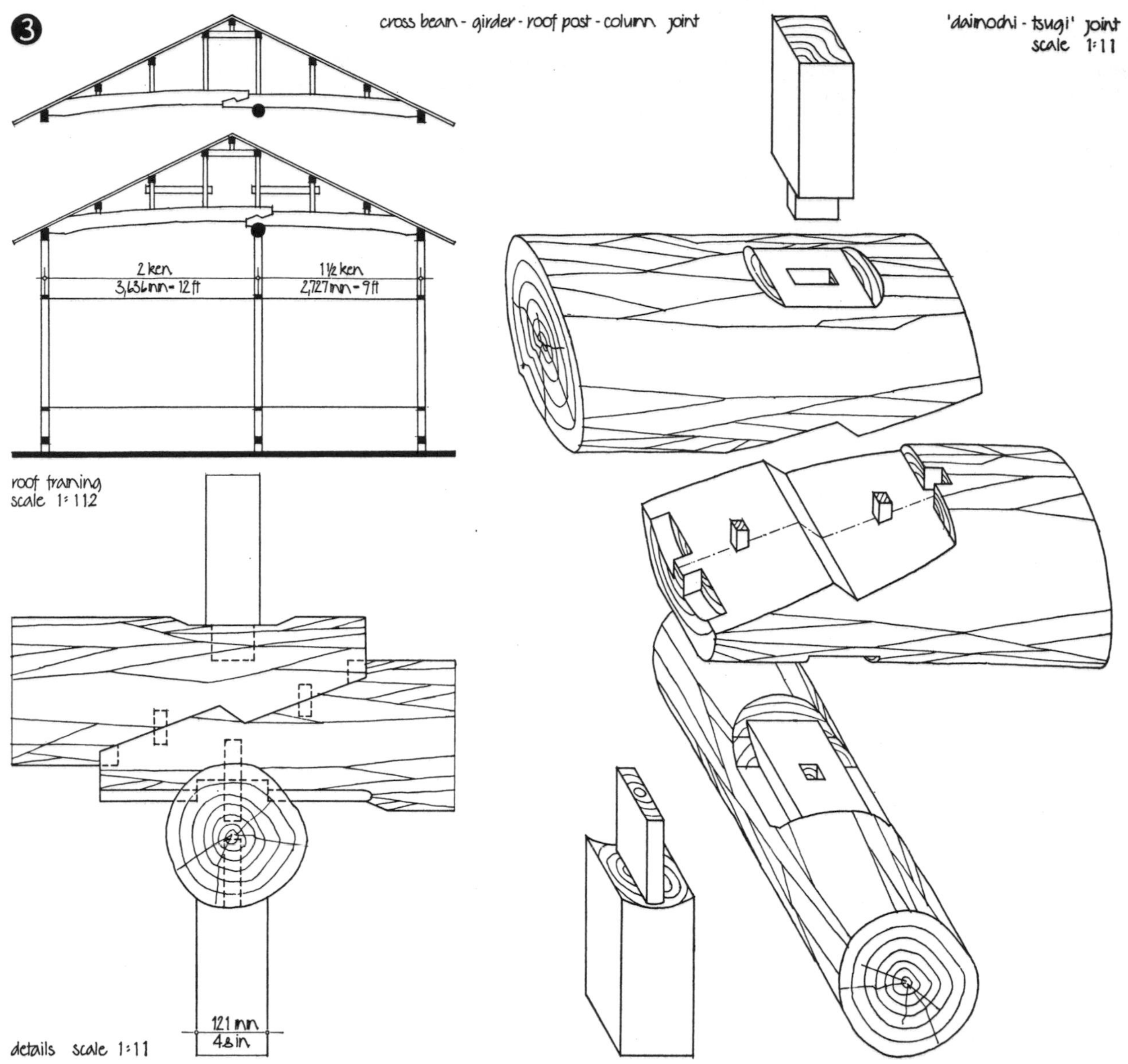

dimensioning of roof post 'koyazuka' according 'kiwari' module: width - breadth - 0.8 x column section - 0.8 x 4.0 sun -3.2/3.2 sun - 97/97mm - 3.8/3.8 in.

FIGURE 33 (continued): Details of roof structure.

ern architecture felt it adequate to cover this important and endangered joint between two roof planes by one row of tiles with a particular shape, the Japanese ridge roofing seems to manifest more concern for its safe insulation. As the illustrations of tile fabric have shown, the joint between two roof planes is not merely covered at the top with ridge tiles, but receives several layers of flat tiles, called *noshi-gawara,* which lift the final ridge tiles to a considerable height and give the ridge a heavy and dominant appearance. It appears almost as if in this instance for once visual concern triumphed over reason, for any layers beyond three of these flat tiles hardly add anything to the watertightness. It might also be possible that the Japanese builders simply followed the Chinese from whom they had originally learned the tile roofing or, more likely, that they felt the need for emphasizing security measures at this very vulnerable part of the roof.

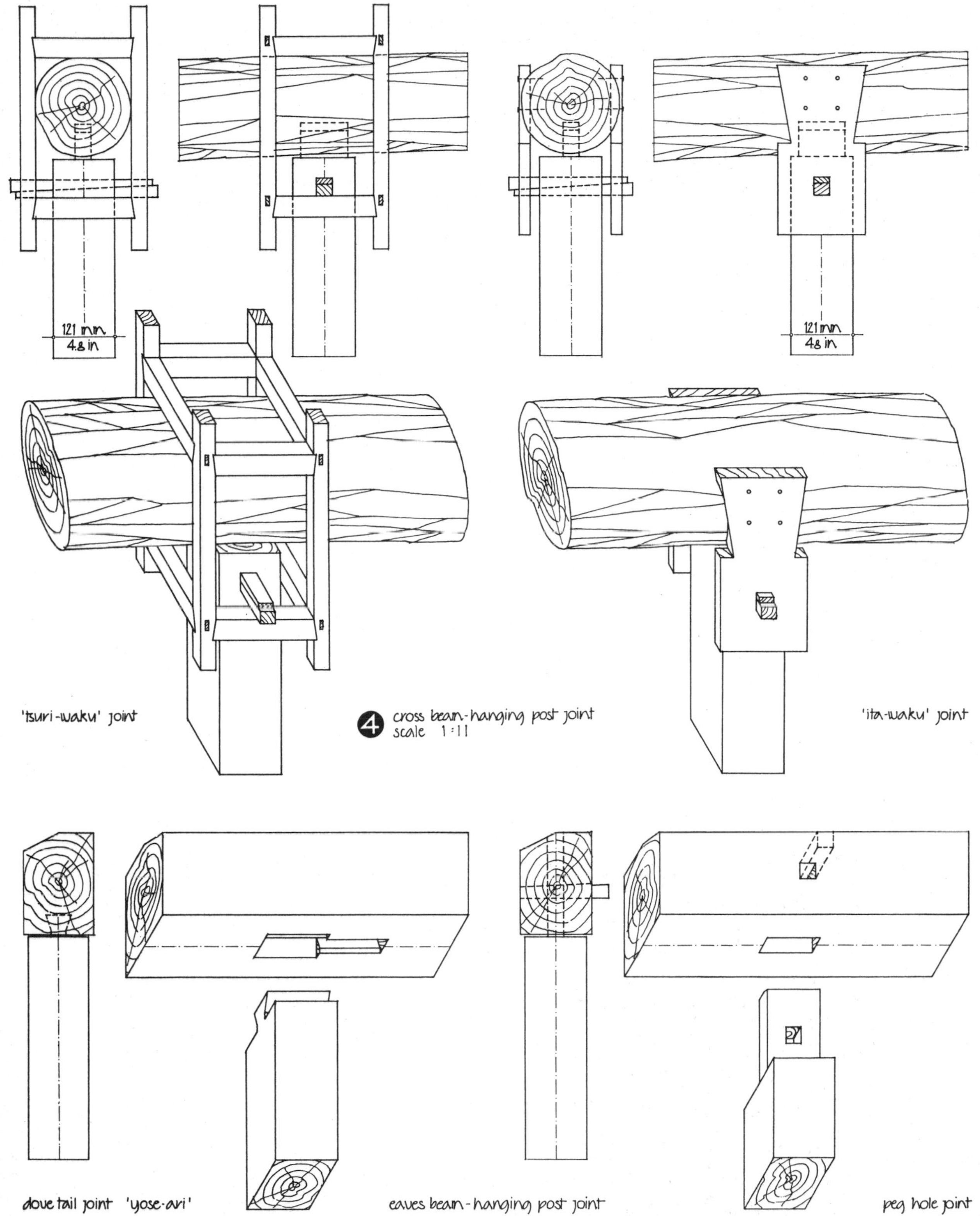

dimensioning of eaves beam 'nokigeta' according 'kiwari' module.: height/width - 1.6/1.1 x column section (-4 sun) - 6.4/4.4 sun - 194/135 mm - 7.6/5.25 in

FIGURE 33 (continued): Details of roof structure.

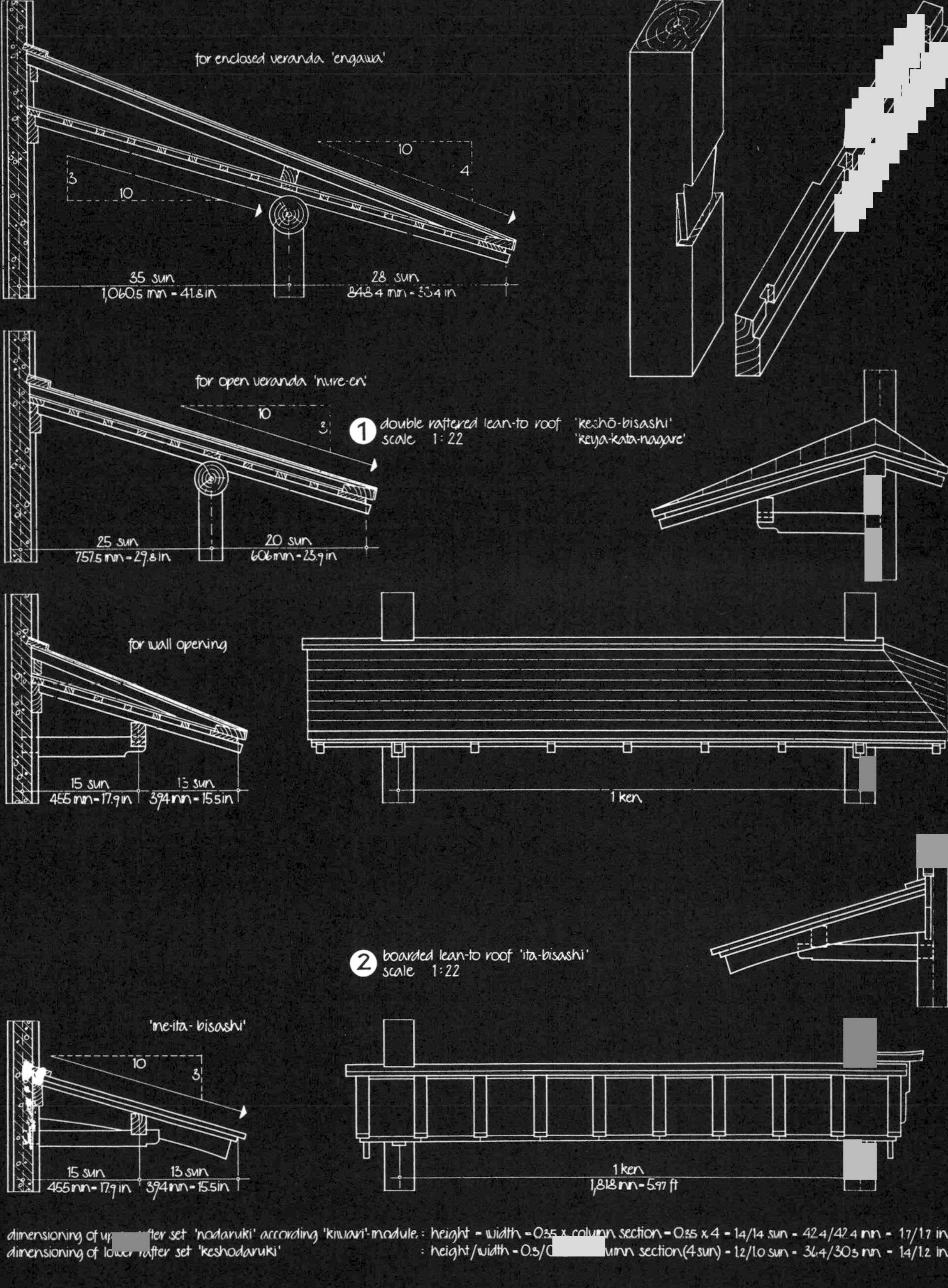

FIGURE 34: Typical forms of lean-to roofs, *hisashi*.

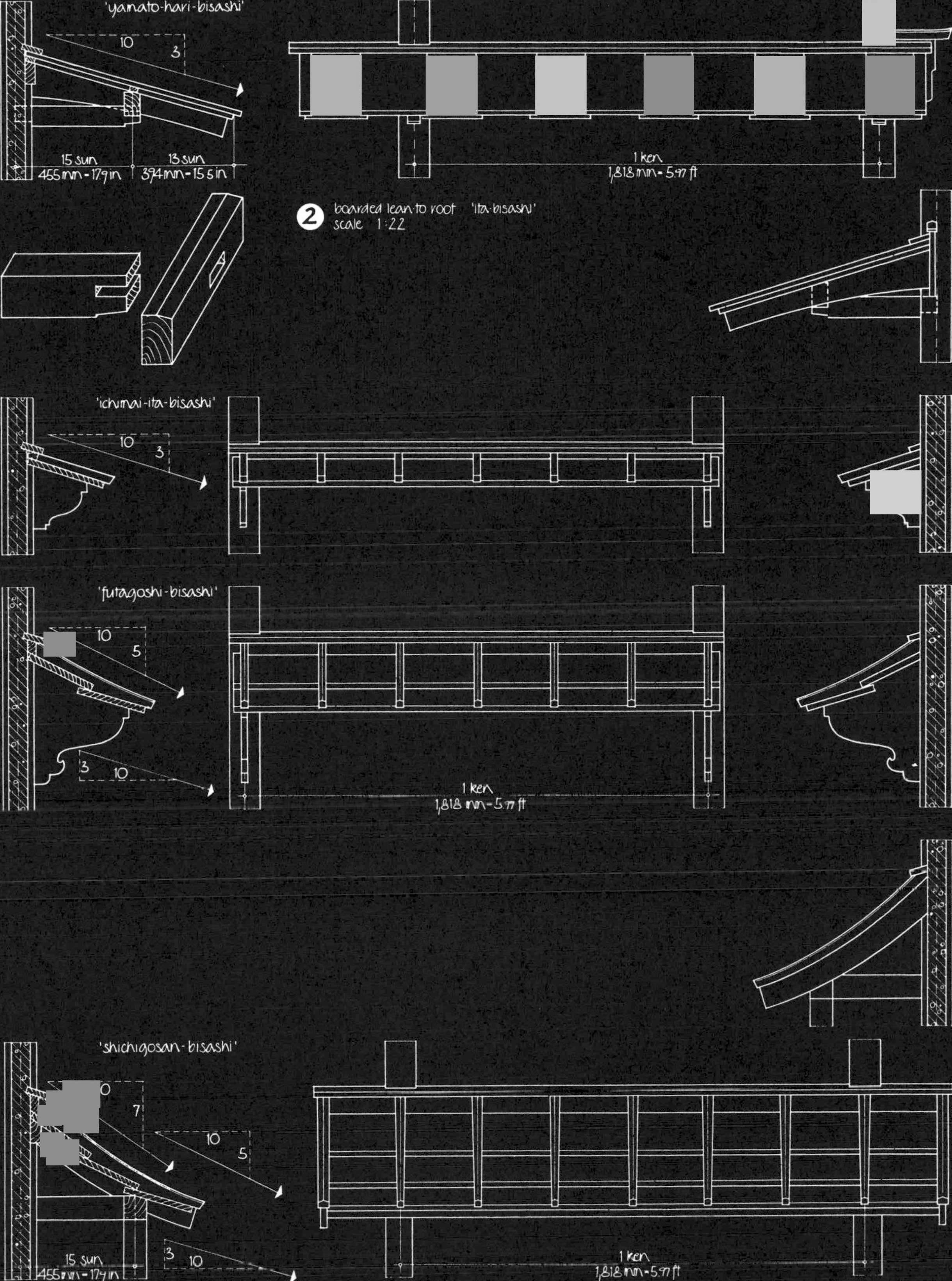
'yamato-hari-bisashi'
10
3
15 sun
455 mm - 17.9 in
13 sun
394 mm - 15.5 in
1 ken
1,818 mm - 5.97 ft
2 boarded lean-to roof 'ita-bisashi'
scale 1:22
'ichimai-ita-bisashi'
10
3
'futagoshi-bisashi'
10
5
3
10
1 ken
1,818 mm - 5.97 ft
'shichigosan-bisashi'
7
10
5
15 sun
455 mm - 17.9 in
3
10
1 ken
1,818 mm - 5.97 ft

Heavy wind ridges along the gable side, accentuated roof hips, particularly shaped tiles at the end of the ridge cover (the so-called demon heads to ward off evil spirits), curving of the roof slope, and other elements of the roof that differ from Western forms do not constitute distinct Japanese features, but confirm only how manifold the architectural motifs and features were that Japan took over from China.

However, the lean-to roof, *hisashi* (or less frequently *kiri-yoke),* does constitute a characteristic feature of the Japanese residence. Its function is to protect the individual wall openings with their paper-covered sliding panels against rain and sun. Yet, such function concerns not only the doors, windows, or verandas, but also such exterior building elements as the shutter compartment, the attached bath, or the toilet. Here, as will become increasingly apparent, a practical device of construction did not remain strictly within the limits of necessity, but in addition became a medium of decorative expression.

For each of the many distinct uses of the lean-to roof a standard type developed, and the number of such types increased with later decorative differentiation. Among them, the double raftered lean-to roof, *keshō-bisashi,* became a dominant feature in the external expression of the Japanese dwelling. Its two sets of rafters have been the subject of much dispute. Since the roof cover could very well have been laid upon the boards of the lower set, the upper set of rafters is superfluous, at least constructionally. Thus it is generally professed that a certain visual intention (though never clearly defined) had effected this additional element. However, since in many cases both rafter sets have an identical inclination or, if not, differ only slightly, neither the presence of the second rafter set nor the difference in appearance is actually recognizable from the normal standpoint of a pedestrian. The assumption that the second set of rafters has a visual purpose is therefore dubious. Instead, it is more likely that the second set of rafters originally served to conceal an unsightly structural member. Such probability also is supported by the fact that in the warrior's house, built in the *shuden* style, the broad roof overhang is achieved by a sloped beam, *hanegi,* carrying a set of rafters on purlins above and concealed from underneath by a second set of rafters. Supposedly this feature, with many others, was introduced into the ordinary dwelling, but since here the rafters themselves took over the constructional function of the sloped beam, the concealment no longer had any meaning. Yet, instead of reconsidering and redesigning according to the new situation, the Japanese carpenter, as in many other instances, apparently submitted himself to habit and tradition.

Another feature of the lean-to roof construction, the intersection of the round veranda beams, *en-geta,* at the corners seems to contradict earlier statements that visual concern never had been an instrumental factor in producing features of the Japanese residence. For here a third piece, a round log with no apparent constructional function whatever, is inserted, obviously to make the two beams appear as if they were penetrating each other. It is true such a measure must at first sight appear formalistic in cause. However, referring back to earlier stages of development, it becomes plain that this device does not actually owe its existence to a creation of pleasing form but rather to a reasonable endeavor to preserve by illusion the architectural form of two overlapping members—the more primitive, though constructionally more logical, method of the past.

This tendency is distinctive of decorative elements in the Japanese dwelling as a whole. For in the Japanese residential evolution, whenever one or another feature shifted its purpose from a utilitarian to a decorative one, an abstraction of form was never resorted to. Instead, an architectural anatomy was developed that maintained the basic expression or even more distinctly manifested what had been the original cause.

5 space enclosures

japanese wall

One of the most expressive features in the Japanese house, though the least regarded as such by Western writers, is the solid wall. In technique and consistency it does not differ much from the old clay wall used in Central European wood-frame buildings, and yet, expressing color, texture, and proportion through its own substance and thus being decorative by itself, it has a character all its own. Thus, it is well justified to use the term "Japanese wall" instead of the more exact Japanese term, *komai-kabe,* literally meaning "wall with small (bamboo) laces."

The aesthetic and cohesive qualities of the solid wall by far outweigh its constructional and resistive qualities. But, as most of its parts are either above the sliding panels or at places hardly exposed to much abuse, such as the picture recess or tearoom, there was no real requirement for constructional permanence, especially as the children in Japan do not consider the house interior a suitable place for strength-testing games. If carelessness does cause damage, repairs can easily be made. And it does not offend the Japanese eye if the repaired part of the wall differs from the adjacent parts. Indeed, the constructional quality of the Japanese wall seems to be consistent with all the other measures taken in constructing the house. For they hardly give the impression of any intention to erect an imperishable monument, but rather manifest the architectural idea of a temporary shelter in those changeable times.

As the columns of the vertical framework are the only bearing members, the wall's sole constructional function is to sustain itself. This is achieved by a wood-bamboo skeleton in which the main horizontal tie members, *nuki,* extend their functional range to keeping the columns in their upright position. While these horizontal members, at an average distance of 2 feet (600 mm.), provide adequate support for the wall skeleton, additional members, *nurigomi-nuki,* need to be inserted vertically in between the columns. The preferred distance is ½ *ken* (909 mm. = 3 ft.), according to the *ken* grid, creating a skeleton pattern of 2 x 3 foot rectangles. Into each opening is tied a bamboo lathwork, consisting of a major frame, *mawatashi-dake* (literally, spanning bamboo), and a grid of bamboo strips, *komai-dake* (literally, bamboo in small laces). They are individually fastened either with rice-straw fiber or rope.

The order of this intermediate skeleton is seemingly insignificant, as it will be covered up later. Yet, it is descriptive of the system that prevails in the overall constructional method. Major order is subdivided into minor, and minor again into minor. Small units are not added, but large units are subdivided again and again into minor orders of continuous subordination.

With this skeleton completed, the wall clay is applied on either side in two, three, or four coats of slightly different consistency, constituting the so-called *arakabe,* the rough wall. Its thickness is about a half to two-thirds of the column thickness, i.e., 2–3 *sun* (60–90 mm. = 2.4–3.6 in.). After its curing process, the finish coat, *uwa-nuri* or *shiage,* is laid on in a very even layer of about 1⁄16 in., with an infinite variety of color, consistency, and texture and thus with infinite expressional possibilities.

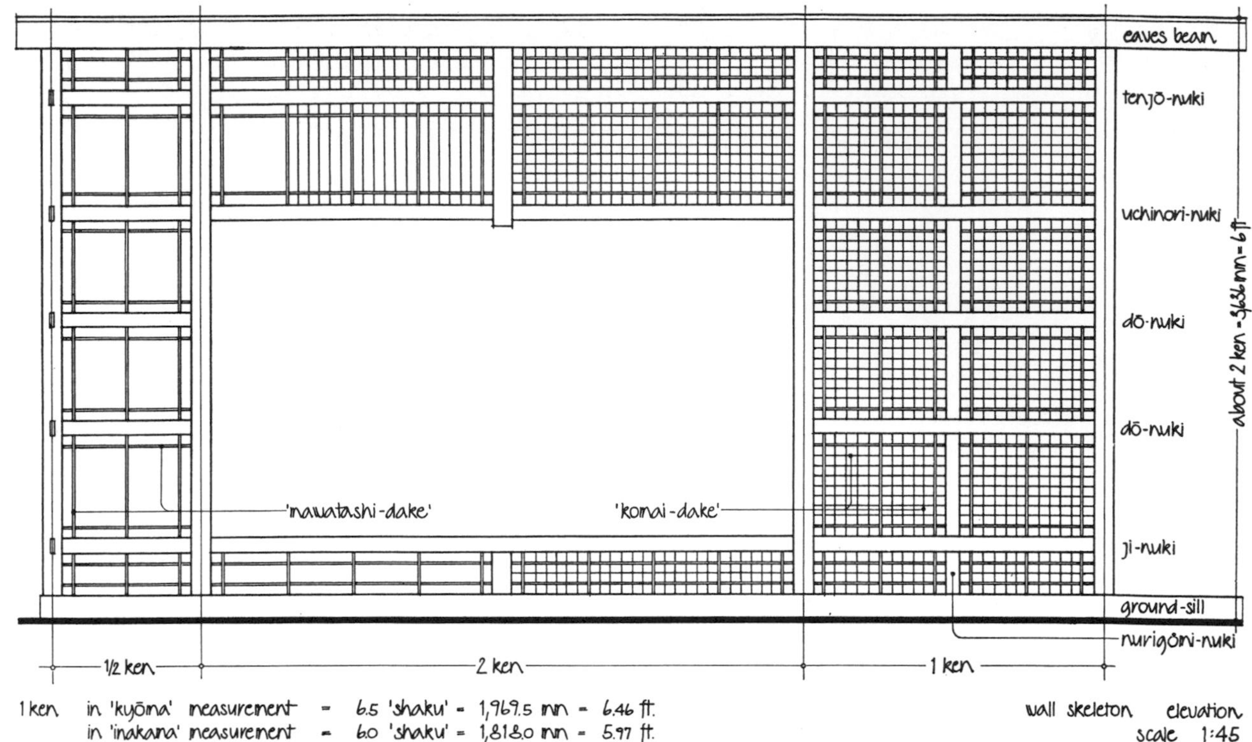

FIGURE 35: Details of walk-skeleton construction.

Yet, constructionally speaking, the most amazing feature of the wall is not the extreme refinement of a basically primitive wall construction but the way the solid wall and column are joined. Although the plaster is simply butted to the wood, no wooden cover detail is used to provide a clean joint or to hide the minute connections which even trained craftsmen find difficult to execute properly. Here, the Japanese carpenter has renounced all trim details that in Western architecture are so necessary and has thus preserved an austere purity of distinction between supporting and non-supporting members.

However, it is certainly too far-fetched to ascribe this method to an active concept that refused the use of members that were liable to efface clarity of constructional definition. The fact is that there simply was nothing that demanded countermeasures with trim details, for there is no shrinkage of either wood or wall clay that could be compared to that in average continental conditions. The reasons for this architecturally favorable circumstance are constructional, climatic, and insulational. The curtain skeleton is tightly connected with the column, thus granting constructional homogeneity; the local climate throughout the year is fairly humid, thus eliminating excessive movement of material; and, finally, the house is neither insulated against temperature or humidity nor is it heated in the winter, thus providing identical climatic conditions for both the interior and exterior. Difference of environmental circumstances, then, is the final reason for this favorable distinction of the Japanese house as compared to its traditional Western counterpart.

Since the wall material is not very resistant to weather, exterior wall parts particularly exposed to rain are frequently covered by thin wooden boards. Characteristically,

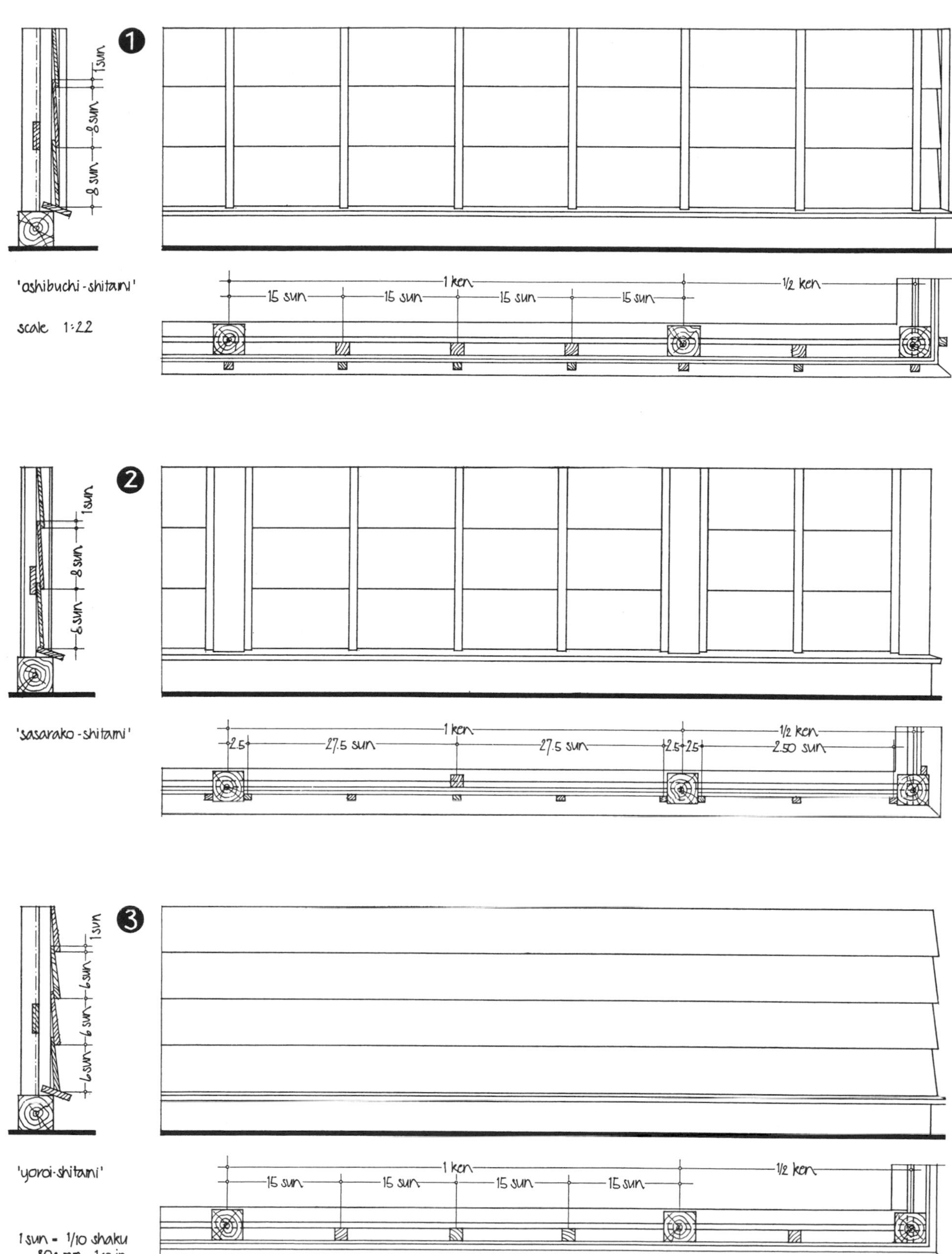

FIGURE 36: Typical forms of exterior wood siding.

this cover does not extend over the clay wall's entire height, as aesthetic considera-tion would suggest, but begins 2 to 3 feet below the roof projection, be it gable or eave. And this is very understandable, because the upper part of the wall, being sufficiently protected by the roof overhang, does not require additional sheathing as does the rest of the wall down to the groundsill.

As a rule, the boards are arranged horizontally, overlapping each other from above in a pattern called *shitami-bari* (literally, underview boarding), which again is performed in several standard methods. In the houses of the wealthier class, boarding is used also for decorative purposes. It usually has a vertical order, *tateita-bari,* and is constructed in the same manner as the shutter compartments, *tobukuro.*

floor

Floor in the Japanese single-storied house is clearly differentiated into three planes. This difference is basic and is more obviously marked than in the usual Western case. For the distinction between the planes is not a mere difference in elevation but a clear definition of the purpose that each of those three planes serves, both in its construc-tion and its utilization. Actually, the height-level difference is only the logical result of the latter. Clarity of definition is further stressed by the three different materials used for floor covering, earth, wood, and mat, which again reflect but the difference of pur-pose. Among them, the matted floor occupies the largest area, living space; the boarded floor is provided for communicative and utilitarian space; and the earthen floor forms transitional space between interior and exterior. A floor covered with bamboo or par-ticularly shaped logs may occasionally be used, yet indicating no other motive than that of decorative concern.

Like all constructional systems in the Japanese residence, the build-up of the floor framework is a succession of subimposed orders, i.e., the constructional system is not derived from the addition of small units as in brick architecture, but is organized in repeated subdivisions of a dominating structural unit. Such a major order is estab-lished by the floor beam, *ashigatame.* The floor beam, being inserted between room-circumferential columns, designates the area to be floored. It is additionally supported by short posts erected upon the groundsill. At the sides where there is no veranda or at interior room partitions, instead of a floor beam, continuous braces, *nedagake,* are tied to the columns. They are in the same height with the floor sleepers, *obiki,* that form the second order. The sleepers are spanned in the direction of the room width and are supported by short posts at standard intervals. The top of the sleeper is lower than that of the floor beam and thus provides space for the third order consisting of joists, *neda,* which again are laid in modular distances. Then follows the last order of floor-support-ing members, the boards that are laid transversely upon the joists. They, finally, are in one level with the floor beam and thus combine major and minor orders, providing a uniform level for the mat cover.

Construction of the floors in the second plane (kitchen, veranda, corridor, toilet, etc.). is somewhat more simple because the span is rather small. For example, in the veranda the forementioned interior floor beam provides support for the transverse joists at the inside, while at the outside another floor beam, *engamachi,* is notched into the veranda post and receives the other end of the floor joists. The joists again are laid at standard distances, providing the base for the floor boards.

The boards of the exposed floor are planed but otherwise are left untreated or only rubbed with a vegetable oil for protection. Continuous use by bare feet or with *tabi,*

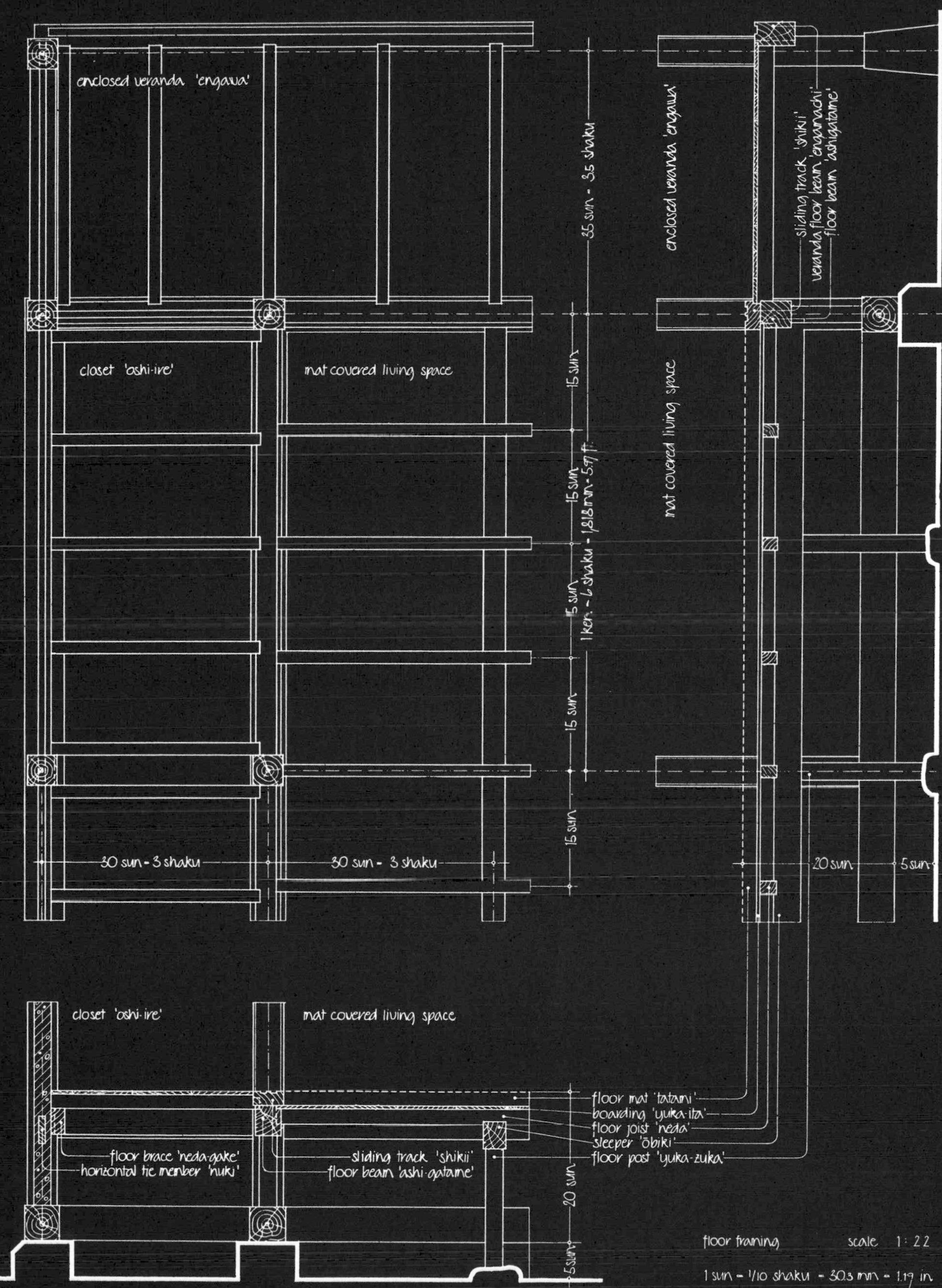

FIGURE 37: Details of floor construction.

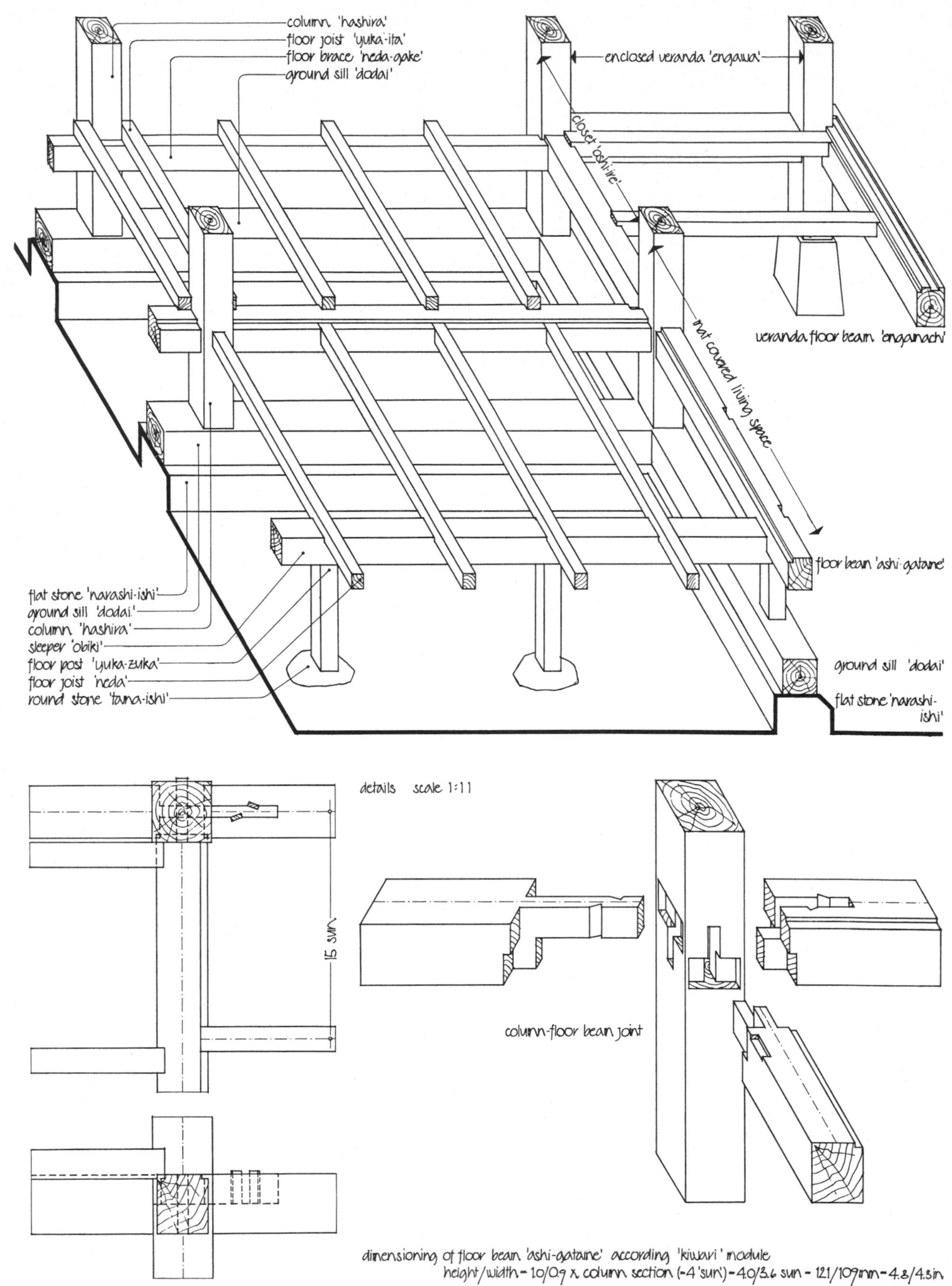

FIGURE 37 (continued): Details of floor construction.

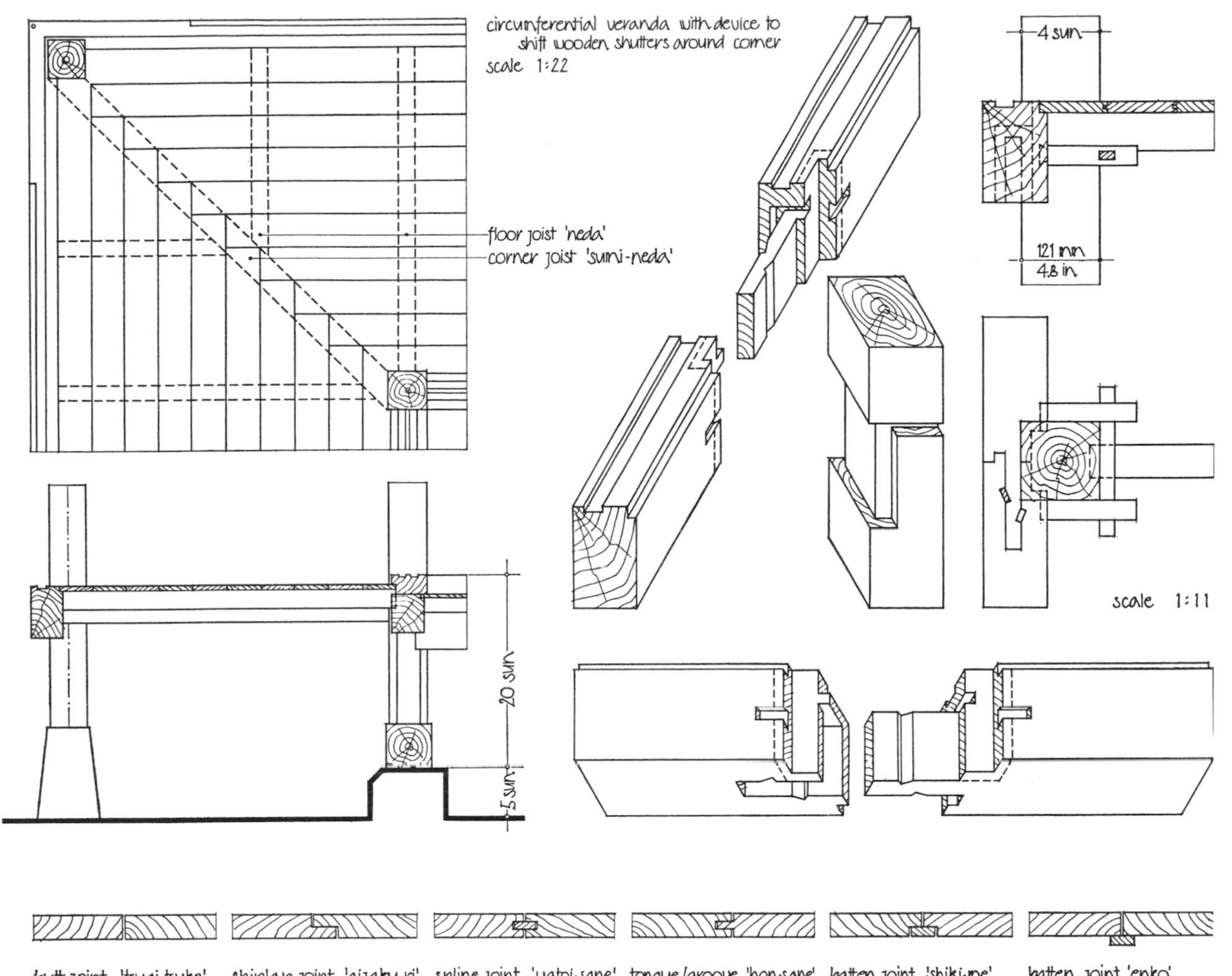

dimensioning of floor joist 'neda' according 'kiwari' module: height/width - 0.5/0.4 x column section (- 4.0 'sun') - 2.0/1.6 'sun' - 60.5/48.5 mm - 2.4/1.9 in
dimensioning of floor board 'yuka-ita' thickness/width - 0.15/0.9 x column section - 0.6/3.6 'sun' - 18.0/109.0 mm - 0.7/4.3 in

FIGURE 37 (continued): Details of floor construction.

the cloth footwear, together with an occasional sweeping (and, no doubt, the aging process too) effects the noted contrasting appearance of the wood's natural texture. In both floor planes, the matted and the boarded, one or two of the boards, *age-ita,* are left loose so that it is possible to get under the floor if repairs become necessary. The boards in this case arc only butted, whereas usually they have overlapping joints.

The floor of the third level, as in the kitchen and in the entrance hall, *genkan,* was traditionally an earthen floor, a simple, though not too hygienic, surface that required no other treatment and care outside of being stamped and occasionally broomed. Today, however, concrete, stone, tiles, and other more resistant fabrics have largely replaced earth in the cities, while rural areas have not as yet parted with this primitive material.

ceiling

The foregoing analysis has already shown that the components of the Japanese house, whether in their origin and evolution or in their treatment and final form, do not manifest a primary concern for visual forms. They have been motivated and determined by constructional-utilitarian purpose, environmental adaptation, and fabric limitation, the latter two, no doubt, in the Japanese case, manifesting passive yielding rather than active response. Realization of their aesthetic qualities followed much later, as did their appreciation and conscious application.

The ceiling in the Japanese house seems to contradict this statement because, clearly, it was prompted by the visual purpose of concealing the roof construction. And yet, the ceiling is no real exception. For concealing the unsightly is one thing and playing with visual forms is quite another. Nevertheless, the stress of the optical purpose of the ceiling was a logical consequence and the step toward decorative treatment was not too great. This is evidenced by the fact that the ceiling is the only component among all elements of the dwelling in which dimensions and organization are still moduled by room size and orientation. The height of the ceiling varies according to number of mats, as does the width of the ceiling boards, which are the main constituent parts (Figure 15). Placement of the rods underneath is determined by the location of columns, and the whole is arranged according to the room orientation.

It is true the ceiling functions as an insulat or against temperature and also as a protector from dust, but since the thin boards are not very tightly connected, and frequently even chink open, both functions are more imagined than real. Its function is to conceal and this aim has been achieved with the least means possible.The purity of this response to a functional demand is décor in itself, and in such simple type of ceiling no additional trim is needed to make it aesthetically pleasing. This is significant insofar as it shows that even the most simple constructional device, if it is approached with austere discipline, possesses distinct expressional-aesthetic potentialities.

The increasing wealth of the townspeople was the reason that the ceiling, until then used only in residences of the nobility, found entry into the ordinary houses—at first only in the reception room, but gradually also spreading into the other living rooms. Yet, there still are many houses in which the kitchen has no ceiling. This somewhat belated appearance of the ceiling in the dwelling, long after all other features had established themselves, has relegated the ceiling to a part that is added rather than incorporated into the constructional anatomy. It thus granted a convenient independence from the total organism that allowed visual adjustment to room size and orientation without additional labor or material. It is noteworthy that now, with roof construction being no longer visible, constructional improvement through use of diagonal truss members did not take place. For it clearly contradicts the common assumption that a particular, inherited Japanese taste prevented the use of structural members other than the horizontal and vertical.

The constructional system of the ceiling is simple. In the ordinary case, the ceiling boards, *tenjō-ita*, are laid upon slender rods, *saobuchi,* which are inserted by their ends into a ledge at the wall, *mawaribuchi*, and are secured by nails along their entire length to another set of transverse joists, *nobuchi,* above the boards. These joists are connected to perpendicular members, *tsuriki,* that suspend the ceiling from the beams above. Usually, the center of the ceiling is lifted about 8 to 9 *bu* (approx. 25 mm. = 1 in.) in order to compensate for eventual sagging of the beams.

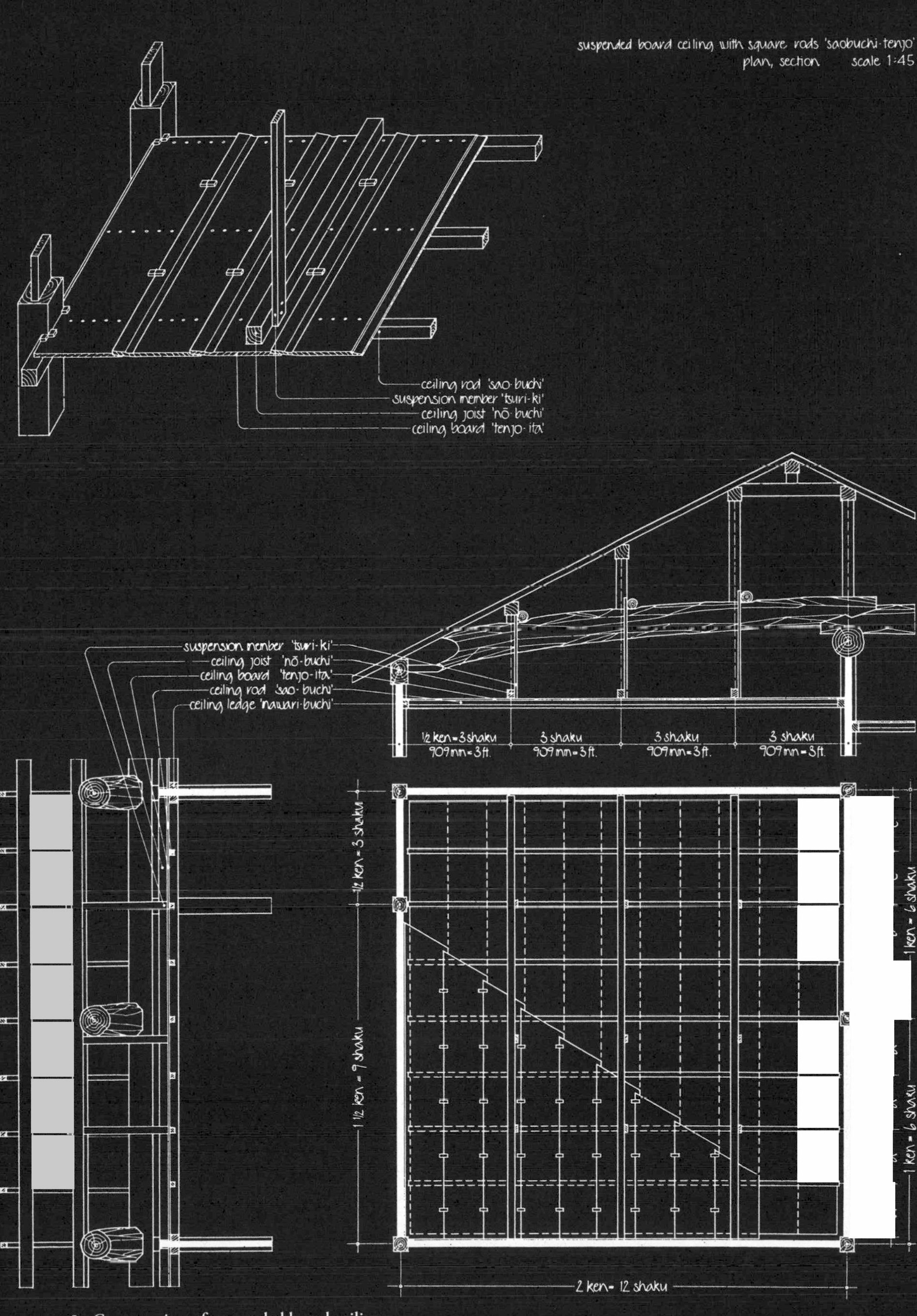

FIGURE 38: Construction of suspended board ceiling.

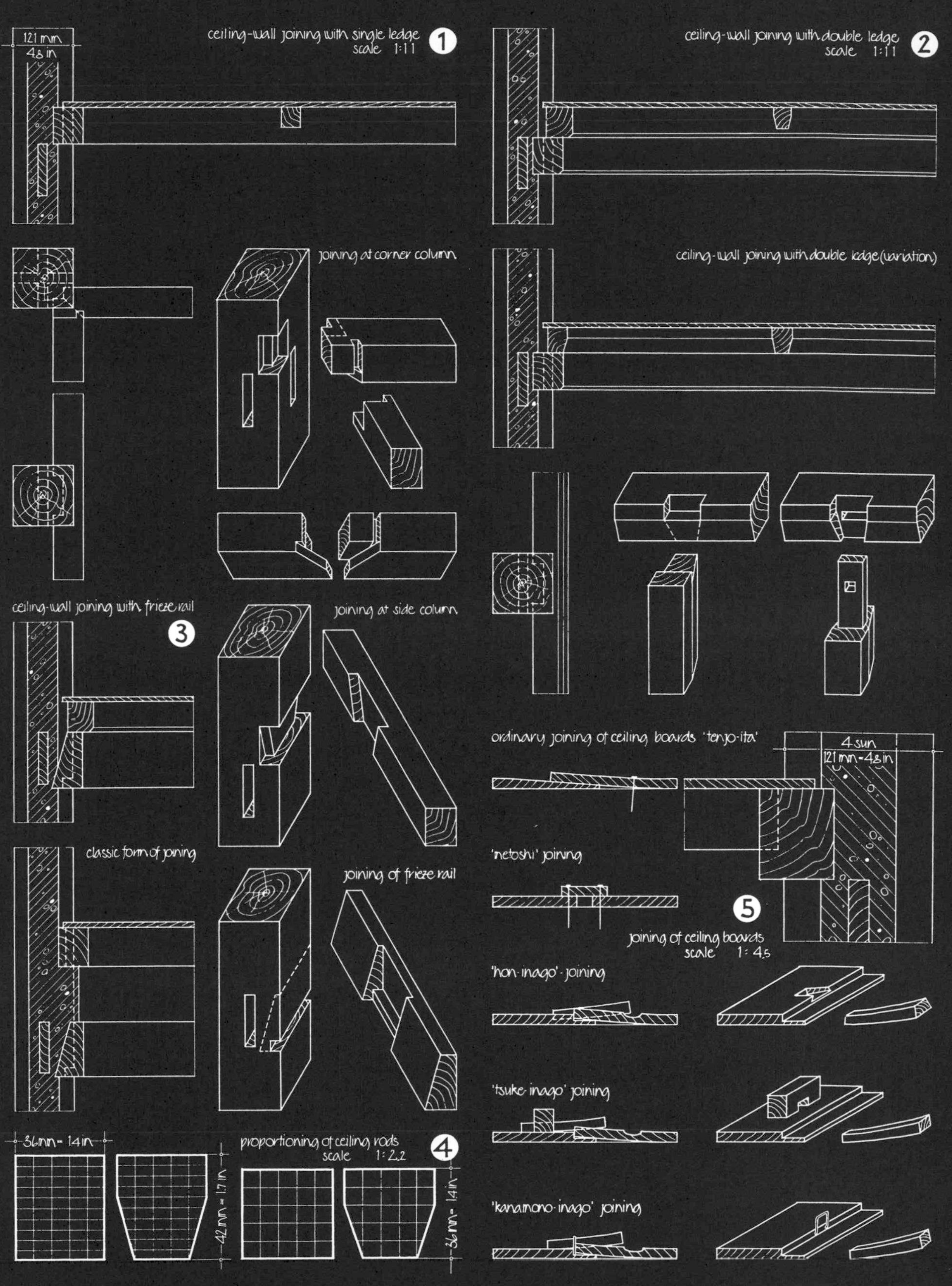

FIGURE 39: Details of ceiling construction.

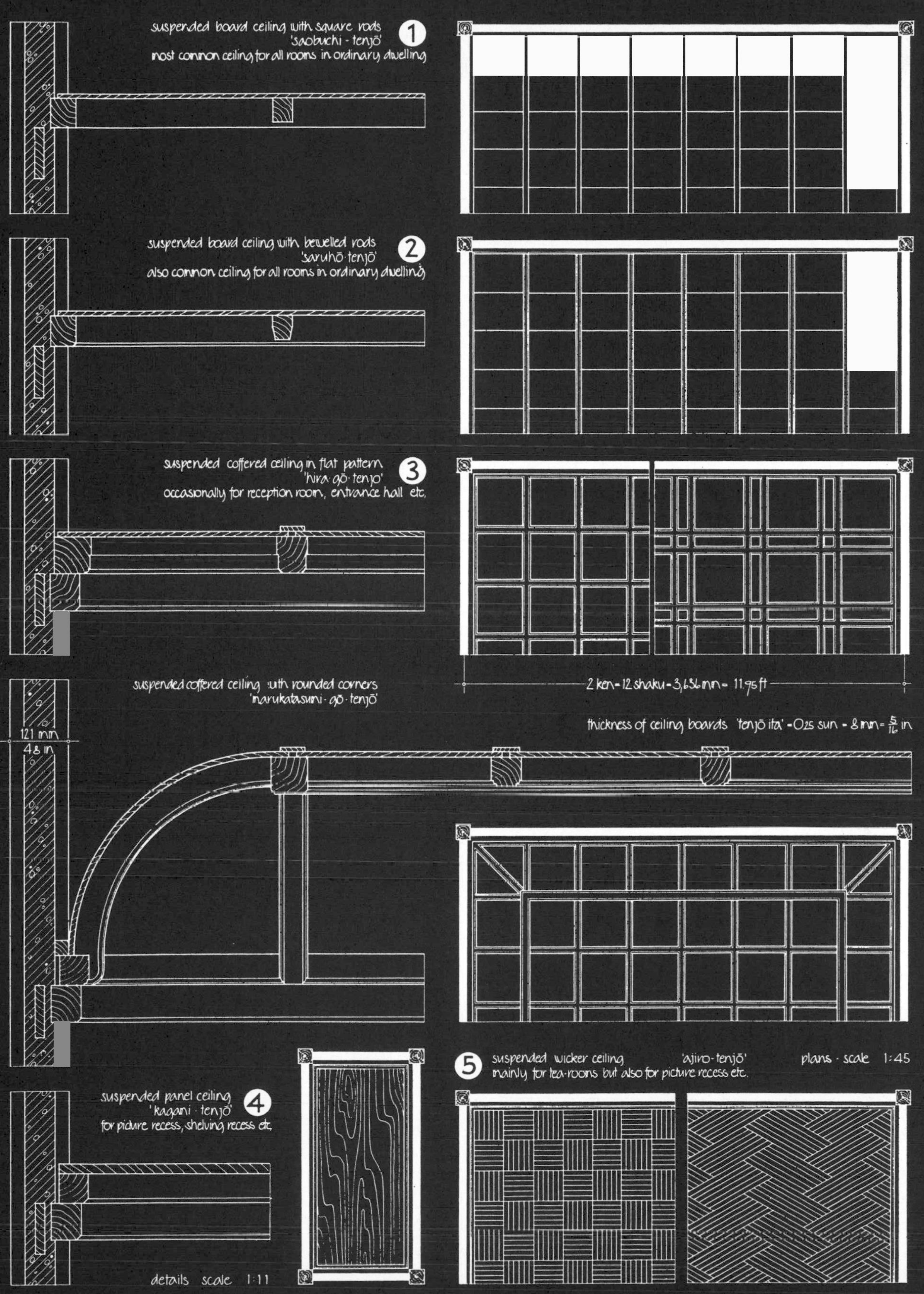

FIGURE 40: Typical ceiling patterns.

The second set of ceiling joists (*nobuchi*) as well as the suspension members (*tsuriki*) are not visible, creating an impression as if the ceiling boards would rest entirely on the square rods (*saobuchi*) which are dimensioned only about 1½ x 1½ in. (40 x 40 mm.). Since these rods would indeed sag by their dead weight alone in the case of a normal span of 12 ft. (3,636 mm.), a twofold illusion is produced: extreme lightness of the ceiling boards and extraordinary strength of the slender ceiling rods. Still it must be doubted whether this unquestionably strong effect was actually anticipated and intentionally sought, or whether this effect was but the result of quite reasonable methods to construct a light suspended ceiling under the given circumstances.

Though the structural principle does not change essentially, both the organization of ceiling pattern and its detailing may show slight variations which in turn may reflect the wealth of the owner. In general, Japanese residential architecture characteristically does not display material wealth through scale, form, organization, construction, or decoration, except for the quality of fabric and size of enclosed space. But in the case of the ceiling, a difference in monetary wealth is more clearly expressed than in other instances, again demonstrating the decorative implication of the ceiling.

Thus, several types of ceiling patterns have evolved, which again are standardized. Among them, the one with square rods, *saobuchi-tenjō,* is the most frequently used. Besides those already depicted, the oblique veranda ceiling, *keshōyane-ura* (literally, underside of the disguise roof), needs mention. This type, which is also called *keshōbisashi-ura,* is not employed in the ordinary interior rooms, but only as a component of the lean-to roof, *hisashi*, and as such, has been treated earlier in the study of the lean-to roof.

Each of these ceiling types again has its variations, both locally and monetarily, but standardization and distribution of carpenter manuals during the Tokugawa era (1600–1867) resulted in uniform application. The wood dimension of each component member is a ratio of the column section, but since the column section in the ordinary house, as a rule, is standardized at 4 *sun* square (121 mm. = 4.8 in.), component members of the ceiling have also become fairly standardized.

Since the main components of the ceiling plane, the ceiling boards, are very thin (1⁄10 roof column section = 40⁄10 = 4 *bu* = approx. 7⁄16 in. = 12 mm.) and thus are liable to curl and chink open, the overlapping edges require additional joinery to at least prevent any major dislocation. The most ordinary procedure is to nail the overlapping board upon the underlying rod, but, in general, additional clips are employed.

Dimensioning and organizing of ceiling elements follows certain rules according to the room size and column placement. In addition, their orientation is decided by visual factors:

1. As the profile of the ceiling is most obvious if the overlapping edges of the boards are seen, the boards are laid with their overlapping edges facing the main direction of approach.
2. If the room has a picture recess, *tokonoma*, the main direction of approach becomes of less importance because it is imperative that the arrangement of ceiling rods, *saobuchi*, be parallel to the opening of the picture recess.
3. In the latter case the overlapping edges of the boards have to face the place of honor, *kamiza*, in front of the picture recess where the guests are seated.

In arranging the boards, there are cases in which the latter rule is ignored. The ceiling is then called *mikaeshi* (literally, reverse facing), indicating that the average Japanese is very well aware of the visual effect of the ceiling's simple order.

6 movable space controls

fittings

In the course of civilization, the development of technology was the reason that increasingly small and convenient metal elements took over the functions of joining, strengthening, and fastening of structural parts, functions that were formerly fulfilled by structural parts of wood, stone, or brick themselves. Accordingly, the word "fittings" in Western architecture has achieved the meaning of additional metal fixtures rather than components that are integrated into, and are part of, the structure. Yet, as "fittings" were originally those structural parts that were shaped "to make fit" the movable parts in the house (the doors, windows, etc.), the designation "fitting" is applicable in the instances discussed below. For all movable parts in the Japanese house, especially the interior and exterior sliding doors and windows, are held in position and kept under control by "fittings" in their original meaning.

In most forms of early architecture, wall openings such as doors and windows were furnished with removable panel-like units that would merely be set in place. But while the West, in defense against the cold, soon took to the more appropriate swinging variety, Japan, favored by a relatively mild climate, retained the original form, and through the centuries, refined what at first had been a simple standing screen imported from China. In the course of this refinement, the screen was set into wooden tracks below, *shikii*, and above, *kamoi*. The lower tracks were sunk into the floor, and the upper tracks were tied to a pair of braces, *nageshi*, which already existed as a constructionally important element even before the advent of sliding panels. Dimensions of the components of the sliding panel were reduced to the minimum and its features exploited as a decorative medium. Of course, the step from portable screen to sliding panel was, technologically speaking, a remarkable achievement. Yet, considering its practical purpose, it was only refinement of what already existed rather than invention of something essentially new. Again in this instance the Japanese house manifests one of its unique characteristics: utmost refinement of what is principally primitive.

Since columns are the only supporting members, the entire space between two columns could easily be furnished with these sliding panels, *shōji* at the outside wall and *fusuma* at the interior wall, or their window-like variations. Minute grooves in a wooden track hold the bottom of these panels in place; they are exposed to the same wear as the floor itself, a circumstance that certainly must have been one of the many motives for the Japanese removing their shoes before entering the interior rooms. For the contours of even the hardest wood could not successfully withstand wear by shoes, especially if they were but ⅛ in. (3 mm.) deep.

As a rule, the sliding tracks have two adjacent grooves, each of which holds one or two sliding panels. Two subsequent panels, therefore, can be slid over each other, reaching a complete overlap. For a two-part sliding wall, this allows an opening of about ½ *ken* width (909 mm. = 3 ft.) and for a four-part sliding wall, an opening of about 1 *ken* (1,818 mm. - 6 ft.). The upper sliding grooves have a height tolerance slightly greater than the depth of the lower grooves. Thus, the sliding panels can be easily removed

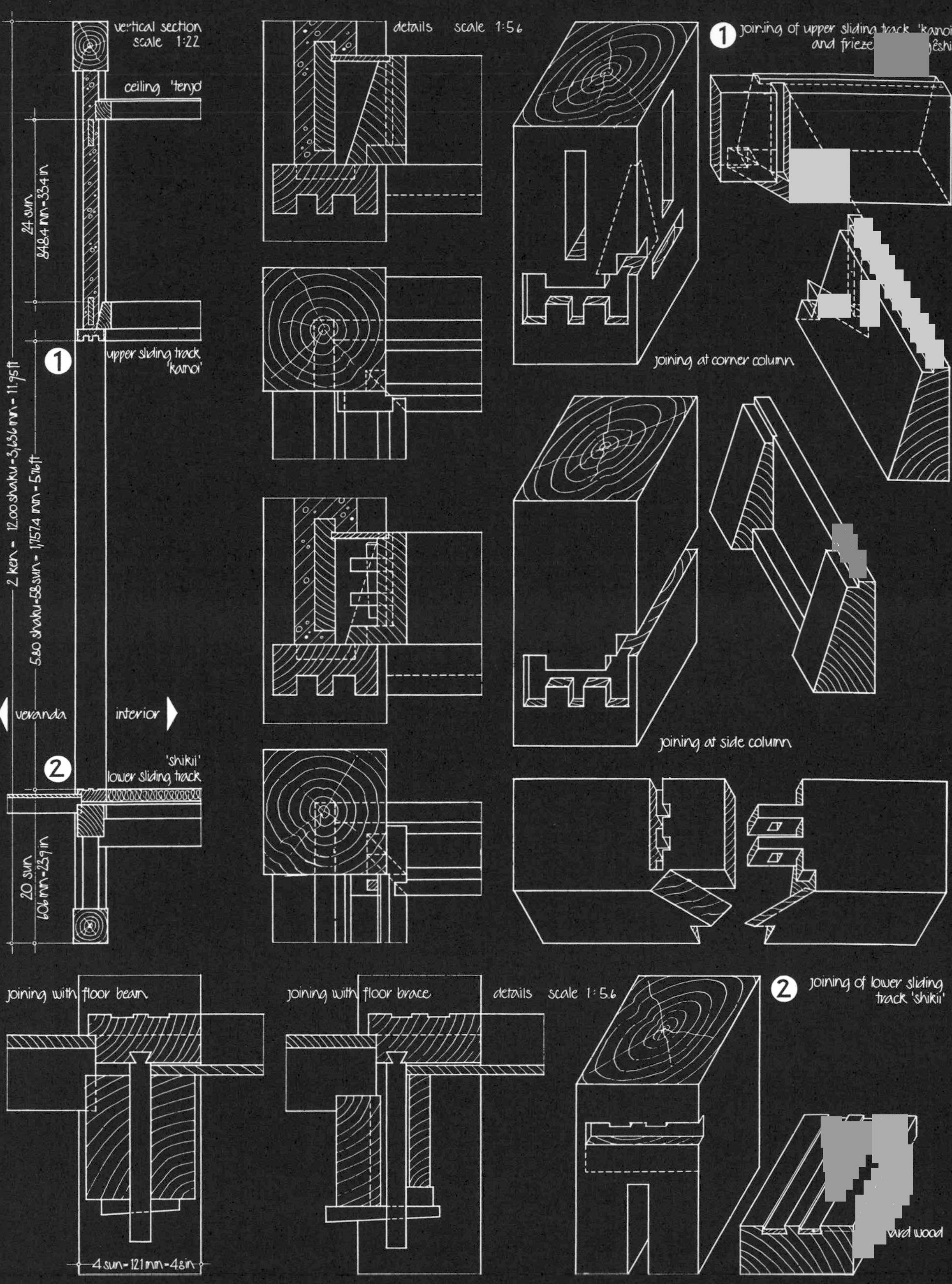

dimensioning of upper sliding track 'kamoi' according 'kiwari'-module: height/width - 0.4/0.85 x column section (=4 sun) = 1.6/3.4 sun = 48/103 mm = 1.9/4.0 in
dimensioning of frieze rail 'nageshi' height/width = 0.9/0.5 x column section (=4 sun) = 3.6/2.0 sun = 109/60.5 mm = 4.3/2.4 in

FIGURE 41: **Details of typical wood fittings and joinings.**

from the wall merely by lifting them from the lower tracks and swinging the bottom out.

The merits of this method of enclosing space have been sufficiently lauded by Western architects. Since the sliding panels can easily be opened as well as entirely removed, stored, and exchanged, interior room partitioning gains a highly desirable flexibility for dwellings with a minimum of space, such as the Japanese house. Moreover, it grants excellent ventilation during the humid summer months and even allows an effortless exchange of sliding panels if season or damage ask for it. Finally, the operation of these panels does not require additional space as in the case of a swinging door, an advantage of which contemporary architecture has become again aware.

On the other hand, there are numerous defects, such as lack of insulation against cold and heat, sound, and dirt and the incapacity to provide privacy for the individual. Though they seriously affect life in many ways, they are hardly mentioned by writers on Japanese architecture—another circumstance that has added to the general confusion of opinion that exists about the potential of Japanese motifs in contemporary architecture. The increasing use of this type of room partitioning in contemporary building is not due to a somewhat belated recognition of the advantages of this system, but is to be attributed to the technical improvement that enables partitioning with sliding units without having to accept the multiple defects mentioned above.

A very controversial part among the components of fittings is the frieze rail, *uchi-nori-nageshi,* which braces the columns just above the upper wooden track, *kamoi,* at a height of about 1 *ken* (1,818 mm. = 6 ft.) and reinforces the latter. Doubtlessly, its origin was due to the necessity of providing lateral bracing to the columns as can be evidenced in many old buildings where these strong lateral bracings are firmly tied to the column in various heights. Yet, since the introduction of concealed horizontal tie members, *nuki* (from 17th-century Sung period architecture of the Chinese), these lateral bracings were no longer constructionally needed for the main framework and instead were only put to reinforcing—quite unnecessarily—the upper sliding track, *kamoi,* at certain points. Thus, controversy exists as to why the frieze rail, *nageshi,* is still used, even in solid walls that do not have sliding panels, and why, upon remaining, it did not follow the general tendency to economize by reducing wood dimensions, but instead retained its original, somewhat heavy appearance.

Since apparently neither constructional logic nor economic reason can account for its continued presence, it is reasonable to believe that visual-aesthetic considerations were instrumental. This assumption seems to be supported by the fact that, optically speaking, the wall above the doors, *kokabe* (literally, little wall), which ranges from 1.8–3.0 ft. (560–900 mm.) in height, needs a beamlike element that would appear to carry the load above. Also, in the case of a solid wall plane without doors, the division of the whole wall height by an intermediate frieze rail in a ratio of 1: 2 to 1:3, combined with the frequently irregular column placement of 1 *ken,* 1½ *ken,* or 2 *ken,* actually does create a harmonious, though asymmetrical, pattern of white wall rectangles, which in its entirety reaches artistic quality.

However, as logical as the previous assumptions may seem, it appears improbable that the ordinary carpenter in building for the lower classes and being provided with a minimum of means, would have concerned himself with such visual effects. Rather it must be assumed that he willingly would have made changes if he could have reduced the costs; and indeed this he has done. There are many houses that do not have a frieze rail, and others wherein the frieze rail has been reduced in size to a bare minimum necessary for reinforcing the upper sliding track, *kamoi.* The only conclusion then is that the retention of the frieze rail and its dimension in the ordinary dwelling is due to traditional custom.

Cases where real structural elements were concealed and instead superfluous ones introduced in order to create a particular visual-aesthetic effect, cannot, even as an exceptional case, be professed to be a feature of the Japanese house in spite of such claims by many Western writers. These cases owe their existence usually to a misunderstood attempt to revive the former *sukiya* architecture in the current so-called new *sukiya* style. The latter, however, is lacking that very structural directness and honesty of the original *sukiya* style, of which an essential component was the *shinkabe* (literally, genuine or honest wall), a wall that honestly shows structural systems.

translucent paper panel

There are two different types of sliding paper panels in the Japanese house: *shōji* and *fusuma.* Both possess a structural skeleton of light wooden strips arranged in a rectangular pattern and framed by somewhat stronger struts. But, while the *shōji* is pasted with translucent paper only on one side, the *fusuma* is covered on both sides with heavy opaque paper. The translucent variety, *shōji,* as a rule furnishes walls either facing directly to the outside or facing across the veranda or corridor. As this panel type is sometimes used also on interior walls where light is wanted, the translation "translucent paper panel" for *shōji* is actually a more appropriate definition than "exterior sliding door," which it is usually called.

The literal meaning of *shōji* is "interceptor," a word very appropriate to indicate its original role in the house organism. The word was first used to designate the portable standing screen, which was the earliest room partition and room enclosure. Then, after being put into tracks, the sliding variety was generally called *fusuma-no-shōji, fusuma* literally meaning bedquilt because its pattern resembles the latter. Yet, after the evolution of the translucent sliding door, *fusuma-no-shōji* was applied only to the opaque variety while the new translucent variety was given the name *akari shōji* (literally, light interceptor). In the process of simplification, *akari-shōji* became just *shōji* while *fusuma-no-shōji* became *fusuma.*

It is understood that *shōji,* like all other components of the Japanese house, has standard measurements. Its width is determined by column distance and its height by distance between upper and lower track, both of which are subject to the horizontal and vertical modular order of the house. Organization of the wood-strip skeleton of the *shōji* is, as a rule, determined horizontally by a process of halving the panel width and vertically by the market size of the translucent *shōji* paper, commonly 9 *sun* (nominal size; actual size 9.2 *sun* = 279 mm. = 11 in.). The paper strips are pasted horizontally on the outside starting from the bottom and continuing upwards, to keep dust from entering if the paper becomes loose. According to the organization of the skeleton of the *shōji,* three major types have emerged (see drawings), each of which has several variations.

In better houses additional wood strips are provided for the frame, and members are beveled. Yet, the simple form, used in the ordinary dwelling, is not only aesthetically better but can also be composed in a greater variety of patterns.

Constructionally, the most astounding feature of both the translucent and opaque sliding panels (*shōji* and *fusuma*) is their extreme lightness. In the case of *shōji,* the horizontal members of the frame measure no more than 12 x 10 *bu* (36 x 30 mm. = 1.4 x 1.2 in.), whereas the vertical frame members are only 8 x 10 *bu* (24 x 30 mm. = 1.0 x

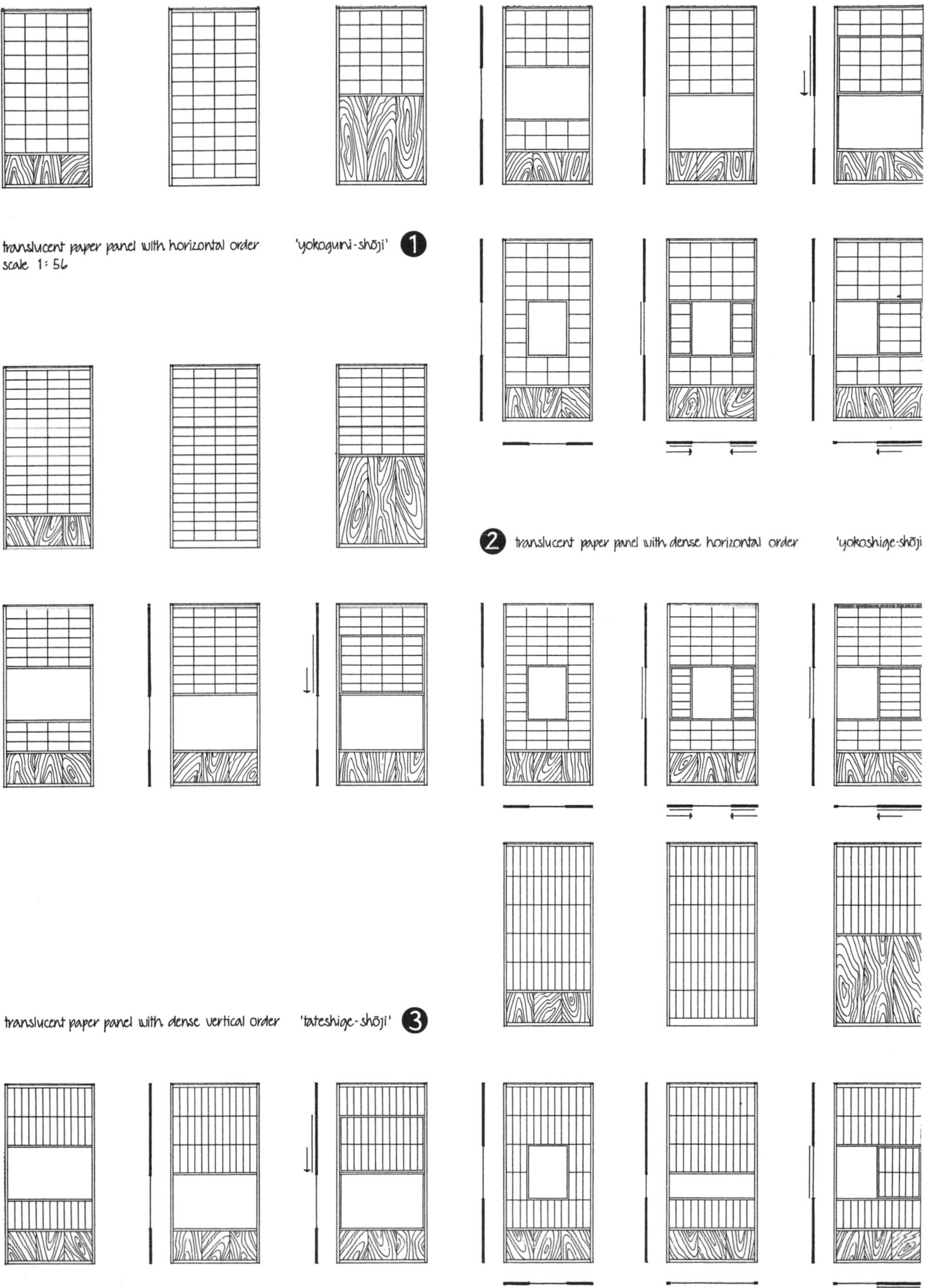

FIGURE 42: Typical forms of translucent paper panels, *shōji*.

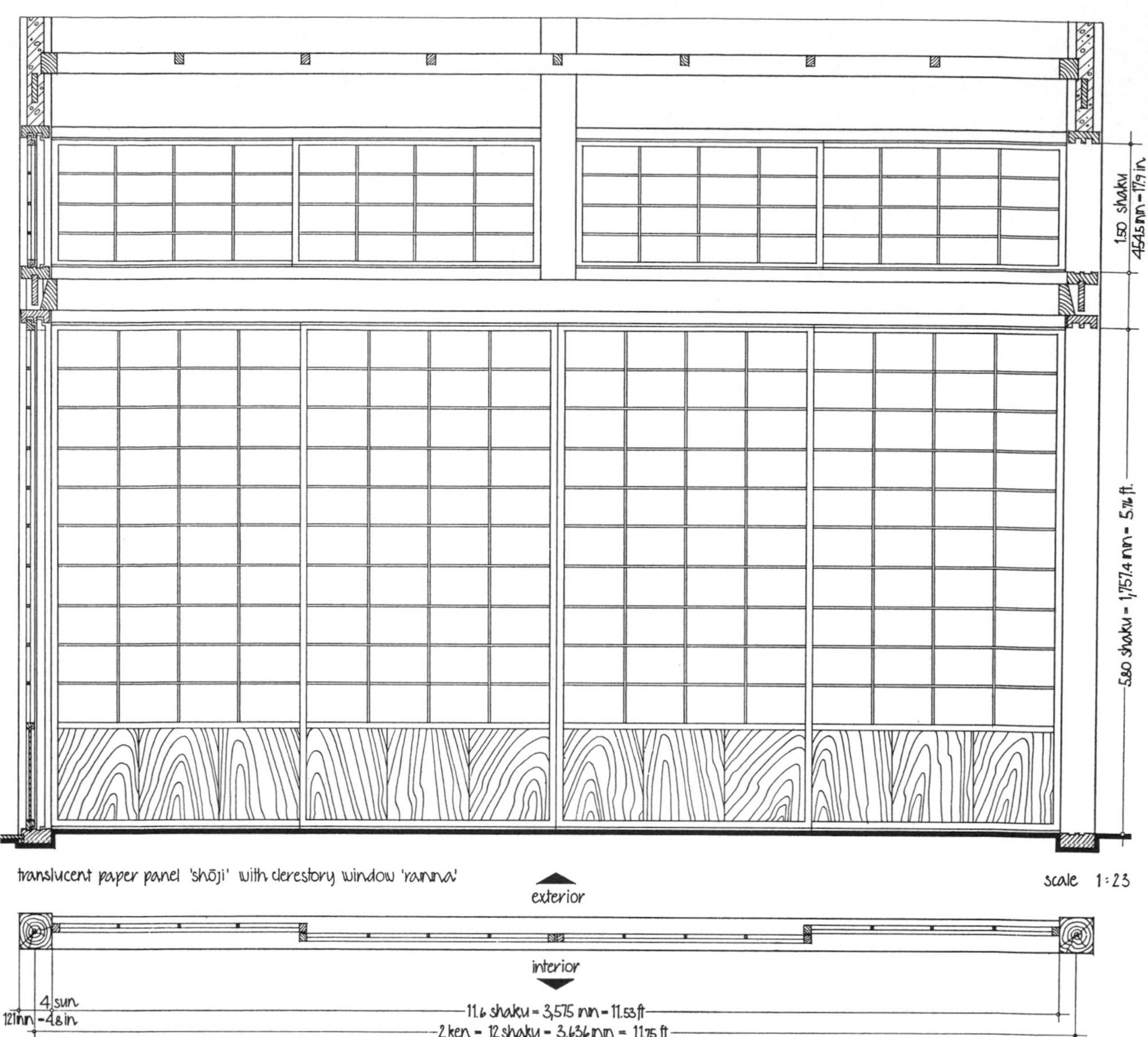

FIGURE 43: Translucent paper panels, *shōji*, in wall opening.

1.2 in.). The skeleton inside the frame then consists of wood strips 2 x 5 *bu* or even 2 x 4 *bu* (6 x 12 mm. = ¼ x ½ in.), and the wooden plate inserted below at the base is but 1.5 *bu* (4.5 mm. = 3⁄16 in.) thick. The single sliding unit weighs but ounces and is so light that rollers to reduce friction in the lower track would be superfluous. All members have rectangular sections, and, as a rule, the edges are not even beveled; no decorative effect is striven for, and expediency and restraint are the only prevailing factors.

And yet, an intimate aesthetic sensation is effected. It is true that the proportions of the *shōji* pattern and the harmony of expression between wood and the translucent paper are partly responsible for this effect, but they only emphasize the actual source of this aesthetic quality: display of the fabric's structural potentialities through the utmost restraint in dimensioning.

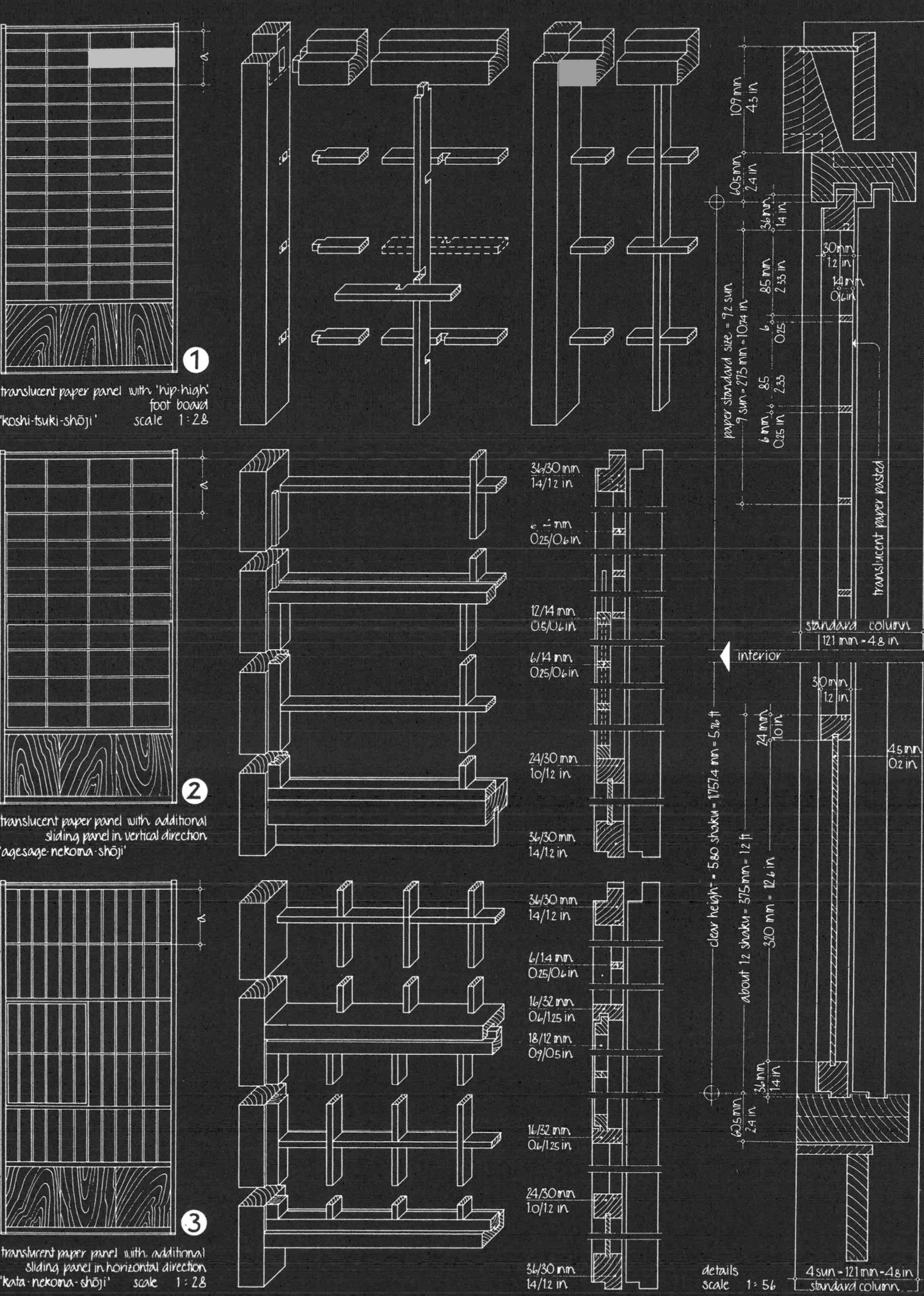

FIGURE 44: Construction details of translucent paper panels, *shōji*.

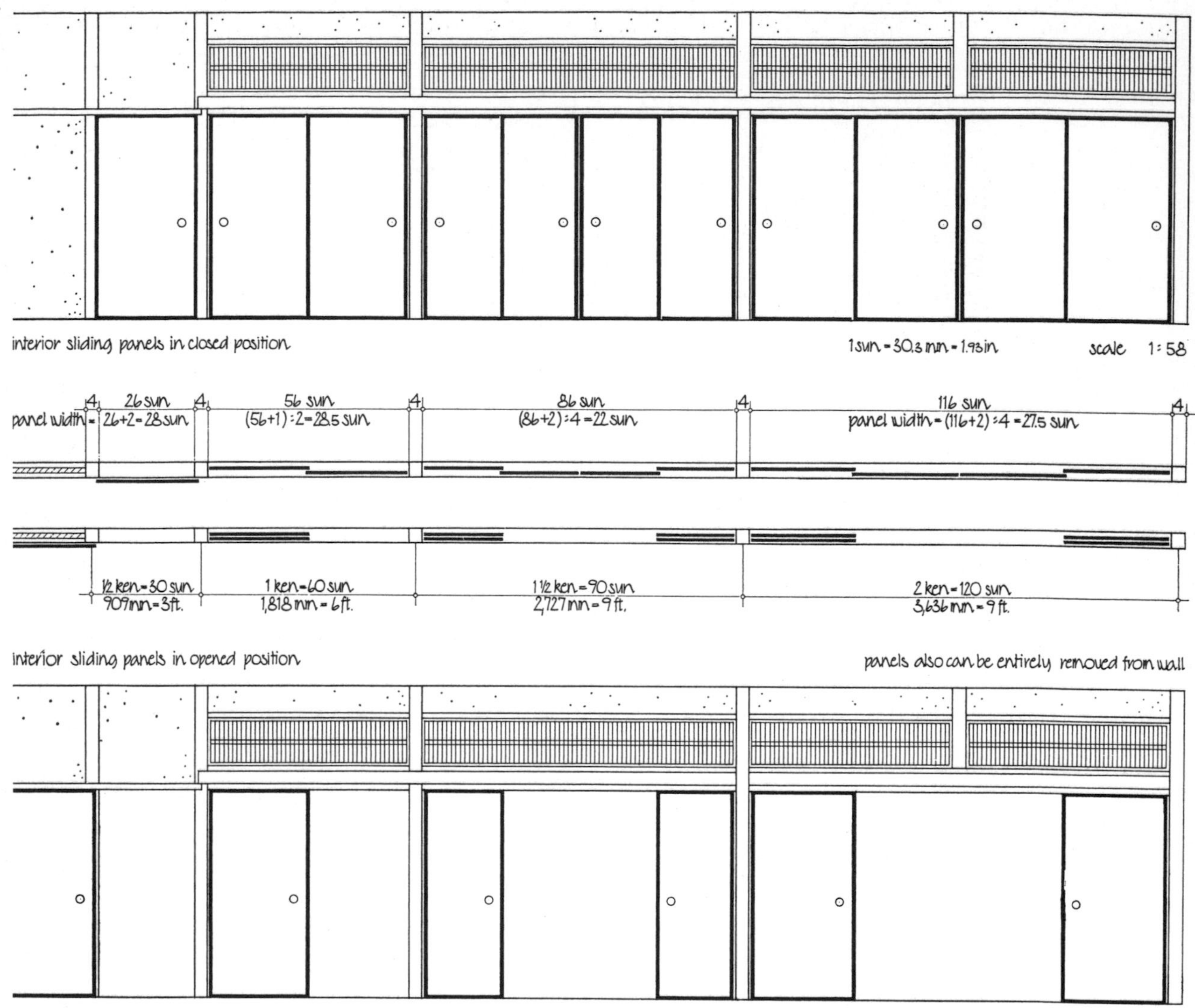

FIGURE 45: Arrangements of sliding panels for different column spacings.

To render possible the reduction of fabric to the minimum, excellent craftsmanship was required, especially since none of the components receive any surface treatment after their assemblage. Yet, even more instrumental for this extraordinary lightness were the prevailing climatic conditions. Without the noted high humidity throughout the year any craftsmanship, however excellent, would prove futile, for unsealed wood of such dimensions would certainly deform in the climatic conditions common to the West. But even with the favorable climate, the wood-strip skeleton, which actually gives the rigidity to the frame, needs preventive measures against deformation, since the members are no stronger than 2 x 4 *bu* (6 x 12 mm. = ¼ x ½ in.). Thus, the wooden strips are notched into each other from alternate sides and thereby effect unexpected rigidity.

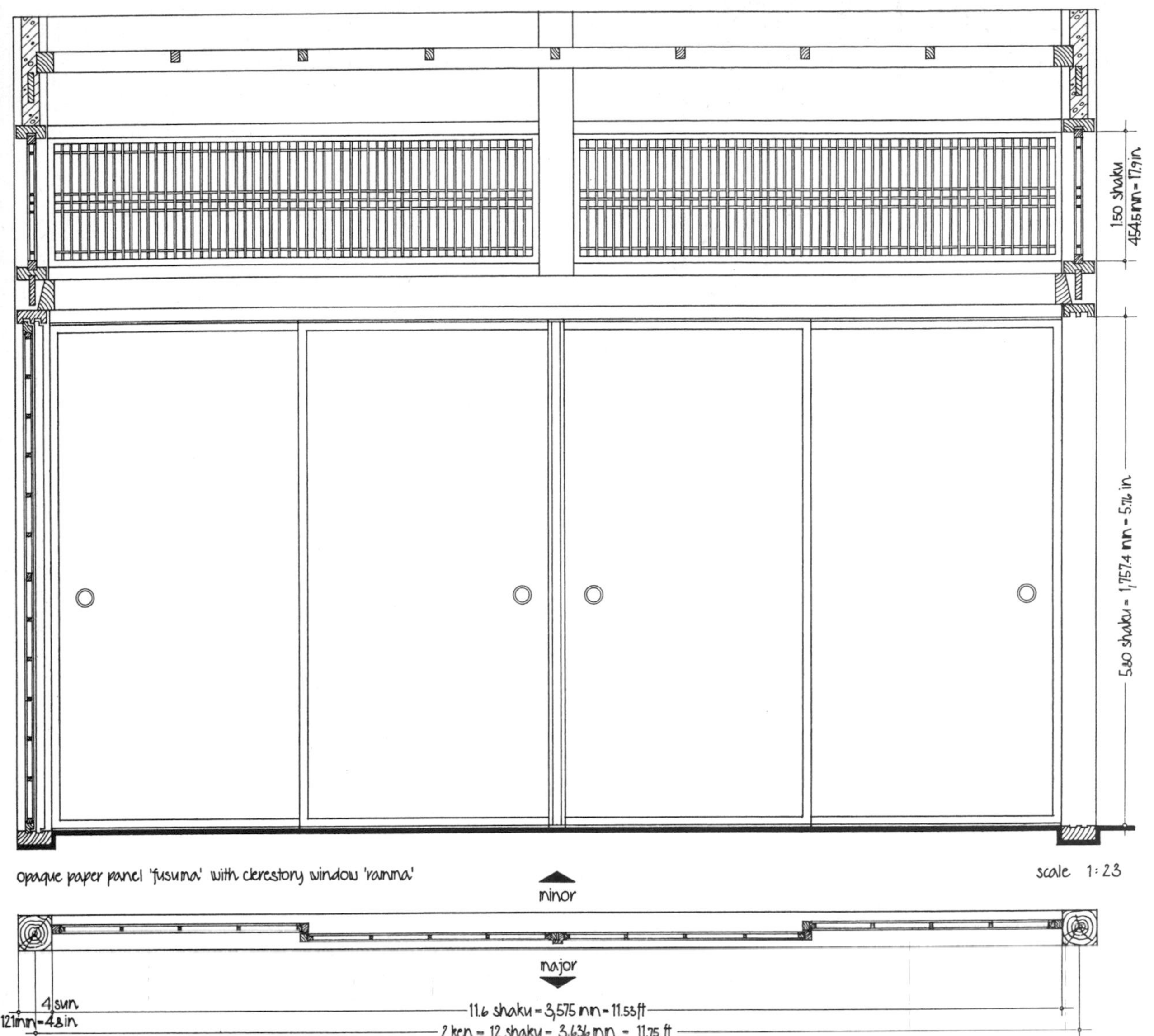

FIGURE 46: Opaque paper panels, *fusuma*, in wall opening.

Simplicity of response to the constructional problem is demonstrated in each detail. Friction from sliding is reduced by having only the sides of the struts in contact with the upper track, and by having the grooves in the lower track just deep enough to keep the panel in position. Additional sliding panels that run in the vertical tracks of the *shōji* frame are joined so exactly that the smaller ones are held at any height by mere friction and do not require more than a light touch of a finger to be moved up or down. Larger units are provided with a simple bamboo spring to increase the friction. Of course, with age and use the minutely dressed joinings wear out; door panels chink open and shake in their track at the slightest breeze. But it is as inexpensive as it is simple to buy a replacement on the market, and there are Japanese who feel emotionally attracted, even touched, at the sight of an old, wornout and fragile *shōji*.

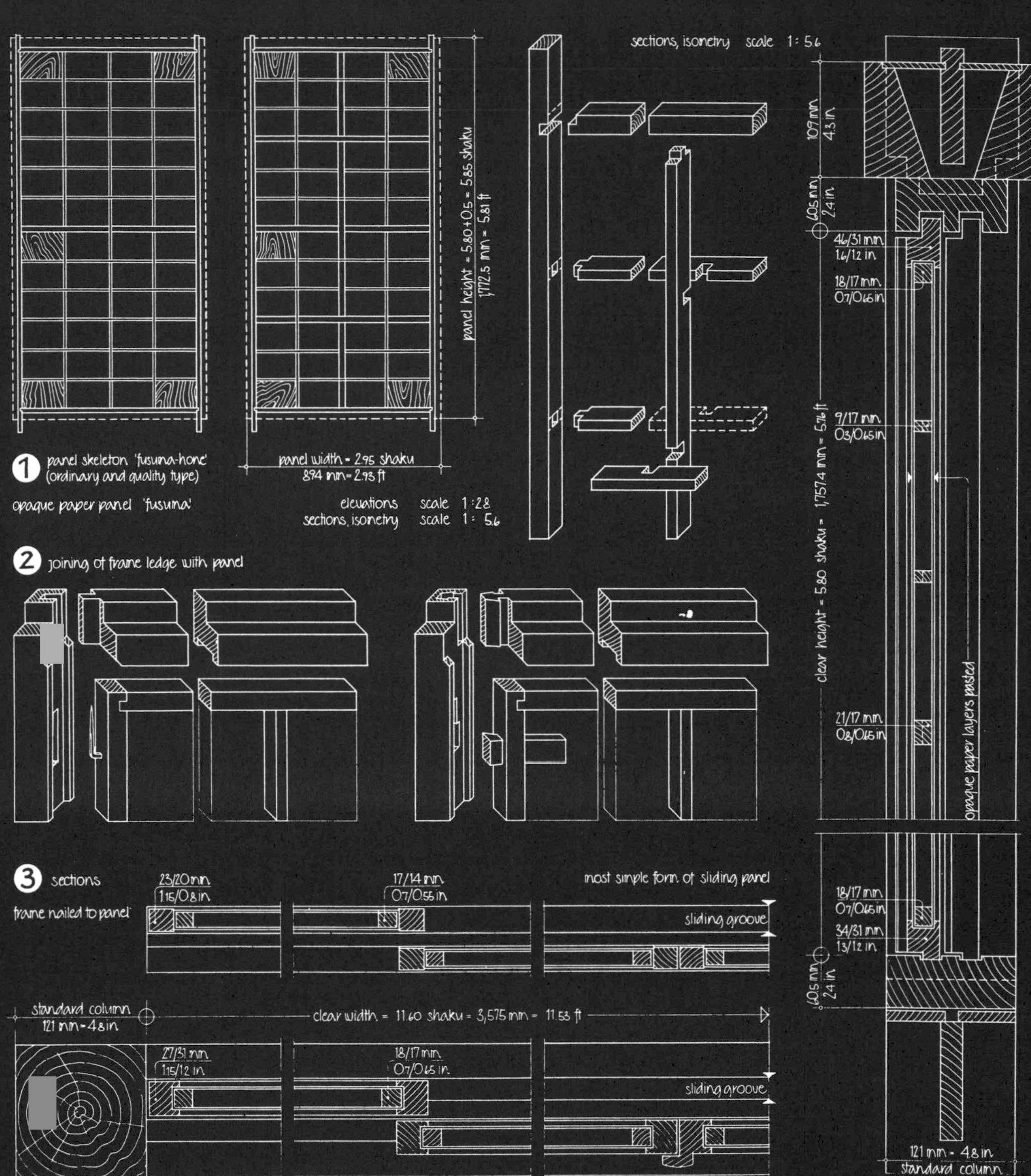

FIGURE 47: **Construction details of opaque paper panels, *fusuma*.**

opaque paper panel

The opaque paper panel which constitutes both room partition and room door in the house organism is called *fusuma*. Its constructional system closely resembles that of the translucent paper panel, *shōji,* in that it consists of a light wooden frame stiffened by thin wooden strips that are arranged in a rectangular pattern. Yet, while in the case of *shōji* this structural skeleton is pasted only on one side with translucent paper, the *fusuma* wood grid is covered on both sides by heavy opaque paper and additionally framed all the way around by a delicate wooden ledge that is frequently lacquered.

Since both *shōji,* the translucent sliding panel, and *fusuma,* the opaque sliding panel, have a common origin, the latter's evolution from standing screen to sliding panel, as mentioned before, does not differ in essence from the translucent variety. But, whereas the translucent paper panel underwent an essential metamorphosis in regard to function and application (and has gained a quality that proved decisive in the evolution of many distinct features of the Japanese residence), the opaque sliding panel, *fusuma,* because of its utilitarian function and decorative role, has preserved the original nature it had at the time it was imported from China. Otherwise, as to standardization of panels, dimensioning of wood, organization of panels together, etc., *fusuma* is modeled after the same factors as is the translucent paper panel, *shōji.*

Outstanding again is the extreme lightness of the structural skeleton. The frame, as a rule, is only 5.5 x 6.0 *bu* but there are also skeletons with frames of only 4.5 x 5.5 *bu* (14 x 17 mm. = 9/16 x 11/16 in.). Rigidity of this light frame is achieved by the same type of interior wooden grid that is used in the *shōji.* The wooden strips are no stronger than 5.5 x 3 *bu* (17 x 9 mm. = 10/16 x 6/16 in.), sometimes even only 4.5 x 3 *bu.* In better-quality panels, rigidity is improved by using stronger members in the middle, both horizontally and vertically. The number of those members is the only means of distinguishing the constructional quality of *fusuma,* a difference hardly worth mentioning as far as Western architecture is concerned, where difference in personal wealth is much more clearly manifested in the quality of construction.

The sliding panels in the Japanese house characteristically demonstrate an unstable state of equilibrium of architectural fundamentals, a compromise between factors opposed to each other in their requirements but again depending on each other for their effects: constructional stability, utilitarian convenience, aesthetic proportion, material economy. Optimum exploitation of each factor has produced a state of unstable equilibrium so liable to topple if one factor just slightly leaves the area dictated by the ensemble of all the others. If, for example, constructional stability were improved, not only utilitarian convenience would suffer because of increased weight, but also aesthetic proportion and material economy would fade. Or if too much consideration were given to utilitarian convenience by reducing the panel weight, then conversely, the quality of all other factors would be encroached upon many times. The highest possible exploitation of all factors concerned and the resulting fragile state of harmony are true refinement for which the Japanese house is justly famed.

As the Japanese also cannot entirely escape the general human ambition of displaying monetary wealth in their dwellings, the *fusuma* offers an opportunity to do so with its thick paper capable of receiving a printed pattern, a mural, or calligraphic work, or through the color of the wooden ledge. In this instance, the Japanese house, which in general lacks any manifestation of wealth distinction other than by the quality of material and the size of building, clearly permits a clue as to the wealth of the owner.

windows

Since *shōji,* the translucent paper panel, principally fulfills the functions ordinarily performed in Western architecture by windows, the relative amount of actual window area, *mado,* is small in the Japanese house. Yet, there are numerous standard types, each of which plays a definite, and occasionally necessary, role in the whole organism, thus contradicting the allegation that the window is but an inferior component. Rather, it might be said that because of its quantitative limitation, it attracts marked attention when used and thus is frequently applied where architectural accentuation is desired. Therefore, in addition to its role as an architectural medium to facilitate ventilation, to provide light, and to allow view to the outside, as the Western window does, it constitutes an architectural feature in its own right, to be seen and appreciated as an object of aesthetic quality rather than as a mere expression of architectural necessity.

The window with low sill, *hijikake-mado* (literally, elbow-rest window), is used on the exterior walls of living rooms and does not differ essentially in construction, organization, appearance, and purpose from the translucent paper panel, *shōji*, except that it does not serve as a passage.

As the interior of the Japanese house is short in providing space (such as shelving) for storing continuously used utensils, bay windows, *de-mado* (literally, projected window) are arranged in the kitchen or living room in order to provide additional surface as table or shelf. The extent of projection varies from I.5 *shaku* to a mere doubling of the width of the lower wooden track beyond the wall plane, and also the height of the lower track is not fixed but ranges from 1.2 *shaku* to 3.5 *shaku*.

The function of the window with high sill, *taka-mado* (literally, high window), is limited to ventilation and illumination. As such, it is used mainly in utility rooms such as the kitchen, bath, toilet, etc., usually on the outside walls but also sometimes on walls toward the corridor. Though much smaller than the *hijikake-mado*, the constructional-organizational system of these translucent sliding panels in tracks is quite similar to that of the *shōji*.

The form of the flame-shaped window, *katō-mado* (literally, firelight window), which is also called *andon-mado*, is almost alien to the whole composition of rectangular planes, linear construction, and geometrically simple forms, and suggests that its major function is of a decorative nature. It is a rather common sight in shrines and temples, while its use in the residence is confined to the wealthier class who can afford to accentuate the place of the picture recess, *tokonoma*, by an ornamental window and a more effective light source than could be provided by a simple sliding door, *shōji*.

The corner pattern window, *tsunogara-mado*, and the circular window, *maru-mado*, also obtained their names because of their distinctive shapes. The shape of the former is a very characteristic feature of Japanese architecture, and with its clear distinction of horizontal and vertical frame members, reflects a very fine sense of structure and proportion. Both these window forms are primarily used in tearooms and sometimes in the entrance hall and reception room.

The lattice window, *koshi-mado* (literally, grating window), exists in three different forms: flush with the wall surface like *hijikake-mado*; projected on cantilevers like *de-mado*; or projected on stilts that perch on foundation stones. Its characteristic feature is a wooden latticework which permits the removal of the translucent sliding panels behind it for ventilation purposes or for viewing, yet without permitting sight from the outside in. This window type therefore is used in living rooms facing the street and, therefore, mainly in the city houses where living rooms often must face a very close roadside.

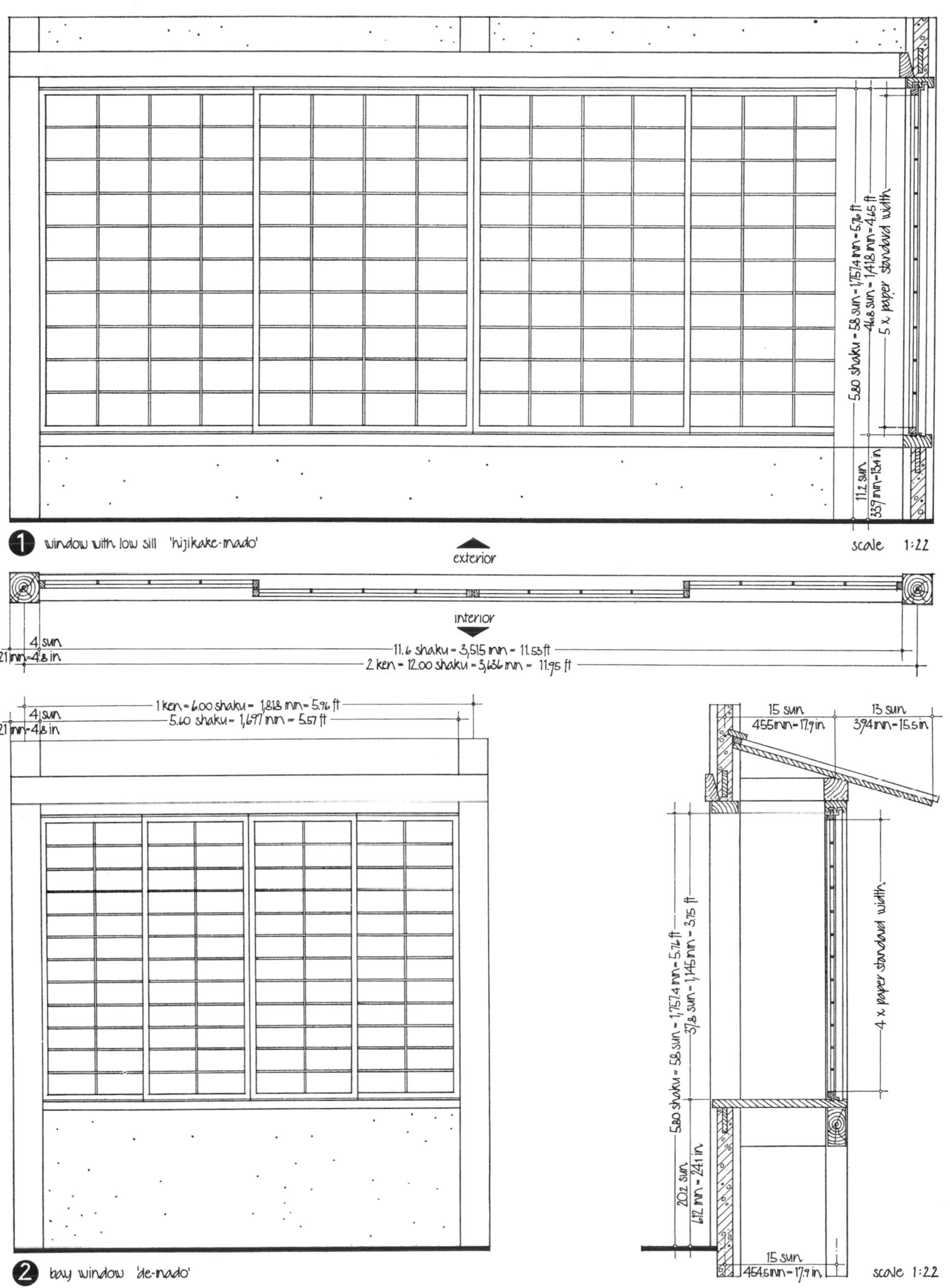

FIGURE 48: Window types and their construction details.

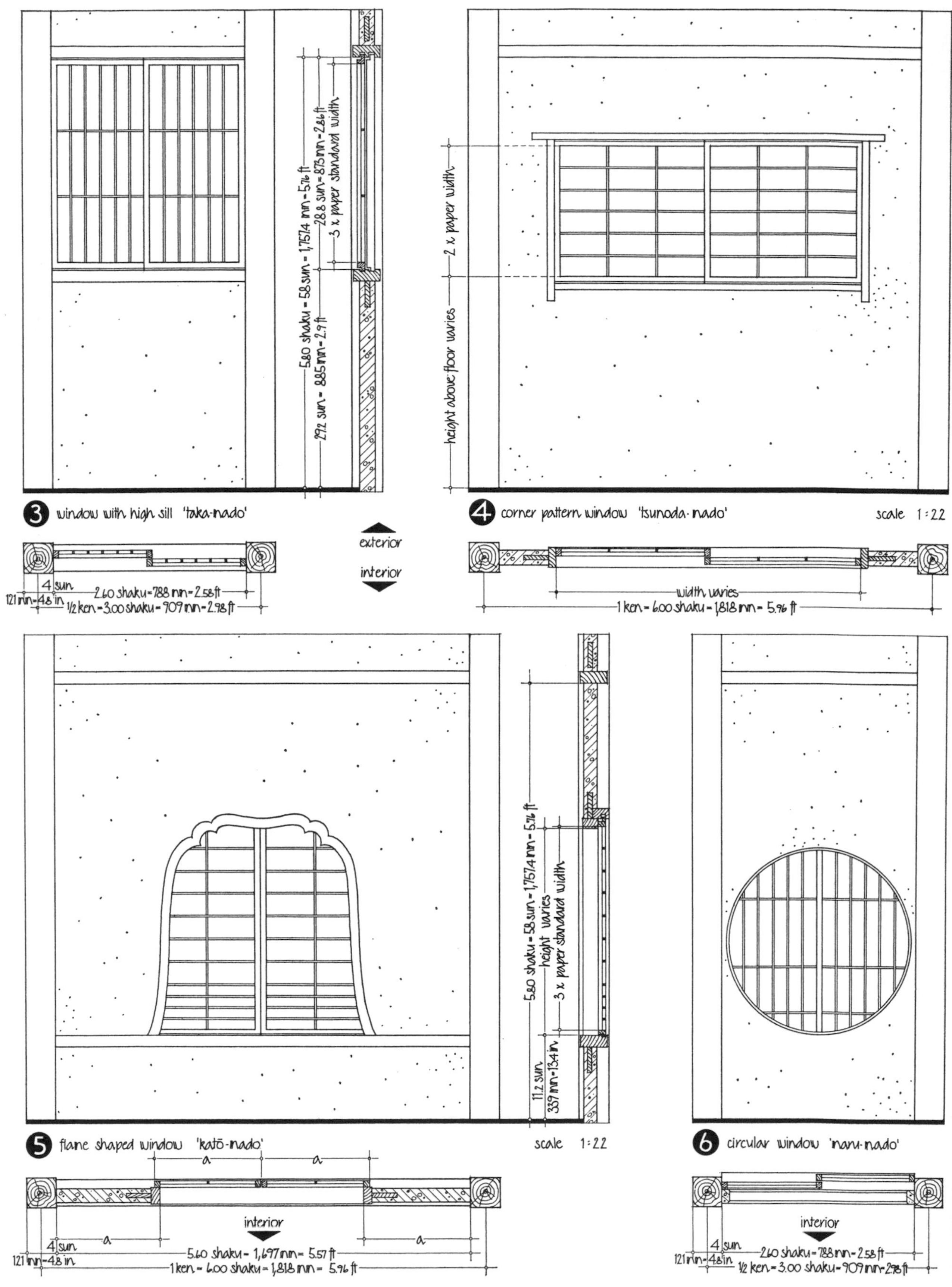

FIGURE 48 (continued): Window types and their construction details.

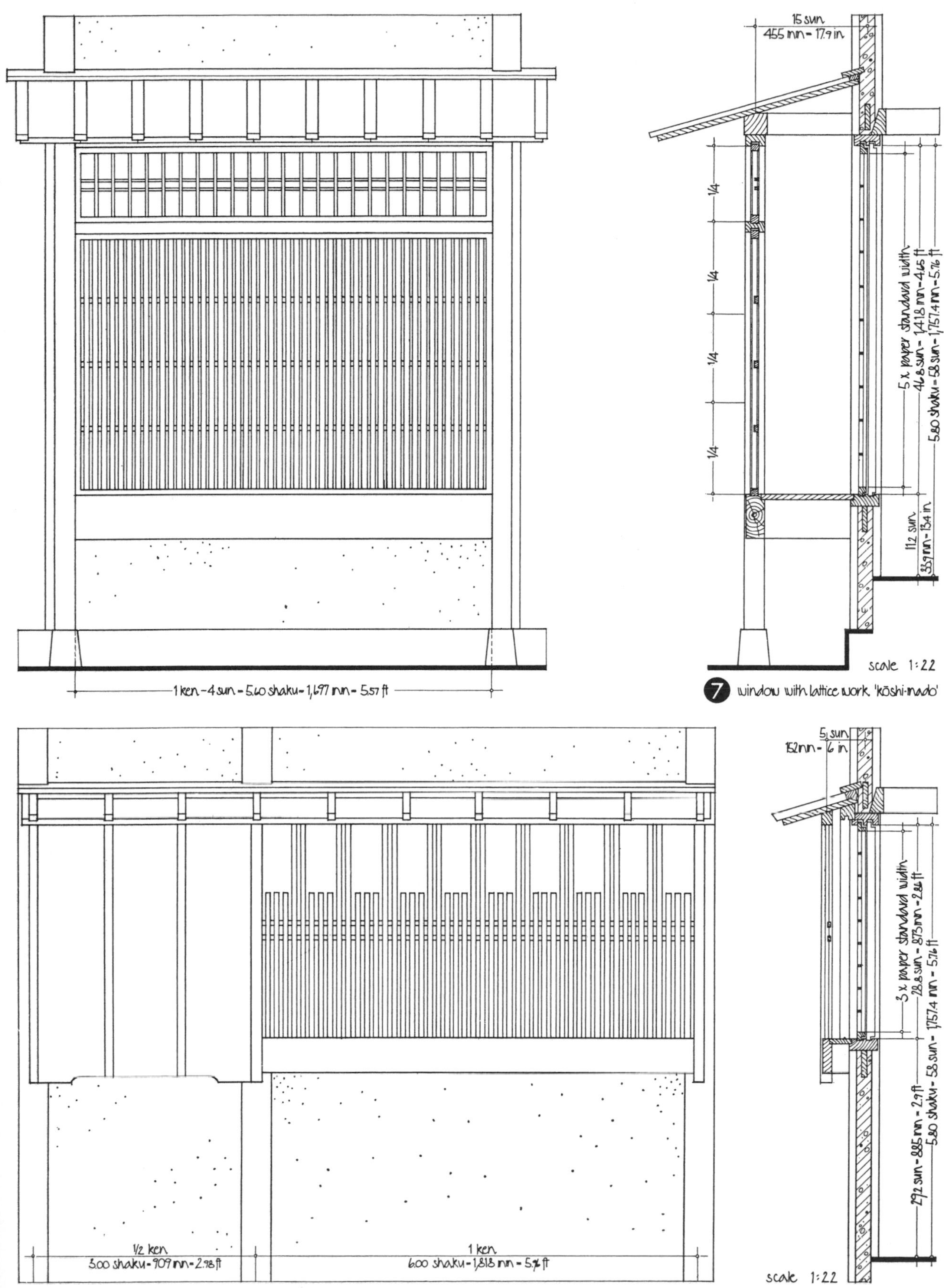

FIGURE 48 (continued): Window types and their construction details.

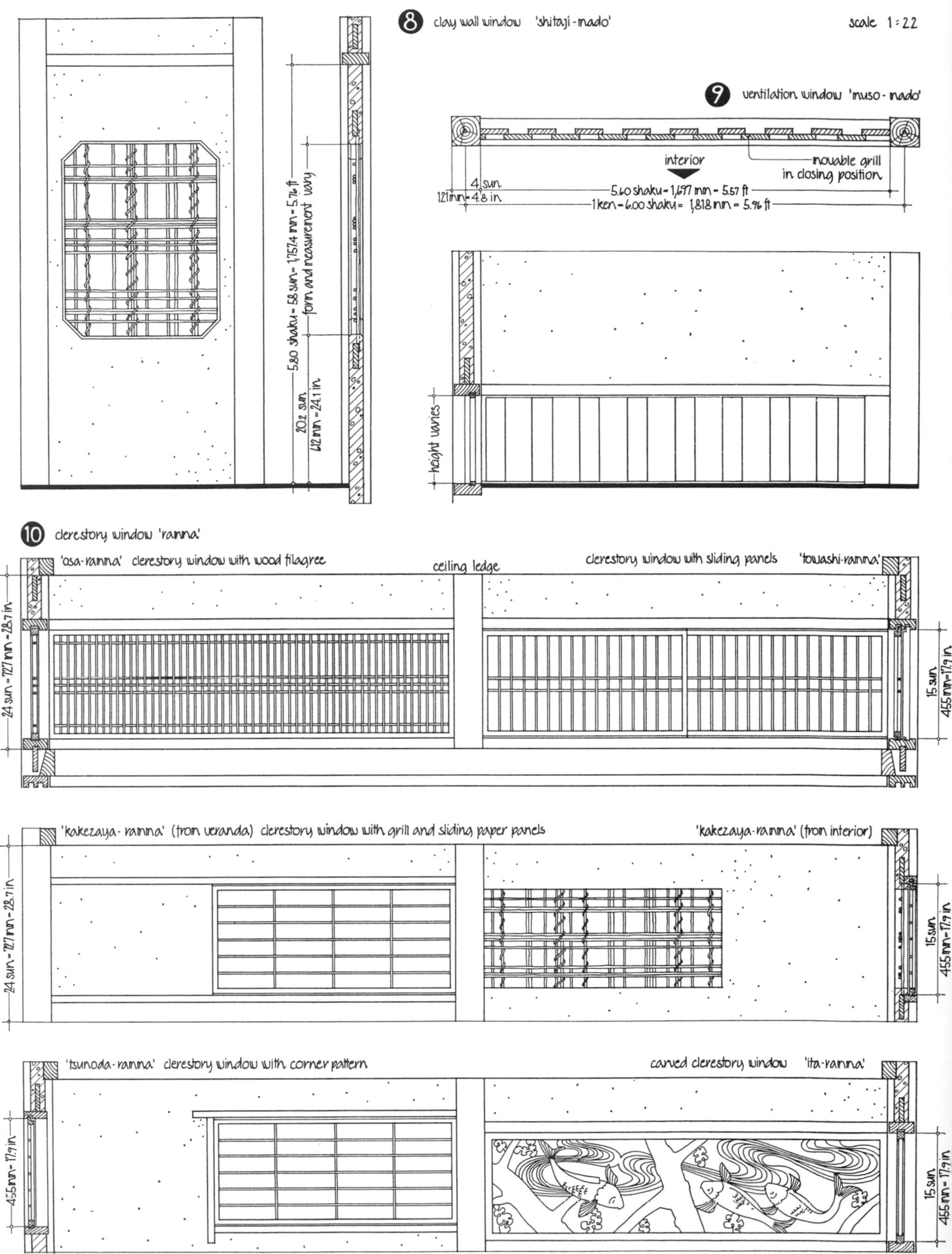

FIGURE 48 (continued): Window types and their construction details.

The clay-wall window, *shitaji-mado* (literally, under the earth window), is modeled into the solid clay wall; the choice of its form is left up to the personal taste of the owner. Geometrically pure forms have evolved that are supplied with an elaborate grill of bamboo, reed, or young branches. It is said that the famous tea master, Sen no-Rikyu (1518–91), developed this type of window for the tearoom after having been stimulated by the sight of a farm hut where the wall openings simply had been broken into the clay wall, exposing the wall's bamboo skeleton. The window is used preferably in tearooms or, with strong decorative accent, next to the picture recess, *tokonoma*.

The functional system of the ventilation window, *musō-mado* (literally, unequal window), also called *renji-mado* (window with parallel batons) or *musha-mado* (soldier window) is based on two grills with vertical wooden strips, the clear space between the strips being equal to the width of each strip. While the exterior grid is stationary in the frame, the interior one can be moved in tracks of the same frame either to the left or right, thereby either closing or opening the slits of the exterior grid. It serves mainly as ventilation in toilet, bath, and storage space, but if used in the exterior shutters, *amado,* it also permits a view to the outside without having to open the protective shutter, an advisable precaution if the night is late and the caller unknown.

Primarily in order to permit air circulation, but also to provide additional light to the farther side of the room, the wall portion between the frieze rail, *uchinori-nageshi,* and the ceiling is frequently left open and provided with a wooden grill pattern, *ramma* (literally, space for *ran,* a type of wood), similar to a clerestory window. Here a constructional, practical device stimulated decorative utilization, and the many forms and formations in which the clerestory window has emerged suggest that the decorative quality is no longer a secondary attribute.

Ramma is employed above the opaque paper panels between two rooms, above the translucent paper panels between living room and veranda, above the main door of the entrance hall, above the glass panels of the enclosed veranda, and above the translucent paper panels of the study-place window. Frequently, in addition to a wooden grill, the opening is furnished with translucent paper panels to check excessive air circulation. Sometimes the clerestory window fills the entire space between the frieze rail and the ceiling, but normally it is inserted into the clay wall.

In addition to the "study-place window," *shoin-mado,* and the "chicken-heart window" of the wooden shutter, *okubyō-mado,* which will be mentioned later at the respective places, there are still other window forms. But they constitute variations of the forementioned basic types rather than variety. The interesting and almost paradoxical fact is that though the application of windows in the Japanese house is limited in proportion to other features, they nevertheless have emerged in so many essentially different types. The reason for this somehow astonishing phenomenon is that the window's function is neither dictated by mere necessity nor is it in each case clearly defined and singular. Rather, its purpose changes with location and produces, together with frequently dominating decorative functions, many differing states of architectural demand, each eliciting a different response.

7 constructions for spiritual spaces

picture recess

It has been stated that the Japanese room, like the house as a whole, lacks accentuation of one side or one direction other than that effected through orientation to sun and environment. Unlike Western residences, rooms are not axially organized by obvious location of entrance-exit and by placement of furniture, nor is the sequence of rooms defined by a gradation from minor to major. Such will certainly be the impression received while passing through a sequence of several rooms, all controlled by sameness of scale, material, feature, and treatment. Yet, to the Japanese the spiritual center of the house is the picture recess, *tokonoma,* or abbreviated, *toko.* Not only does such a focusing of esteem exist psychologically, but as is evidenced in the construction of the ceiling, this orientation of room and house to *tokonoma* is also physically manifested through spatial organization and constructional detail. Here, as a single instance in the Japanese house, additive decoration is displayed in the form of a hanging picture scroll, *kakejiku,* and a flower in a simple vase below it, giving an excellent example of the increase in effect through limitation of motif.

While the undisputed aesthetic significance of the picture recess and its controversial historic background will be examined later, at this time it only needs to be mentioned that *tokonoma* is not a mere form of décor with a questionable architectural integrity, but is simply a part of the basic stuff of which the Japanese residence is composed. Indeed, it is a strong statement of the spiritual-aesthetic significance of building and dwelling, which is unique for Japan. Just as the origin of *tokonoma* is multiple—varying with the eager opinion of the scholar—so too its conclusive meaning in the ordinary dwelling is not but one. Display place for a piece of art, sacred place of an admittedly uncertain relation to Buddhism, honorable place for defining the seat of the distinguished guest, all of these have supposedly in the past had their separate architectural expressions but have streamed together and, each of them contributing its own significant distinction to one singular statement, have resulted in one of the most dynamic achievements of Japanese residential architecture.

The *tokonoma* is also subjected to the modular order of design (based on 1 *ken* = 1,818 mm. = 6 ft.). It is usually recessed ½ *ken* and extends over a length of 1 *ken,* thus occupying a bay of 3 x 6 feet (909 x 1,818 mm.). The floor of this recess is differentiated from the room's mat floor either by a separate level or a different material, or both. In case the difference is in level, the recessed space is marked by a raised threshold, *toko-gamachi,* which in its traditional execution is lacquered in black. Since the floor area behind the threshold corresponds with the standard mat size, the flooring may consist of a single mat, but more frequently a boarded floor, *ita-datami,* slightly lower than the threshold, is provided, which is covered with a thin straw carpet, *usuberi;* or the boarding itself remains the final floor surface, either in one single piece or several joined together. The height of the crossbeam above, *otoshigake,* differs markedly from the standard height of all the other wall openings, sharply interrupting the circumferential frieze rail, *uchinori-nageshi,* and effecting through a bold break of continuity an architectural accentuation which could not be stronger if more elaborate and extensive means were employed. It supports the wall above and has, as a rule, a square section.

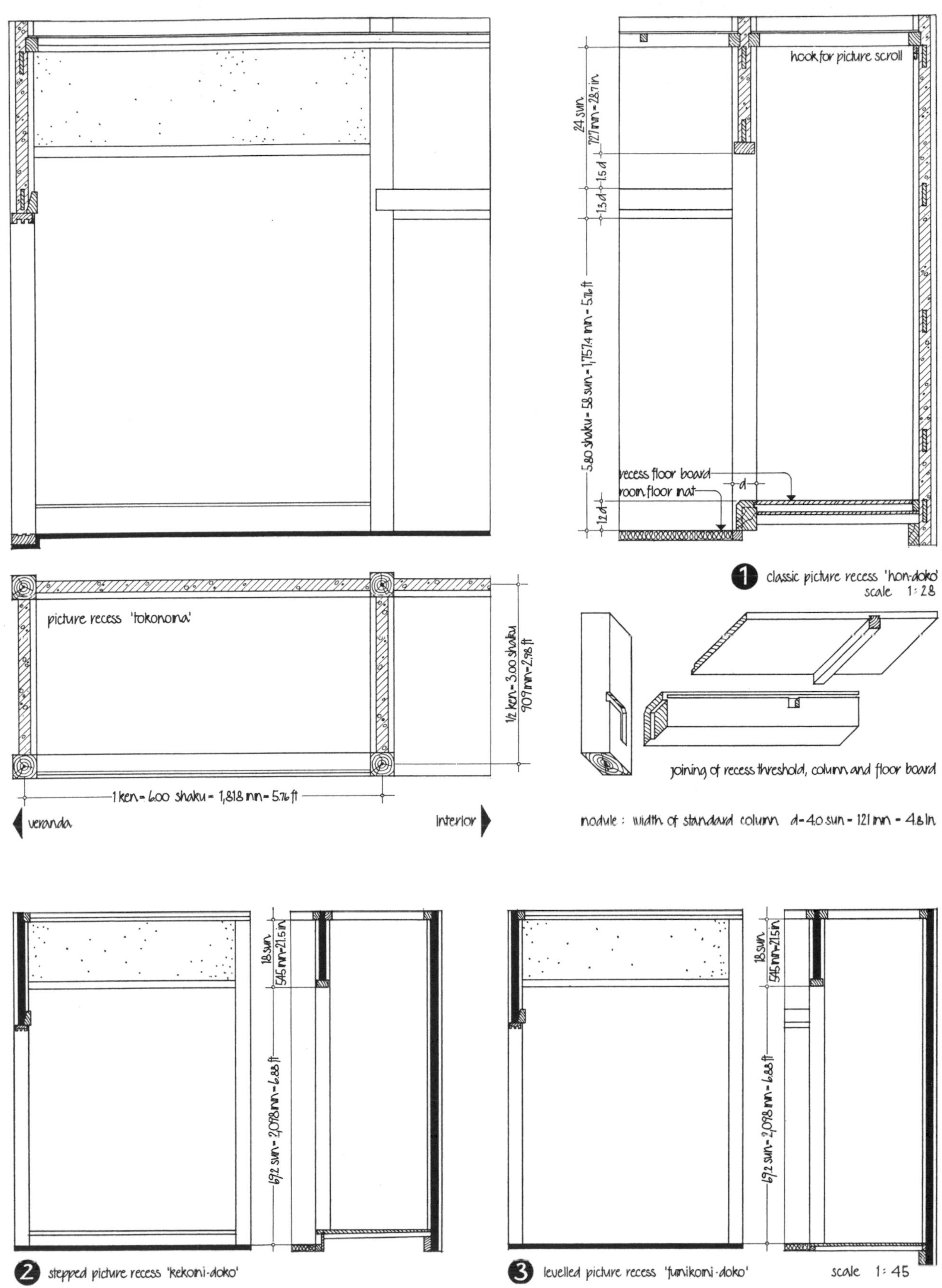

FIGURE 49: Typical forms of picture recess, *tokonoma*, and their construction.

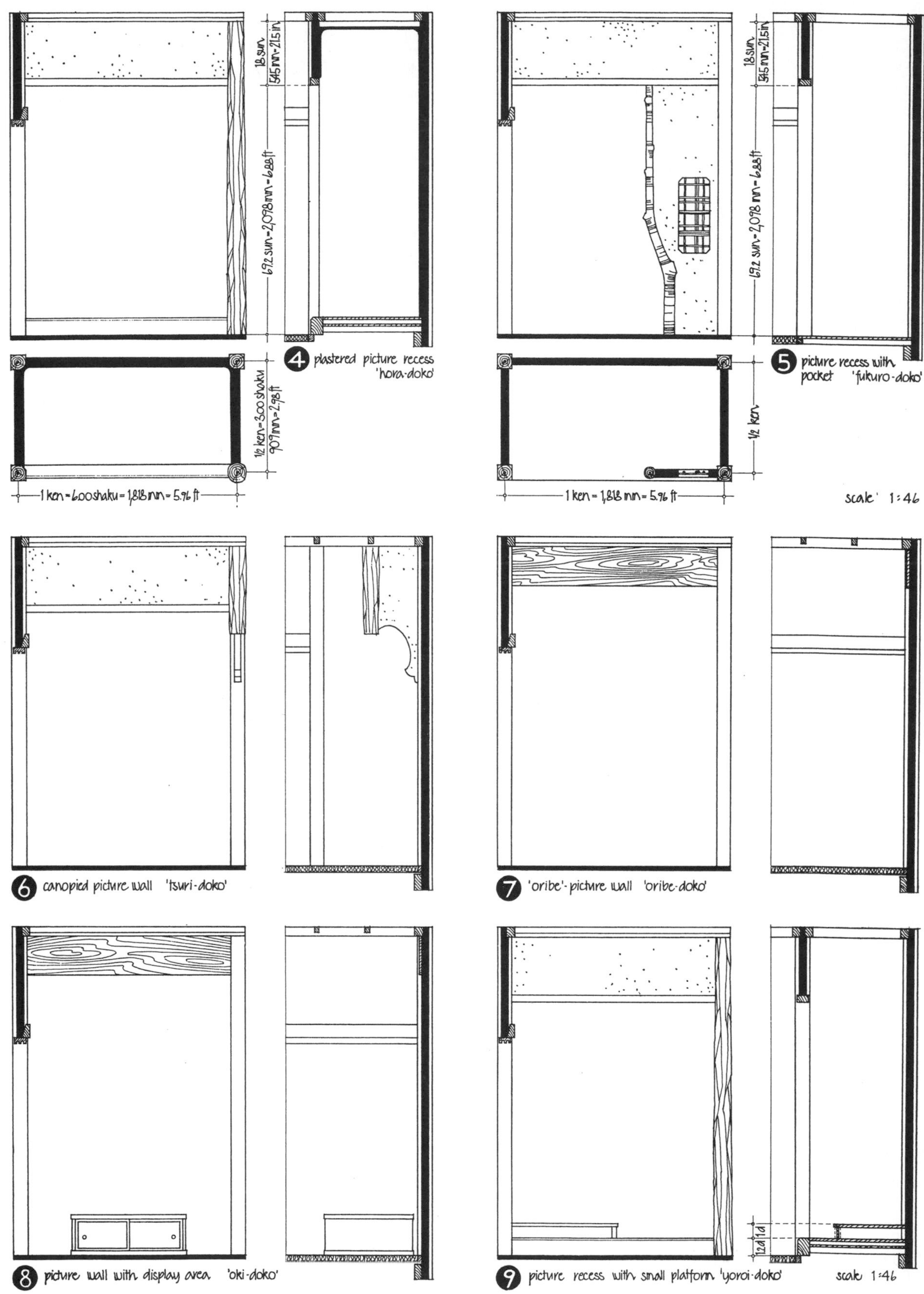

FIGURE 49 (continued): Typical forms of picture recess, *tokonoma*.

One side of the recess borders the outside wall of the room through which light enters, while on the interior side another recess, *tana* or *tokowaki,* which contains wall shelves and cabinets arranged in various ways, is aligned. The partition between the two recesses consists of a solid wall piece with a column, *tokobashira,* at the front. In the archaic performance, the section of this recess column is square and is of identical material and appearance to that of the other columns in the room. However, occasionally this member, like many another in the *tokonoma,* is altered for satisfaction of a personal liking, although hardly to the improvement of expression; and exquisite woods of particular grain and shape are widely used. At the back wall directly under the ceiling ledge, a minute wooden strip is attached which contains a metal hook for hanging the picture scroll, *kakejiku.* While the walls of the recess are formed by materials and methods identical to those of the solid walls of the room, the ceiling of the *tokonoma* is distinct from the room ceiling, thus completing the multiple measures taken to distinguish this place from the rest of the room.

Like all components in the Japanese house that have a certain optical-decorative implication, such as the window and the ceiling, so too the *tokonoma* has emerged in various forms. Again, all the variations, as could be expected, have been largely standardized, although the *tokonoma* in the tearoom has always remained the object of invention and innovation.

In addition to the types depicted, there are also many other variations which may produce new details, but hardly new aspects. However, the archaic, and probably most pure, design of the *tokonoma* employed materials and forms of a kind not different from those used in the entire dwelling. The architectural task, so to speak, was to create additional space reserved solely for a piece of art and to distinguish the spiritual importance of its location. The immediate and bold-simple way of responding to this demand in the classic way without any elaborate artistic means was architectural accentuation in its best and strongest form. Yet, man's wish for individuality and his inclination toward extravagance wherever means permit did not exempt the Japanese, and the use of exquisite woods along with a preference for odd shapes has somewhat falsified that pure effect of the classic *tokonoma.*

shelving recess

Since the picture recess, *tokonoma,* as a rule does not occupy the entire room width, another recess, which is usually furnished with decorative shelves and cabinets, is placed to one side. Adjoining the *tokonoma* at the end toward the house interior, this shelving recess is to be interpreted as an integral part of the picture recess rather than as an independent architectural feature. Yet, there are houses in which the decorative shelving recess is replaced by the more useful closet, the *oshiire.*

The decorative shelving recess is called *tana,* a name that was given to it because the recess contains built-in shelves called *tana* in Japanese. Frequently the name *chigai-dana* is also used. This, however, refers to a particular order of shelving most commonly used in the ordinary houses. Another identification, *tokowaki* (literally, side of the *toko*), designates its adjoining location to the picture recess. It is separated from the latter by a shieldlike solid wall of clay which is defined at the front by the previously mentioned column, the *tokobashira.* The parting wall has, as a rule, a bamboo grid window admitting light from the outside across the picture recess and into the shelving alcove, which otherwise would be left quite dark.

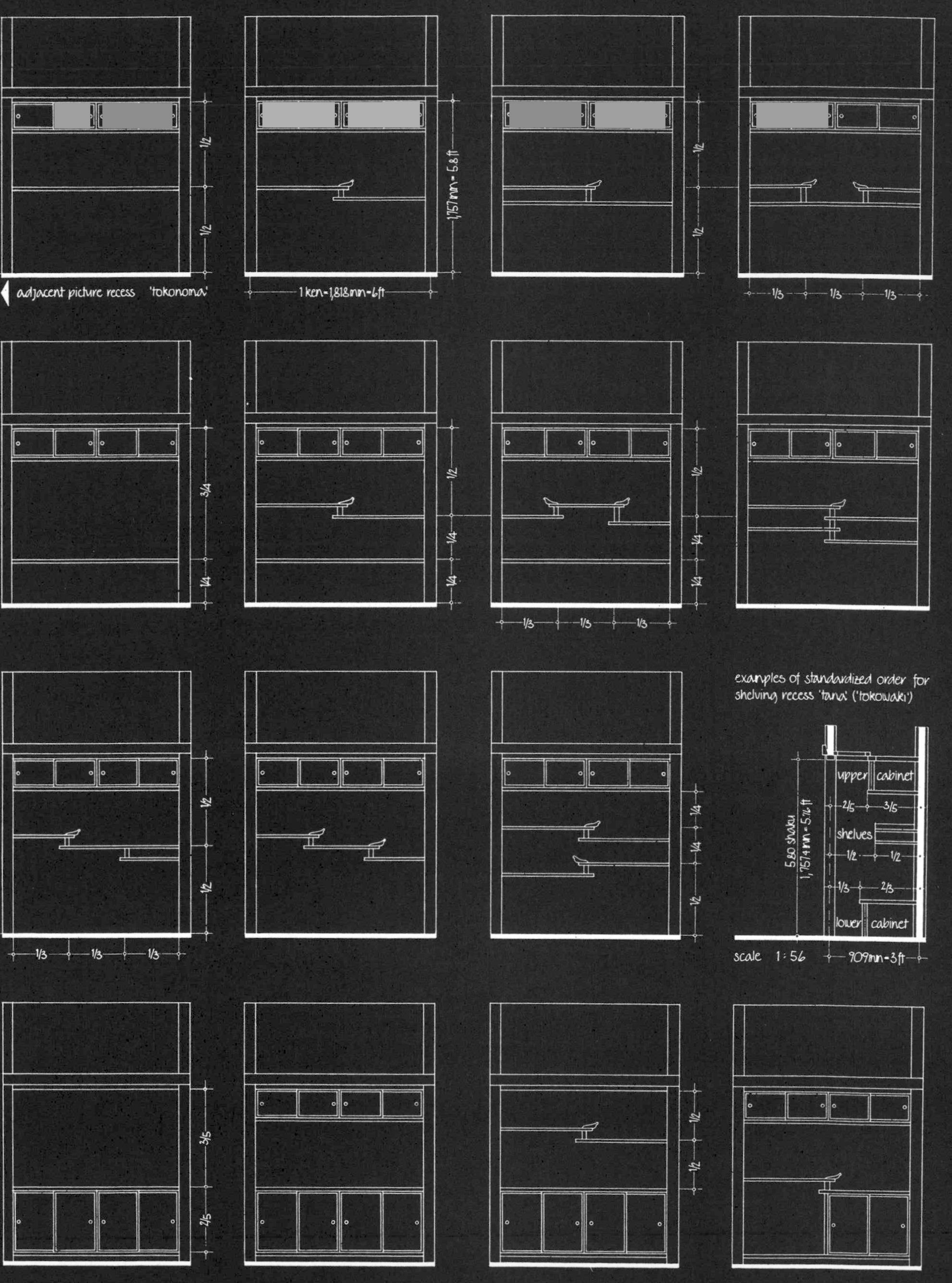

FIGURE 50: Typical forms of shelving recess, *tana*.

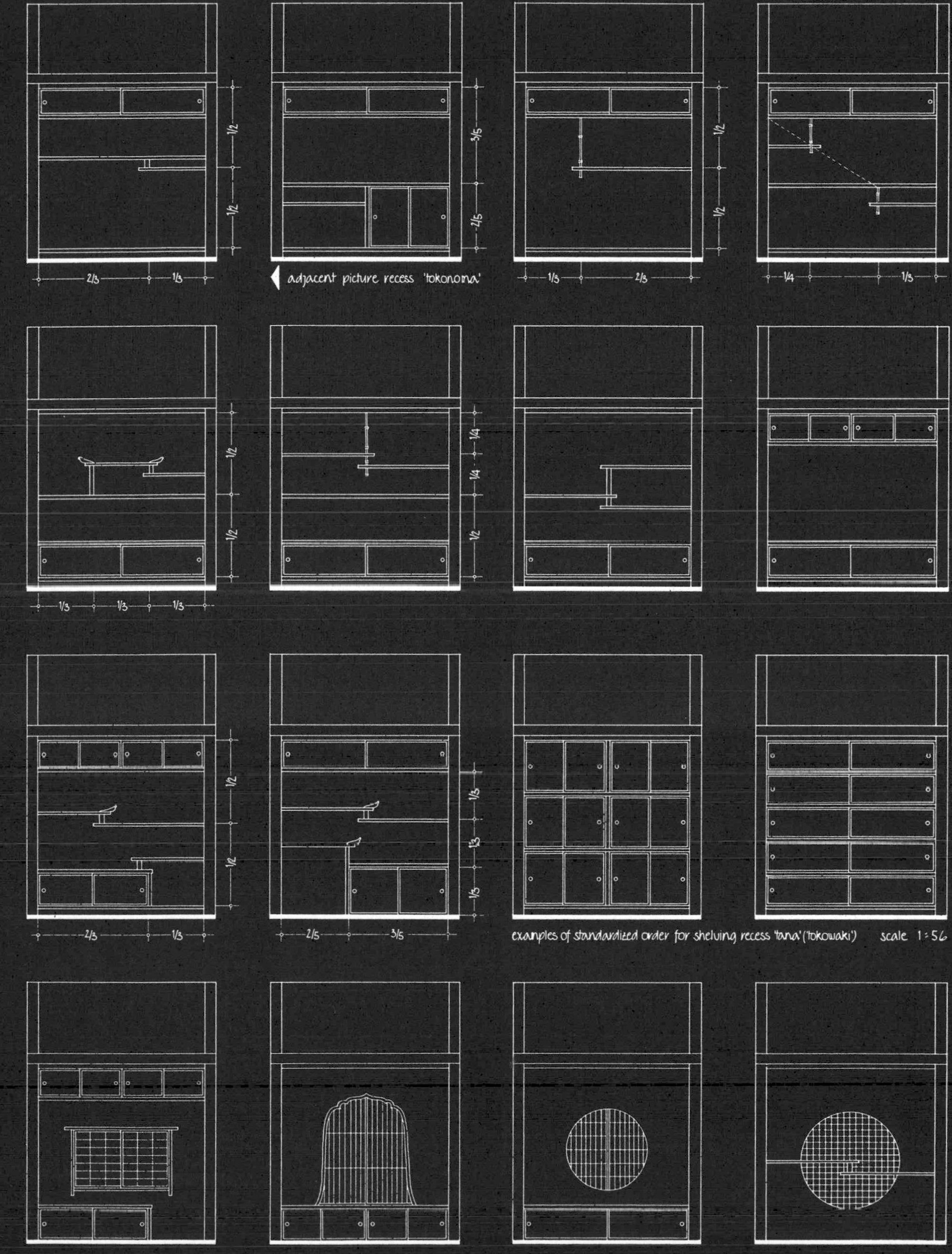

FIGURE 50 (continued): Typical forms of shelving recess, *tana*.

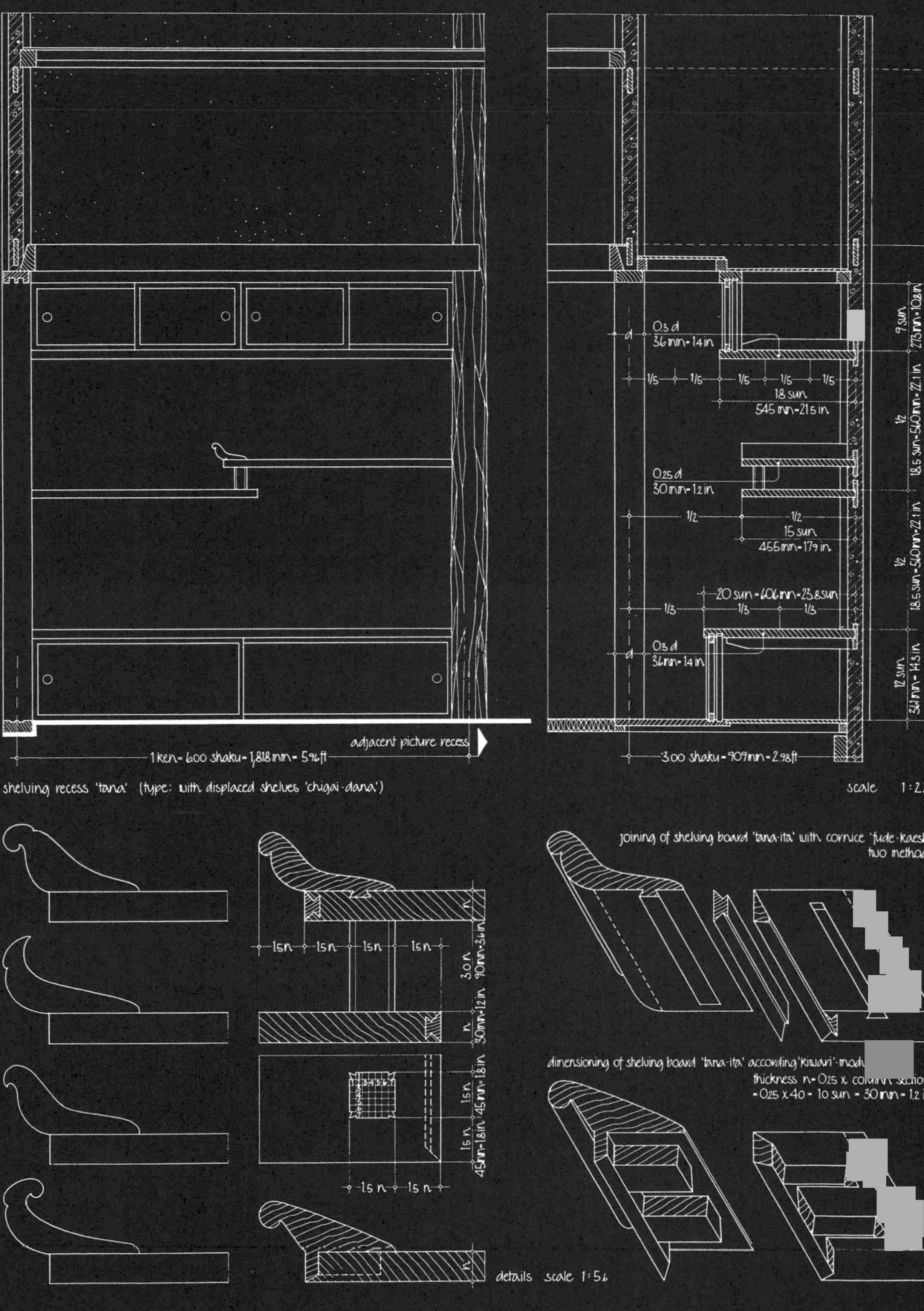

FIGURE 51: Construction of shelving recess, *tana*, and cornice details.

It is said that the origin of the *tana* dates back to the 10th and 11th centuries, at the time of the *shinden* style, when a similar kind of cabinet which was not yet built-in but was designed as a portable unit was already in use. Although utilitarian in origin, the shelf arrangement, by being placed at the picture recess and by becoming combined with the latter, inevitably changed into a decorative element, while its original function as a container for utensils was no longer of primary concern.

Thus, having changed not in form but in function to a decorative piece, the shelving recess, *tana,* has produced more organizational varieties than any other feature in the house. All of them have been classified, denominated, and put into woodblock prints at the disposal of every carpenter in the country. Yet, such a particular concern for the *tana* does not necessarily imply an affirmation of its architectural quality. On the contrary, in many cases the wish for originality led design to petty absurdities which harmed the unity of expression that distinguished the interior of the Japanese dwelling.

The shelving recess, usually covering an area of 3 x 6 ft. (909 x 1,818 mm.), is, like the picture recess, incorporated into the house organization by being synchronized with the universal beat of the *ken* module. Yet, contrary to the picture recess, it is tied to the room order by being assimilated into the circumferential frieze rail, which also braces the top of the door and window tracks. Thus, the *tana,* as a physical feature, is to be considered a component adjusted to its neighborhood rather than a component contrasting to it as some *tana* patterns tend to suggest.

Both floor and ceiling consist of a wooden plank, the latter at the same height as the frieze rail, while the back and side walls consist of the same clay used in the room itself. Constituent parts of *tana* are cantilevered shelves attached to the back wall. If cabinets with sliding panels are incorporated, they are fixed in height of the frieze rail above or below at the floor, or both. These members extend to only a part of the depth of the recess, thus preserving the effect of one niche. Their dimensions and relationship to each other are standardized to the minutest detail in a precise ratio to the standard column section (4 *sun* = 121 mm. = 4.8 in.) and are coordinated with the *ken* module. Exactness and accuracy of joinery ranks with the finest cabinetwork. Sculptural treatment is given in particular to the wooden cornice, *fude-kaeshi* (literally, writing brush returner), which accentuates the end of the upper shelf when the freely projecting form is employed. Here also the profiles have become standardized, and the carpenter makes use of them rather than engaging in the development of new forms.

The most distinct and probably most frequently employed type of *tana* is the *chigai-dana,* the recess with displaced shelves. More than one hundred different types of *tana* have emerged, all catalogued, yet hardly requiring complete recording at this place. It suffices to state that in spite of austere limitation of space, motif, and means such a variety of standard forms could be produced, for such a phenomenon surely contradicts the commonly held opinion that standardization strangles creative design and renders narrow the scope of architectural possibilities. On the contrary, it is evident that standardization of a basic feature and the resulting clear definition of its architectural role in the house organism was the very requisite for freeing all creative forces from entanglement with mere practical-constructional factors, thus allowing full exploitation of architectural potential and development of new form.

However, it must be pointed out that once standardization had exerted its eliminative and sobering effect and had encompassed the entire house the Japanese failed completely in developing new standards, both for living and building, leaving the standards in a medieval state, too perfected and too remote to permit organic transfer to contemporary living and building. Western civilization and technology, although bringing

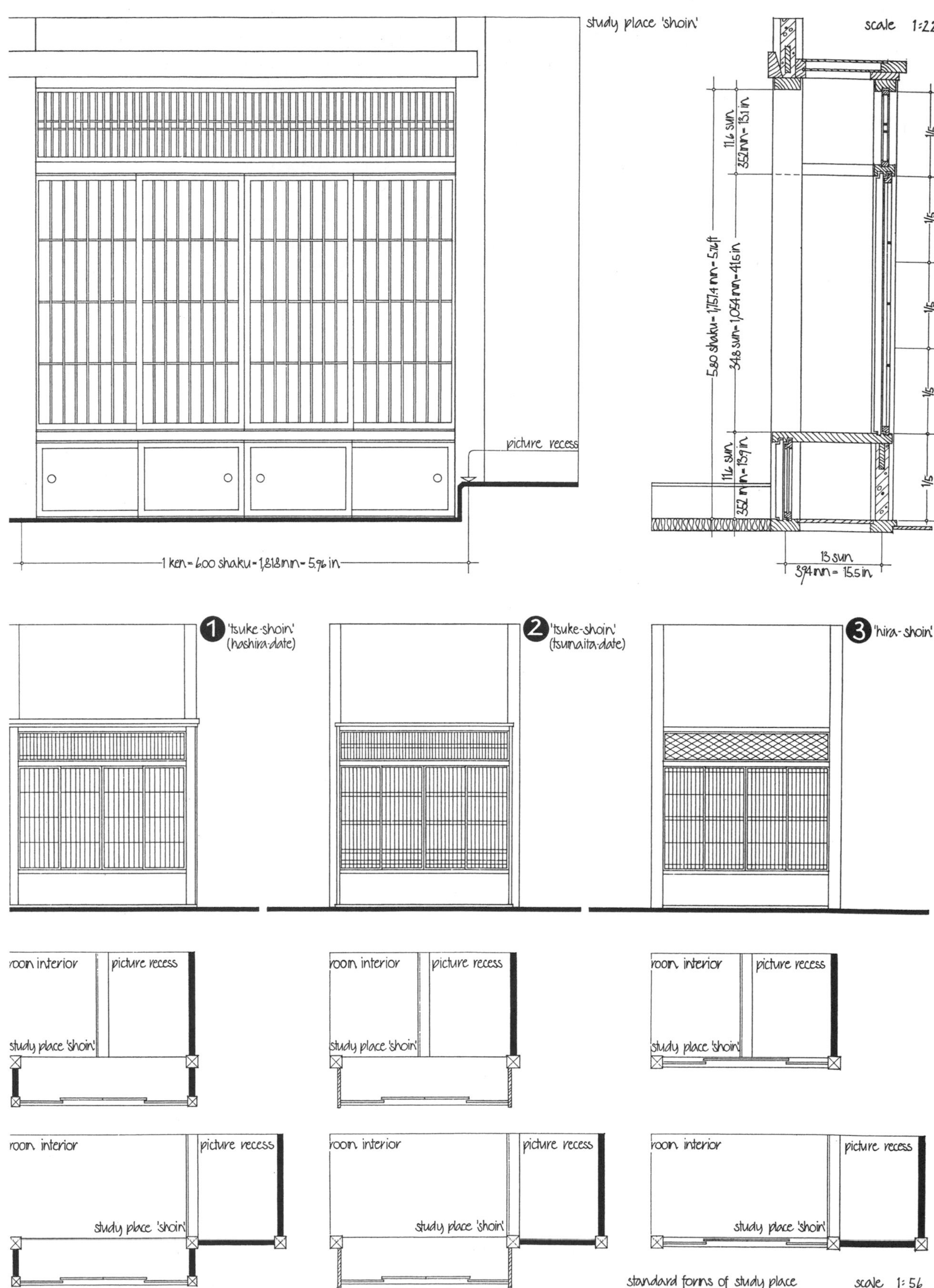

FIGURE 52: Typical forms and construction details of the study place, *shoin*.

conveniences into the house in the form of electric and sanitary installations, furniture, and the like, only created architectural discrepancies in the formerly unique expression and could not satisfactorily bridge the gap between the past and present. On the other hand, the same technology also provided the means for enabling a radically new approach to a contemporary form of dwelling, which Japan's domestic architecture has yet to see.

study place

As utilitarian or even indispensable as devices and components generally are in the Japanese house, some of them have not remained true to their original functional motive. As the picture recess, *tokonoma,* and shelving alcove, *tana,* have exemplified, the Japanese, also, could not quite escape the common architectural trend to decoratively exploit a constructional-utilitarian necessity, gradually bringing about a shift of emphasis from utilitarian to decorative in a manner that preserved the original meaning only in form, but not in function.

A similar transformation can be observed also in another distinctive component in the Japanese residence, the study place, *shoin.* Also here a formerly practical device has become a decorative feature without essentially changing its form. As is the case in the picture recess and shelving alcove, the evolutionof the *shoin* reflects the close architectural interchange between the various social strata—nobility, clergy, warrior, and commoner—which distinguishes the growth of the Japanese residence, and plainly manifests the various backgrounds to which the Japanese house owes its extraordinary character.

Originally a reading place in the house of Buddhist priests of the Zen sect, the *shoin* was projected into the veranda for better light conditions and was elevated for convenient reading. But when re-enacted in the mansions of the nobility and the military; the *shoin* left the private sphere of the house and was performed in the reception room which was reserved for official occasions. With the effacement of the feudal rank distinction in buildings, the merchants adopted this feature for their own representative space in the house and thus made it accessible for the houses of the common people. Here, *shoin* is but a window attached at right angles to the picture recess, *tokonoma,* to which it provides light, and being harmoniously incorporated into the spiritual, decorative organism of *tokonoma* and *tana* (the two recesses) it no longer primarily serves its original purpose as a study place. Still, one can occasionally see the master of the family sitting at the bay and contemplating life while viewing the garden, not unlike the priest who hundreds of years ago wrote his scripts in the *shoin.*

Although exposed to many influences and resulting alterations, the study place, *shoin*, has essentially preserved its original features. The modular grid of *ken* determines the main dimensions of height and width, whereas the baseboard is elevated approximately 1.2 ft. above the floor. The upper frame piece, then, corresponds to the circumferential frieze rail and integrates the bay into the room composition. The upper fourth of the opening is provided with a lattice grill, *ramma*, while the remaining three-fourths of the opening is furnished with four translucent sliding panels, *shōji*. In case the *shoin* is projected as was its original form, the side wall consists of clay or of a thick wooden board, while the space under the table board serves as storage with access through wooden sliding panels either from the inside or from the veranda. In the simplified execution, the *shoin* window is in the same plane as the rest of the wall. Usually it adjoins the picture recess, *tokonoma*, directly in front of the latter's opening to the room, but often the opening of the study place begins at the back wall of the recess and extends ½ *ken* (3 ft.) into the room. Another variation consists in reduction of width; thus, the opening is occasionally only ½ *ken*, with only two sliding panels.

8 house enclosures

wooden shutters

Since the translucent paper panels, *shōji,* which close the various forms of the outside wall openings, actually constitute only a screen against sight but do not extend their shielding function to other unwanted exterior elements, be it wind, cold, and dust, or man with his not always respectable intentions, each opening that leads directly to the outside has, in addition, wooden shutters, *amado* (literally, rain door), which safely and efficiently lock the entire house.

The smallest of the shutters are used for individual windows and during the day are swung up to the rafters if they are hinged, or if suspended by hooks; are simply hung onto other hooks adjacent to the opening. Larger openings are furnished with shutters that run in a single groove next to the translucent paper panels. During the day these shutters, *amado,* are slid back and kept in wooden compartments, *tobukuro* (literally, door container), which are arranged conveniently at one side of the wall opening or at the end of a panel sequence. With fading daylight, these units are drawn from the compartment and are slid along the tracks, sometimes even shifted around corners, to again close the opening. Since they run in a single groove and are all in one plane, the entire wall can be closed by manipulating the panels from the storage space. To lock the panels safely in place, only the last unit taken from the container needs to be bolted into the tracks above and below, thereby arresting the entire sequence of panels. But, since the panels are light and actually could be lifted individually out of their grooves from the outside, they are frequently all bolted to each other.

This is especially advisable in the case of the simple application, when the panels are merely butted to each other. In a better execution, the joining has either a shallow profile or is slightly overlapped. At the bottom, the panels run in grooves of hardwood, and, in the ordinary type, no other means are utilized for reducing friction than an occasional waxing of the grooves. But since the introduction of Western methods, rollers of hard rubber or metal are very common, permitting heavier and stronger shutter construction without affecting maneuverability.

Since in the summer months even at night there is hardly any relief from the moist heat, some of the wooden shutters are provided with a ventilation window, *musō-mado,* which can be opened and closed at will. Another device is a square opening of less than 1 foot width, arranged about 2 feet above the floor level and provided with a wooden sliding panel at the inside. It is called *okubyō-mado,* meaning "chicken-heart window." Being inserted into the entrance shutter and into the panel next to the interior toilet and exterior handwash basin, it is welcomed by the timid who at night do not like to leave the protection of the locked house, whether to see a caller or to wash the hands after having used the toilet. Provision has also been made for leaving the enclosed house during the night without undergoing the fussy and noisy process of unlocking the shutter panels. Especially in traditional houses, where toilet and bath often are under a different roof, such a device in the form of a swinging door of 2 x 3 ft. (610 x 1,068 mm.)inserted in the first shutter next or the shutter compartment, has proven

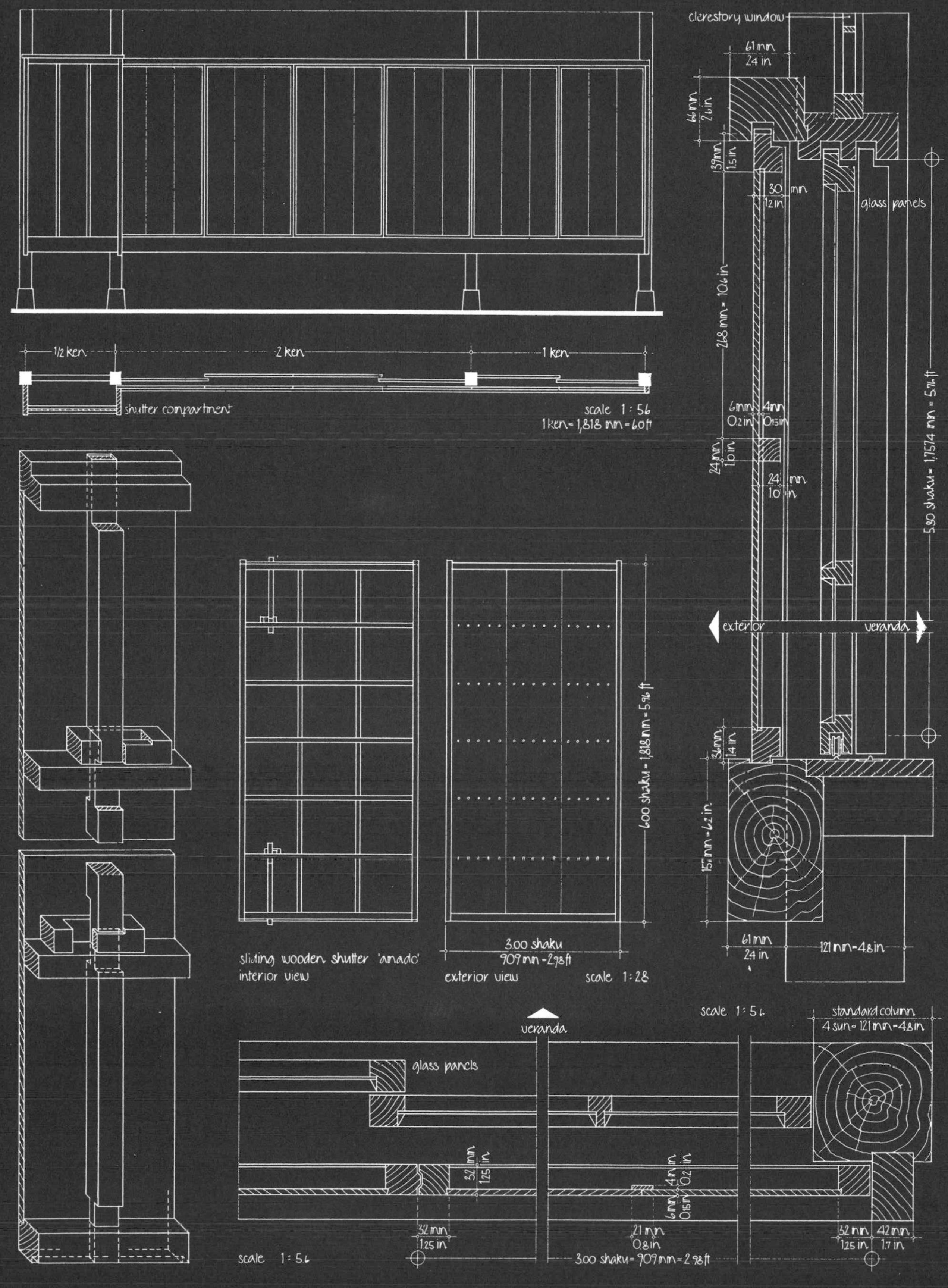

FIGURE 53: Arrangement and construction details of typical shutters, *amado*.

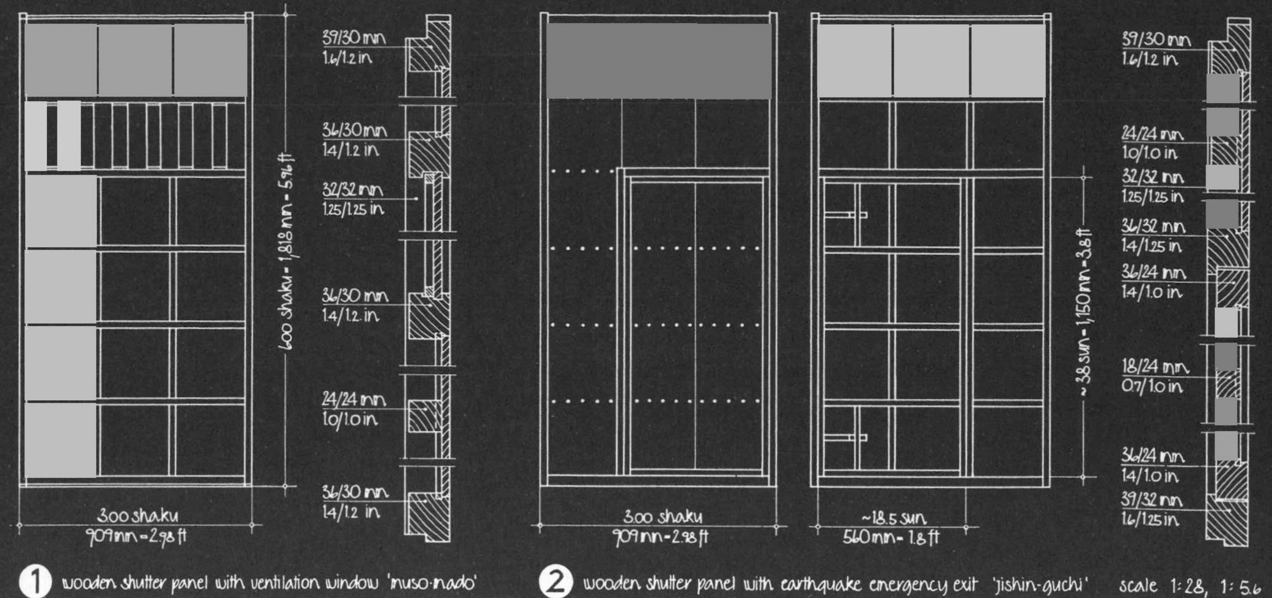

FIGURE 54: Special forms of shutters, *amado.*

very convenient. Its name, *jishin-guchi* (literally, earthquake exit), suggests that it was originally a kind of emergency exit for leaving as quickly as possible a place that was not safe against the frequent earthquakes.

shutter compartment

The method of how to secure the extensive openings of the Japanese house—and for that matter the opening of any building—against the possibility of forcible impact by weather or man is not so much a constructional-static problem as it is a functional dynamic one. That is to say, the architectural challenge is less a question of how to join solid wooden panels with openings and how to keep them in their position, than it is a problem of how to move them to and from an opening (which might be the entire house front itself) and how to store them in the simplest way possible. The task of enclosing a front of 36 feet would present the Western architect with quite some difficulties in regard to the constructional system and functional manipulation, not to mention the economic or aesthetic aspects. The problem is solved by the Japanese very ingeniously. At the end of each shutter sequence a boxlike door compartment, *tobukuro,* is provided where all shutters can easily be slid to and fro. Naturally the size of this compartment corresponds to the height, width, and number of shutter panels, this being the only matter that actually requires some thought, since the length of front to be enclosed is of no direct concern. In cases where placement of the shutter compartment, *tobukuro,* on either side of the house front would be detrimental to the view, a particular construction at the house corner is provided which permits shifting of shutters around the corner.

The constructional-functional system of the shutter compartment, *tobukuro,* is as appropriate as it is simple. The high part of the upper and lower sliding track on the exterior side is taken away inside of the compartment so that the shutters, after being

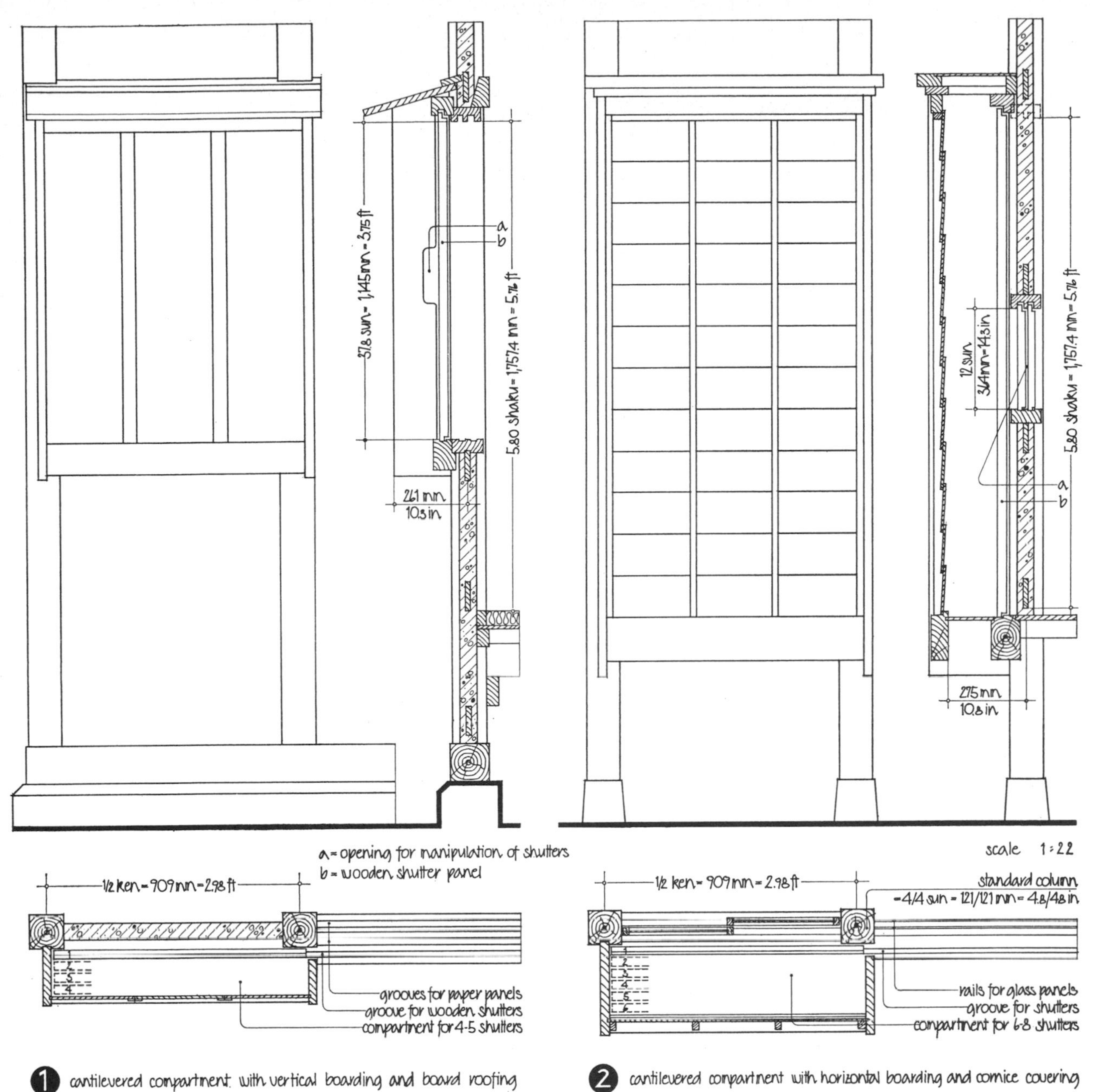

FIGURE 55: Typical forms and construction details of shutter compartments, *tokukuro*.

led into it, bend over to the outside, so they can be pushed aside by the following panel, thus gradually filling the compartment. In taking out the shutters, each panel must be set into the upper and lower tracks and the whole sequence moved along, one panel pushing all the rest. Since the width of the entry into the compartment is just the thickness of a single panel, a particular opening needs to be provided so that one can reach into the compartment. It takes either the form of a widening of the entry slit at its center or else a small sliding window at the interior wall of the shutter compartment. Since both upper and lower track are attached from the outside to the veranda post, shutters can be moved and arranged independently of placement of exterior column.

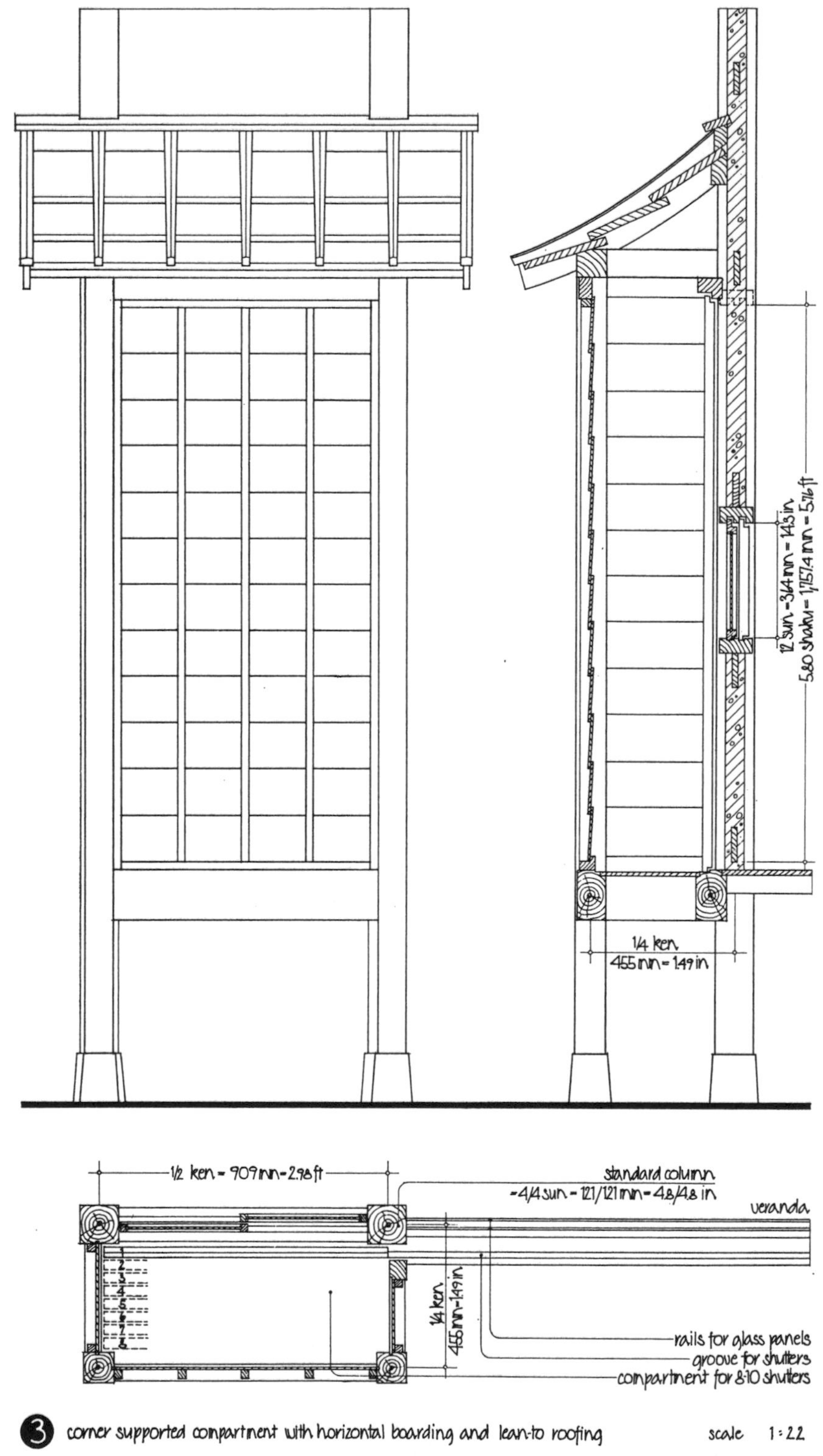

FIGURE 55 (continued): Typical forms and construction details of shutter compartments, *tokukuro.*

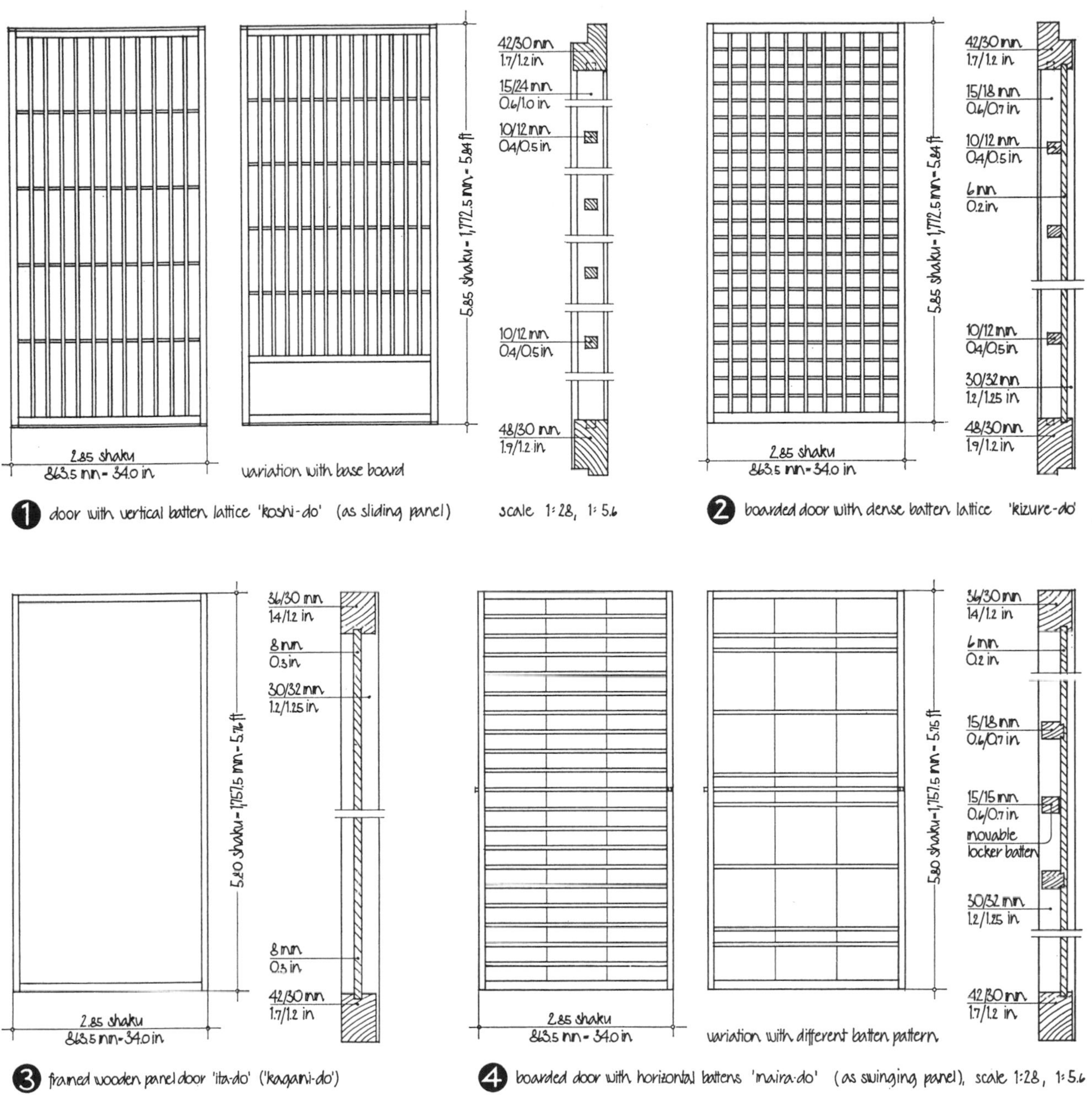

FIGURE 56: Typical forms and construction details of doors.

The shutter compartment is but a device of necessity and thus differences in performance are limited to systems of construction, means of boarding, and methods of roofing. These differences can be applied in various combinations and are defined each by their respective names. For openings of up to eight shutter panels, the compartment is simply projected from the veranda and suspended by two vertical flanking boards, which simultaneously constitute the side walls of the compartment; if more panels are used, the compartment requires additional posts at its corners, which rest on foundation stones.

doors

Besides the translucent and opaque paper panels, *shōji* and *fusuma,* two other types of sliding doors are employed in the house. One of them, the glass sliding panel, *garasu-shōji,* though but recently introduced into the house composition, has achieved increasing popularity. Being a better insulator against cold and more resistant to weather, it gradually has replaced the translucent paper panel, which was the original device for closing all exterior openings such as in toilet, bath, veranda, etc. Yet, in spite of this popularity it should be understood that glass is actually alien to the Japanese house. Its texture and consistency do not possess the common denominator that encompasses all other constituent fabrics, and its weight makes the panel's sliding system, with its simple grooves, inappropriate and difficult.

As doubtful as the integrity of the glass sliding door must be in the pure performance of the Japanese house, just as unequivocal is the homogeneity of the wooden doors in the fabric of the traditional house. They are used in the ordinary houses mainly for practical purposes in utilitarian rooms and serve as door panel from corridor to closet, kitchen, bath, etc., but also perform a refined aesthetic task as the main entrance to the house, *genkan-iriguchi,* as a partition between the entrance hall and the interior of the house, *genkan-agariguchi,* and as an access from the corridor to veranda, *engawa-totsuatari.* In these instances, the wooden door is not only a practical device but accentuates the importance of the place and thereby constitutes decoration.

The panel's dimensioning is submitted to the same controlling factors as are all the other sliding units described previously. Outstanding again is the extreme lightness so essential to the whole functioning of the Japanese house mechanisms. In connection with the entrance hall, panels are used as sliding doors, framed and joined into the fittings in the same way as all the other sliding units in the house. Yet, the swinging type is frequently employed for toilet, bath, corridor, etc. In this case, the panel is butted and hinged in simple pin fittings of metal. The frame is made rigid by wooden lattice, or by boards, or by both, giving rise to multiple patterns of form and system, of which only the major types are depicted.

conclusion

for contemporary architecture

The development of technology in the last century has brought about revolutionary changes, not only technically but also socially and hence politically. To architecture, it meant a change from handicraft methods to machine-craft methods for the manufacture of materials and components and also for the procedure of construction. This transformation, however was not confined to the mere technical-practical aspect of building. Just as civilization as a whole entered a basically new phase, each architectural factor, its content and its proportional contribution in the total creation, is drawn into the whirlpool of this revolution.

It is true that both the manufacture of materials and the procedure of construction have for a long time realized the potential of machinery and are largely, though far from completely, following the principles of technology in their activities. But it is erroneous to assume that with this the period of technical transformation belongs to the past. Instead, as the conflicting viewpoints regarding the meaning of technology in building prove, the intellectual argumentation and ideological discussion among those who actually design and control all this building, the architects, is only in its very early stages. Thus, a portion of them works on the basis of the theory that modern technology has changed only the productional method and not the product itself, its entity, its function, and its expression. Whereas the other group indiscriminately surrenders to technology and does not consider architectural form and space the primary aim, but only a secondary consequence dictated by structure: constructivism. Common to both the first underestimation of technology and the second overestimation, is the dogmatic interpretation of construction in building, and thus its very narrow leeway. The result is that the transformation of building by technology so far has remained but a physical affair, outside of human comprehension or sympathy, and therefore frequently with inhuman tendencies.

Against this trend of oversimplification and intolerance, the role of construction in Japanese building is a favorable, and therefore instructive, contrast. Far from affirming constructivism, it nevertheless states clearly that the very medium of creating architectural form and space is construction. With construction, space is spanned, is enclosed, and enriched; and human space is created. With construction, human emotions are also addressed. Yet, never is the spatial-utilitarian requirement encroached upon by constructional dogma, and never is the expression of building dictated by constructional demonstrativeness and structural exhibitionism, as so often is the case in contemporary building, where either ignorance or indifference on the part of the architect has obstructed full intellectual comprehension and hence excludes the full mastership of handling structure in building.

The value for contemporary architecture lies in the realization of the fact that a residential architecture—standardized in element and system as no other before and after—still succeeded in exercising a tolerance, both physically and conceptionally, in the application of construction. For it can be concluded that even mechanized and industrialized building does not necessarily mean constructivism. Certainly, constructional systems, such as thin shells or post-lintel construction, do impose their respective orders upon the plan, space, and form of building. But if they thereby obstruct or limit human requirements, both physically and emotionally, the construction itself is not at fault, but its initial choice. There is an infinity of constructional systems and forms available in contemporary technology, assuring a ready and exact constructional answer for any possible human requirement. There is no justification for ever limiting utilitarian, visual, or even emotional needs of man because of the constructional system.

The Japanese residence reveals most of its constructional members to the inside and outside and distinguishes the component parts of building, support and non-support, crisply and without cover pieces or unnecessary detail. The structural system, except that of the roof, is therefore exposed to the eye of the beholder and, no doubt, effects a strong intimacy with the anatomy of house, both from within and without. However, such an aesthetic expression is not a conception in the sense of something previously conceived, but is a logical result of architectural methods to enclose human space in the simplest way, with the least means possible. The Japanese have by no means intended to make their dwelling a constructional showpiece, as the frequent identification with contemporary trends suggest. Exposure of construction in the Japanese house was never a matter of intellectual principle, but was the result of very reasonable architectural measures that suggested themselves. In fact, previous analysis has not given the slightest evidence that constructional regularity, though seemingly the inevitable result of modular design, has ever been considered by the Japanese more important than man's comfort.

Still, there is no question that the structural system is likely to become the dominant source of form expression in contemporary architecture. Because increasingly building will become an assembling of prefabricated parts, as effected by the industrialization of building; and consequently physical distinction between structural and non-structural screening members will be inevitable, as is also the case in Japanese residential architecture.

Yet, in the Japanese house the function of construction is not confined to spanning space or to revealing the structural forces of the building or, as in the best examples of contemporary architecture, to displaying pleasant proportion and texture of material. Its range extends also to areas that are still occupied in Western architecture by other agencies. Thus, construction also constitutes decoration itself. Structural members are employed in awareness of their aesthetic meaning. Constructional device is exploited as ornamental form. And even non-functional construction is introduced to serve as décor. It is by this reason that decoration in the Japanese house is essentially architectural, i.e., it is not additive but is structurally integrated. Form (in the sense of color, shape, and texture), therefore, the mediatory element of décor, is a derivative of construction, i.e., it is not alienated from its *raison d'être,* as was the trend in each architectural period in the West, and therefore has not taken to abstraction. Even the spiritual center of the house, the picture recess, *tokonoma,* is but a niche differentiated from all other room components by change of floor level and a bold interruption of the frieze rail that horizontally circumscribes the Japanese room.

Furthermore, Japanese construction functions as the interpreter of religious philosophic values that characterized the epoch. The aestheticism of the tea cult and the religion-philosophy of Buddhism recognized, in the unsophisticated and humble construction of the ordinary dwelling, a singular opportunity to demonstrate their own spiritual values and bring them to the consciousness of the common people. It may even be that both tea cult and Buddhism obtained decisive motifs and stimuli from a constructional order which, better than any words, directly stated life, the simple life of man in its basic and true meaning. Through such linking of physical structure with the spiritual values of the epoch, the cultural standard of the lowest classes was elevated to a level that shows a keen awareness as to the presence of art and religion in living and thus contrasts favorably with that of the comparable social class in the West.

This successful employment of construction for the multiple functions which architecture performs as a necessity of life, as a symbol of era and as a form of art, is of revelation for contemporary architecture. For not only does the Japanese example show that the medium for all architectural efforts is construction, but it also unveils the enormous potential of structure in building. Just as art and philosophy, the one through material means, the other through intellect, are apt to interpret the life of the contemporary epoch, to establish the relationship of the individual to the universal, and thus to stimulate cognitions as to the ethical values of the epoch, so too the physical structure of a building does possess the potential of being an artistic and philosophical instrument that identifies architecture, symbolizes era, and interprets life.

Yet, this intellectual recognition would remain without purpose and meaning, if not followed by a plan for action. The practical conclusion to be drawn, then, is the imperative of employing structure in building not only as medium of spanning space but also as medium of substantiating man and his time. Through such spiritual interpretation of structure, the intellectual basis would be established for concealing obtrusive structure, changing ill-sized (although economical) structure, employing decorative structure, and inserting symbolic structure. That is to say, justification would be gained for breaking the mere technical-dogmatic supremacy of constructivism in contemporary building to pave the way for a more universal, more tolerant, and more valid application of construction in building—a prime requisite for making building a true expression of the total meaning of technique, as it determines the contemporary epoch not only physically, but even more so spiritually.

While this would be primarily the task of the architect-designer, the other imperative would concern the architect-educator. For it could hardly be expected that the general public is sensitive a priori to this multiple and profound significance of construction in building. Rather, an education of the general public is required in the form of an introduction to the vocabulary of contemporary architecture, and the symbolic, aesthetic, and anatomic meaning therein occupied by construction. While admittedly it is the architect's privilege to address society directly with his buildings and not with words, it must be questioned whether in the present state of alienation—between man and art, man and science, man and architecture—the advanced performance of any individual architect can still reach the sentiment of the masses.

Rather, as the increasing emotional indifference of the general public to contemporary art, science, and architecture proves, there is an urgent need for basic intellectual education. In the case of building, this task has to be performed by those who actually carry the social responsibility in matters of the physical environment, the architects. And it is due in no small part to either the architects' ignorance of the cultural mission of architecture or to their inertness in matters of public opinion, that the level of culture, characterized by the psychological relationship of man to the man-made environment, is at such an all-time low.

Although the constructional system of the Japanese house has never really evolved from its primitive pattern and is defective in many ways, it nevertheless reaffirms the truth, which is also apparent in all architectures of the past, that no period has built less skillfully than it knew how, regardless of the current taste. Thus, if it is accepted that regularity in the historic occurrence of a distinct feature proves that this feature is an essential and characteristic quality, then, contemporary building can only make the claim of being true architecture if it consciously and consistently applies the latest recognitions provided by science. There is no excuse for designing and building unscientifically because of an obsolete preference of the general public for the form expressions of backward beliefs, thoughts, or methods.

To build scientifically, yet, does not only concern the technical-mechanical aspect of building, but distinctly means use of, and strict compliance with, the scientific facts of sociology, hygienics, optics, and psychology. With such intellectual foundation, construction in building would be given its proper role in the organism and, instead of being irreconcilable and authoritative as it is at present, it could again become a rich source of expression, in no way inferior to the human-spiritual role of construction in past building, be it Gothic or Japanese.

Yet, again, such scientific design is not to be considered a mere mathematical function that would solve all constructional problems and make structure expressive in the widest meaning. Instead, it is only the essential directive that guides the thought and action of the designer for an effective approach, and excludes the danger of either wasteful subjective searching or direct misuse. However, it requires the creative intuition of an artist to grasp this multiple potential of construction in its total scope and make it as well a unique expression of its spiritual significance. Only then will industrialized and mechanized architecture be the materialization of human life itself, as handicraft architecture has been before, and only then will it be able to stir in return the most varied human emotions. The constructional system of a building then would be no longer the inevitable result of a mere rational-mathematical equation. Instead, both the creation and experience of structure would possess features that are the characteristics of true art.

index

Numerals in italics refer to pages on which illustrations appear.

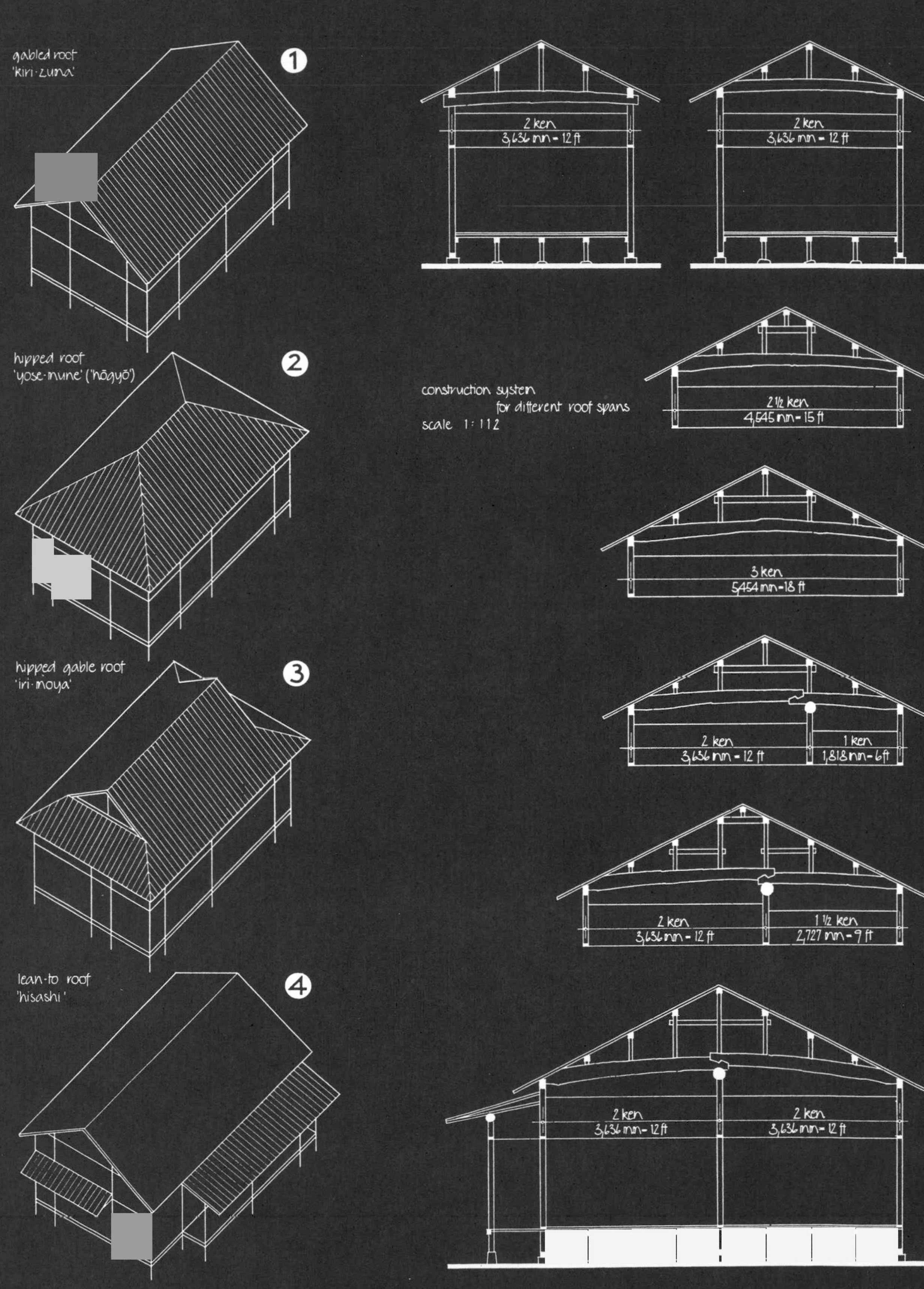
gabled roof
'kiri-zuma'
1
hipped roof
'yose-mune' ('hōgyō')
2
hipped gable roof
'iri-moya'
3
lean-to roof
'hisashi'
4
2 ken
3,636 mm - 12 ft
2 ken
3,636 mm - 12 ft
construction system
for different roof spans
scale 1 : 112
2½ ken
4,545 mm - 15 ft
3 ken
5,454 mm - 18 ft
2 ken
3,636 mm - 12 ft
1 ken
1,818 mm - 6 ft
2 ken
3,636 mm - 12 ft
1½ ken
2,727 mm - 9 ft
2 ken
3,636 mm - 12 ft
2 ken
3,636 mm - 12 ft